The Politics
of Industrial Change

The Politics
of Industrial Change

*Railway Policy
in North America*

R. KENT WEAVER

THE BROOKINGS INSTITUTION
Washington, D.C.

Copyright © 1985 by
THE BROOKINGS INSTITUTION
1775 Massachusetts Avenue, N.W., Washington, D.C. 20036

Library of Congress Cataloging in Publication Data:
Weaver, R. Kent, 1953–
  The politics of industrial change.
  Includes bibliographical references and index.
  1. Industry and state—United States. 2. Industry
and state—Canada. 3. Railroads and state—United
States—Case studies. 4. Railroads and state—Canada—
Case studies. I. Title.
HD3616.U47W355 1985   338.973   85-24274
ISBN 0-8157-9260-3
ISBN 0-8157-9259-X (pbk.)

9 8 7 6 5 4 3 2 1

THE BROOKINGS INSTITUTION is an independent organization devoted to nonpartisan research, education, and publication in economics, government, foreign policy, and the social sciences generally. Its principal purposes are to aid in the development of sound public policies and to promote public understanding of issues of national importance.

The Institution was founded on December 8, 1927, to merge the activities of the Institute for Government Research, founded in 1916, the Institute of Economics, founded in 1922, and the Robert Brookings Graduate School of Economics and Government, founded in 1924.

The Board of Trustees is responsible for the general administration of the Institution, while the immediate direction of the policies, program, and staff is vested in the President, assisted by an advisory committee of the officers and staff. The by-laws of the Institution state: "It is the function of the Trustees to make possible the conduct of scientific research, and publication, under the most favorable conditions, and to safeguard the independence of the research staff in the pursuit of their studies and in the publication of the results of such studies. It is not a part of their function to determine, control, or influence the conduct of particular investigations or the conclusions reached."

The President bears final responsibility for the decision to publish a manuscript as a Brookings book. In reaching his judgment on the competence, accuracy, and objectivity of each study, the President is advised by the director of the appropriate research program and weighs the views of a panel of expert outside readers who report to him in confidence on the quality of the work. Publication of a work signifies that it is deemed a competent treatment worthy of public consideration but does not imply endorsement of conclusions or recommendations.

The Institution maintains its position of neutrality on issues of public policy in order to safeguard the intellectual freedom of the staff. Hence interpretations or conclusions in Brookings publications should be understood to be solely those of the authors and should not be attributed to the Institution, to its trustees, officers, or other staff members, or to the organizations that support its research.

Foreword

THE U.S. and Canadian governments have been challenged to help
their industries adapt to increasing competitive pressures. In this book,
R. Kent Weaver examines the political barriers the two governments
confront in this effort. He argues that their constraints are different—
notably, fragmentation of governmental power in the United States and
intense regional conflict in Canada. But the impact of these constraints
is similar: an unwillingness or inability on the part of the government to
impose concentrated, visible losses on well-organized producer, consumer, and labor groups. As a result, the two governments tend to delay
rather than aid industries' adjustment to changing markets. He concludes
that these constraints are so fundamental to the two political systems
that neither government has much prospect for improving its ability to
help industries adjust in the future.

In reaching this conclusion, Weaver examines three tasks that are
crucial for executing effective industrial policies: selecting policies that
promote rather than prevent sectoral adjustment, choosing policy instruments (for example, regulations, loans, and subsidies) that are
appropriate to an industry's problems, and implementing those policies
once they have been selected. For this last task, he focuses on problems
associated with the use of public enterprise.

The author illustrates his general arguments with a comparative case
study of U.S. and Canadian federal policies toward the railroad industry.
In particular, he looks at the establishment and subsequent operation of
the four major government-owned firms: the Consolidated Rail Corporation and Amtrak in the United States, and Canadian National Railways
and VIA Rail Canada in Canada. Weaver argues that railway policies in
the two countries have differed significantly in recent years. Canada,
though more protectionist than the United States, has had more freedom
in choosing policy instruments. But both governments have attempted
to delay needed adjustments in the rail industry much more than they

have tried to promote them. And when they have attempted to speed change, they have had little success.

R. Kent Weaver is a research associate in the Brookings Governmental Studies program. He wishes to thank Martha Derthick and Paul E. Peterson, who offered encouragement and suggestions as the manuscript developed, and Hugh Heclo and Raymond Vernon, who directed the author's doctoral dissertation at Harvard University from which this book was adapted. He also received helpful comments from Vinod Aggarwal, Michael Denning, John Gratwick, George Hilton, Theodore Keeler, Robert Z. Lawrence, Lloyd Musolf, David Olson, and Harold Seidman. Alice Keck Whitfield provided research assistance, computer analysis, and much valuable criticism. Barbara de Boinville and Alice M. Carroll edited the manuscript; John Clark, Karl Knapp, and Joel Ostrow verified its factual content; Pam Harris provided typing assistance; and Gerry Drysdale, Brenda Esson, and others at the headquarters of Canadian National Railways assisted the author's research in Montreal. Many people in both countries were interviewed for this study, and they gave their time generously. All were promised confidentiality in exchange for a candid expression of their experiences and opinions. The author received financial assistance from the Danforth Foundation and the University Consortium for Research on North America.

The views in this book are those of the author and should not be ascribed to the persons or organizations whose assistance is acknowledged, or to the trustees, officers, or other staff members of the Brookings Institution.

BRUCE K. MACLAURY
President

October 1985
Washington, D.C.

Contents

Figures

CHAPTER ONE

Industrial Adjustment

THE ECONOMIC malaise of the 1970s and 1980s has given rise to a variety of proposed solutions. Supply-side economists call for reduced government taxation to release the dynamism of private enterprise. Other critics of the status quo, advocates of what they call *industrial policy,* believe a reduced government role is precisely the wrong response. They argue that government must intervene more directly in specific sectors of the economy, using public enterprise, loans, selective subsidies, and tax incentives to promote the development of "sunrise" industries, ease the demise of dying industries, and revitalize those in danger of failing.[1] Failure to do so, they contend, will lead to a decline in U.S. competitiveness on world markets and to a drop in U.S. living standards. John Zysman and Laura Tyson, for example, suggest that governments can, by astute investment policies, create a permanent competitive advantage for their countries in specific investment-intensive industries.[2] Critics of industrial policy, on the other hand, argue that while such interventions may be successful in other countries, they would be a disaster in the United States. One prominent critic asserts that the "U.S. government . . . is inherently incapable of doing a decent job of picking and choosing among individuals—be they individual regions, firms, or people."[3]

The proponents of an activist industrial policy are certainly correct in at least one respect: government is already heavily involved in determining the fate of many American industries, although it may not be doing so purposely, let alone effectively. Too often, however, they fail to

1. See, for example, Ira C. Magaziner and Robert B. Reich, *Minding America's Business: The Decline and Rise of the American Economy* (Vintage Books, 1982); and Lester Thurow, *The Zero-Sum Society* (Basic Books, 1980).
2. John Zysman and Laura Tyson, eds., *American Industry in International Competition: Government Policies and Corporate Strategies* (Cornell University Press, 1983), p. 27.
3. Charles Schultze, "Industrial Policy: A Solution in Search of a Problem," *California Management Review,* vol. 25 (Summer 1983), pp. 5–15.

recognize the logical implication of their own argument—namely, that the successes or failures of current policies may shed light on the ability of the U.S. government to carry out constructive industrial policies. Both the proponents and critics of industrial policy have failed to examine carefully the American experience. Proponents have stressed the success of other countries and have suggested that because an active industrial policy is necessary it is feasible. They imply that the United States could implement a successful industrial policy if policymakers were more aware of the need for and principles of such a policy and developed a government bureaucracy committed to those principles.[4] Critics of industrial policy, on the other hand, have relied largely on anecdotal evidence to support their contention that the United States is incapable of imitating the industrial policy successes of other countries.

The debate on industrial policy has been deficient in another respect: the industrial adjustment problem should not be viewed primarily as a trade problem. Constraints on an effective policy are in large part domestic political ones. Moreover, many industries that are not subject to stiff international competition—for example, dairy farming and railroads—face the same adjustment dilemmas as trade-threatened industries and will experience many of the same protectionist outcomes.

What is needed is a theoretical understanding of how (if at all) the United States is different from other Western industrial countries in its ability to intervene in specific industries and evidence that applies this analysis in a cross-national setting. What follows is an effort in this direction. This book compares the United States and Canada, focusing on the impact that political constraints have had on policy choice. Although the two countries are by no means identical, their cultural heritage, level of economic development, and private sector dominance of economic production are similar. But they differ dramatically in their political institutions (congressional versus parliamentary systems) and in the strength of regional identities (much stronger in Canada). Comparing the U.S. government's response to industrial adjustment crises with Canada's throws into relief crucial determinants of policy choice that might otherwise go unexamined.

This book considers three questions central to the industrial policy debate. Part one asks how capable the U.S. and Canadian governments

4. Magaziner and Reich, *Minding America's Business*, pp. 370–74.

are of accelerating industrial adjustment rather than delaying or preventing it. Part two asks what factors constrain governments' choice of
policy instruments in dealing with specific sectors of the economy and
whether those constraints prevent the U.S. and Canadian governments
from choosing the most appropriate instruments. Finally, part three
addresses the constraints political systems place on the implementation
of sectoral policies.

This study concentrates on a single policy instrument, public enterprise, to give these very broad questions a more manageable focus. Each
of the three parts opens with a chapter developing a general set of
arguments concerning the political constraints on industrial policy.
These arguments will then be tested and refined by chapters analyzing
the railway industries in the United States and Canada.

The central thesis of the book is this: national variations in political
constraints give countries differing comparative advantages in pursuing
particular governmental activities, just as variations in economic resources create comparative advantages in specific industries. In simple
terms, not all governments are equally capable of using the same policies
or the same policy instruments. Government policies to accelerate
industrial adjustment within individual industries almost always require
governments to impose concentrated costs on politically powerful actors. The political structures of the United States and Canada, for
somewhat different reasons, make it particularly difficult for these
governments to overcome the obstacles to such policies. Learning by
policymakers is not sufficient to overcome these deeply rooted political
constraints.

If governments wish to stimulate economic growth, they should
choose instruments and policies that they can use most effectively,
rather than copy other governments with differing capabilities. Although
policies that accelerate economic growth may be the best option in other
countries, market-oriented policies generally will be superior in the
United States given the political constraints against successful operation
of accelerationist policies. Similarly, while public enterprise may be an
effective policy instrument in other countries, political constraints in the
United States limit its usefulness here and require that exceptional care
be devoted to its design when it is employed.

In Europe, and to a lesser extent in Canada, industrial adjustment
policy and the extension of government ownership have been closely
intertwined. European nationalizations occurred under conservative

governments as well as socialist ones.[5] During the 1970s public enterprises were created or expanded in a number of troubled industries
across Europe—for example, British Leyland (autos), Rolls-Royce
(aircraft engines), and British Aerospace in the United Kingdom. Foreign
public enterprises also made their presence known in the United States
not only by competing with U.S. firms but also by purchasing them.
Renault bought a controlling stake in American Motors, and Elf Aquitane
purchased Texasgulf, to cite two of the best-known examples.

   In the United States little serious consideration has been given to
public enterprise as an instrument for dealing with industrial adjustment
problems even though such enterprises are widely used by state and
local governments. Alternative instruments—for example, loan guarantees to Lockheed and Chrysler, contract arrangements in defense and
other "high-tech" research, a private sector government-sponsored
corporation in communications satellite development—clearly have
been preferred to public enterprise. Indeed, in the primary case where
public enterprise has been used to respond to an industrial adjustment
crisis—the railways—nationalization of Amtrak and Conrail evolved
rather than being consciously chosen, as chapter 4 explains. Moreover,
public enterprise has been limited in scope to the most troubled sectors
of the industry.

   The Amtrak and Conrail lessons are nonetheless indicative of the
probable direction of any future U.S. industrial policy. As additional
U.S. industries, and the communities that depend on them, seek assistance to grow or to avoid decline, many of the same questions—and very
likely some of the same answers—arrived at in the Amtrak and Conrail
cases will resurface. The United States has been relatively fortunate in
its adjustment efforts so far: for example, Lockheed and Chrysler were
able to repay their loan guarantees. What follows is an analysis and a
cautionary tale of what is likely to happen if and when future Lockheeds
and Chryslers cannot.

Studying Industrial Policy

   The term *industrial policy* has been used to describe a broad range of
government goals and actions; it will be used here to describe policies

   5. For an overview of these trends, see R. Joseph Monsen and Kenneth D. Walters,
Nationalized Companies: A Threat to American Business (McGraw-Hill, 1983),
chap. 1.

intended to promote the economic efficiency and viability of a specific domestic sector. More specifically, industrial policies attempt to help an industry adjust to changing patterns of technology, competition, and consumer demand. This adjustment might necessitate changes in the number of firms or the level of employment. But adjustment goals are likely to be included on the public agenda only when the industry is facing a crisis, and government responses to industrial adjustment objectives will often be short-term, although possibly quite radical, interventions.

Policymaking for industrial adjustment is complicated by the fact that these goals compete with a range of other sectoral policy objectives— for example, maintaining employment, providing an adequate industrial base for defense needs, promoting industrialization in underdeveloped regions, lessening pollution, and avoiding monopoly power abuses. These latter goals may be labeled *public needs goals* because they are more concerned with the needs of consumers, employees, and other groups than with those of the firms in the industry. Unlike adjustment goals, public needs goals are usually relatively stable items on the public agenda, and government responses to these objectives may be quite different: long-term programs of financial assistance, ownership, or regulation.

Adjustment goals and public needs goals may be compatible or even complementary. Indeed, the cases cited by proponents of industrial policy as evidence that the United States can carry out such a policy effectively (for example, aircraft manufacture) are instances where government was pursuing public needs goals (for example, national defense), and successful industrial adjustment policies emerged as a byproduct. At other times, however, industrial adjustment and public needs goals will conflict. Forcing steel and other heavy industries to pay their pollution clean-up costs and stop polluting may threaten the survival of some firms in those industries. In industries such as shipbuilding, cutbacks in domestic production due to foreign competition affect employment and defense goals. Over time, an accommodation is likely to be reached between the financial needs of the industry and other government objectives. If this balance is upset by an adjustment crisis, however, some new accommodation must be reached. But new policies to promote sectoral adjustment cannot be written on a blank slate. These proposed solutions may conflict with existing public needs policies. Governments will have to choose between them.

Types of Industrial Adjustment Policies

Governments can pursue three broad types of policies to deal with sectoral adjustment problems: market-oriented policies, protectionist policies, and accelerationist policies.[6]

Market-oriented policies, as the term implies, rely on market signals and general macroeconomic and social policies to address industrial adjustment problems rather than on sector-specific solutions. Governments exercise a wide variety of instruments to influence industrial growth, such as education and training to develop a more highly skilled work force, unemployment insurance to ease the costs to workers of job changes, currency devaluations to make exports more competitive, and tax and monetary policy to influence the supply of credit. Supply-side economics, for example, calls for cuts in tax rates to stimulate savings and investment. Enterprise zones are another market-oriented policy proposal designed to facilitate economic growth. Although the package of tax and regulatory incentives included in the design of a zone may affect some industries differentially (for example, loosening of environmental restrictions would be particularly attractive to industries that are heavy polluters), enterprise zones are not directly industry- and firm-specific.

Protectionist policies are generally sector-specific, but not firm-specific. (Commodity-specific tariffs are a classic example.) They attempt to avoid the imposition of concentrated costs on any domestic group—most notably, firms within the industry, their customers, suppliers, and employees. This is impossible in practice, of course, but protectionist policies may ease, disguise, or diffuse such costs.

Accelerationist policies, on the other hand, attempt to speed up industrial transitions when the market appears unlikely to produce efficient outcomes or when it produces adjustment too slowly. These situations may arise as a result of classic market failure (for example, monopoly power, high transaction costs, poorly developed capital markets) or when political markets overwhelm economic ones (for example, when firms and employees in a declining industry have the political power to force a bailout). Accelerationist policy attempts to ease economic and political barriers to change. This includes buying off

6. A fourth option, of course, is to eschew even general market-oriented adjustment policies.

opponents when necessary. Because firms within an industry may not be equally viable, accelerationist policy is likely to be firm-specific as well as sector-specific.

Because both protectionist and accelerationist policies may involve compensation of "losers" in industrial adjustment crises, differences between the compensation practices of the two options must be spelled out carefully. Accelerationist compensation, first of all, is limited in time, with benefits being phased out as soon as practicable so that labor and capital resources can be redeployed quickly into efficient uses. Temporary assistance programs may prove difficult to dismantle, being subverted in practice into long-term subsidies that create perverse incentives for producers and consumers. Accelerationist compensation should also be limited in size and scope to those whose claims are current and substantial. For example, creating a set of transitional benefits for firms and workers may speed shrinkage in a declining industry, but it makes no sense to allow participation by future entrants, who may be attracted by the level of benefits established by the compensation program.

Adjustment Policies and Industrial Life Cycles

The precise goals and content of these three policy options differ substantially depending on the particular stage of an industry's life cycle. Table 1-1 outlines these responses to industrial adjustment problems in three phases of an industry's life cycle: "sunrise" or growth, maturity, and "sunset" or decline.

SUNRISE INDUSTRIES. In an industry's sunrise phase, demand for a product or some range of related products is increasing, but potential entrants to the industry may face high barriers. International competition may lead late developing countries to protect "infant industries" from competition from foreign imports (which can take advantage of economies of scale and greater technological expertise) until their own industries can become competitive.[7] Governments may also intervene when a private firm cannot generate a commercially viable rate of return because a sufficient market for the product has not yet developed. (This

7. For a review and critique of infant industry arguments, see Robert E. Baldwin, "The Case against Infant-Industry Tariff Protection," *Journal of Political Economy*, vol. 77 (May–June 1969), pp. 295–305.

Table 1-1. *Industrial Adjustment Policies and Industry Life Cycles*

	Policies		
Industry	*Market-oriented*	*Protectionist*	*Accelerationist*
Sunrise	Provide incentives for research and investment (for example, investment tax credits) and development of efficient capital markets.	Provide assistance to all firms entering an industry on an equal basis as a mechanism for promoting growth.	Promote development of selected firms to encourage growth; discourage excessive entry.
Mature	Allow market forces to decide prices and market shares except where there are serious market failures (for example, externalities or natural monopoly).	Cartelize industry to stabilize competition among firms; diffuse adjustment costs among broader public.	Encourage exit of least efficient firms to develop a more efficient industry.
Declining	Allow exit of weaker firms as determined by market forces; utilize society-wide programs (for example, unemployment insurance) to ease transition costs.	Preserve employment and productivity by assisting firms (especially weaker firms) through regulation or direct assistance.	Promote exit as a mechanism for lowering excess capacity in industry; restructure existing firms to develop a more competitive industry.

is known as *premature enterprise*.)[8] Transportation and communications systems in unsettled areas, for example, may not be able to earn a commercial return until there has been an increase in population, which may be highly dependent upon prior provision of the product or service. Moreover, the start-up costs of such projects may be huge. Governments are thus faced with a choice of waiting for private enterprise or assuming part or all of the risk themselves.

A market-oriented policy in the sunrise phase would suggest reliance on private capital markets to promote industrial development. The primary responsibilities of the government are to ensure that these markets operate efficiently (for example, by preventing securities fraud) and to encourage productive investment (for example, by providing investment tax credits).

Alternatively, governments can pursue a variety of protectionist policies that are generally sector-specific but not firm-specific—for

8. See Robert Fogel, *The Union Pacific Railroad: A Case in Premature Enterprise* (Johns Hopkins Press, 1960), pp. 18–24.

example, tariffs for firms facing international competition—and tax incentive or subsidy programs for all firms meeting a specified set of eligibility criteria. The costs imposed by these programs are likely to be widely diffused. The danger of such protectionist policies is that they will promote excessive entry and lead to the development of numerous relatively small firms that are dependent upon government assistance. If government attempts to phase out such assistance, some or all of the firms may fail.

Accelerationist policies in the sunrise phase attempt not only to encourage the growth of an industry but also to improve its prospects for long-term viability. They require that governments have the capacity to discriminate not only among sectors but also among firms, giving assistance only to those that are likely to survive, while other firms are encouraged to exit or merge with the "winners." Thus European countries have attempted to develop "national champions" (and in some cases European champions) to compete with U.S. multinationals in high-technology fields such as aerospace and computers.[9]

MATURE INDUSTRIES. Governments face different industrial adjustment problems when an industry is capable of generating sufficient capital to meet replacement and growth requirements. A first set of policy disputes may focus on competition within an industry, with weaker firms trying to use government policy to avoid being forced out of business. Second, there is competition between the industry and other industries (or foreign competitors) producing substitutable goods or services, with industries trying to use government power to gain an advantage over their competitors. The U.S. dairy industry's long-time success in preventing the use of yellow coloring in margarine (which makes it a more attractive substitute for butter) is an example. Finally, there may be conflict between firms in an industry and its customers and suppliers. Members of the industry may again attempt to use government power to limit competition among themselves and to eliminate new entrants, enabling existing firms to earn above-market profits.[10] Consumers and suppliers, on the other hand, are likely to seek limitations on these firms' market

9. On European efforts to create national champions, see Raymond Vernon, ed., *Big Business and the State: Changing Relations in Western Europe* (Harvard University Press, 1974); and John Zysman, *Political Strategies for Industrial Order: State, Market and Industry in France* (University of California Press, 1977).

10. See George Stigler, "The Theory of Economic Regulation," *The Bell Journal of Economics and Management Science*, vol. 2 (Spring 1971), pp. 3–21.

power. Adjustment crises may occur when business downturns, supply disruptions (such as the oil shocks of the 1970s), or technological changes upset the existing competitive relations among these groups.

The market-oriented response to these conflicts is straightforward: government intervention should be resisted unless the industry has special characteristics indicating serious, permanent market failures (for example, natural monopolies or significant externalities). Protectionist responses, on the other hand, involve replacing market-generated outcomes with government-mandated ones, easing or spreading the burden of an adjustment crisis. Weaker firms in an industry may be provided with government assistance or, under a regulatory regime, given business opportunities denied their more profitable competitors. Entry, pricing, and exit restrictions can be used to prop up an industry or segments thereof. (The Civil Aeronautic Board's pre-deregulation policies of tightening entry and price restrictions during traffic downturns and limiting new entry on lucrative routes to struggling air carriers is a clear example of such protectionist policies.) Competition among industries producing substitutable goods can be eased by regulatory or subsidy regimes that attempt to preserve existing market shares and price structures (generally by passing on higher prices to consumers). After the Interstate Commerce Commission's regulatory authority over railroads was extended to interstate trucking in 1935 and to some barge traffic in 1940, the commission developed "umbrella ratemaking" policies that attempted to divide traffic among competing modes while providing adequate revenues to each.[11]

The same techniques can be used when relationships between an industry and its suppliers and consumers are disturbed. The petroleum price regulations instituted after the 1973–74 oil embargo are a classic example of a protectionist response to an adjustment crisis. Through an extraordinarily complex cross-subsidy scheme, government attempted to keep down prices for consumers while simultaneously equalizing the crude oil prices of refiners that did have access to low-cost domestic oil and those that did not. The costs of the program—increased demand leading to higher world oil prices, disincentives for domestic production, and incentives for inefficiency in the refining industry—were less con-

11. See George W. Hilton, *The Transportation Act of 1958: A Decade of Experience* (Indiana University Press, 1969), pp. 22–34, 47–78.

centrated and less visible than those resulting from a market solution. Because the costs were hidden does not make them any less real, however.

Accelerationist policies, on the other hand, attempt to speed up the attainment of a new market-based and market-sustainable equilibrium. Government may pick up some of the transitional costs to ease resistance to change. Intervention is likely to be intermittent (at the time of adjustment crises) rather than constant. Thus in the energy example cited earlier, government assistance for weatherization and short-term energy assistance for low-income households might ease political barriers to oil price deregulation; over the longer term, government funding for research into more efficient auto engines could help to accelerate change of an energy-inefficient capital stock.

DECLINING INDUSTRIES. Industries can decline for a number of reasons, including product obsolescence (for example, buggy whips), development of substitutes preferred by consumers (for example, automobiles instead of interurban railways), increased foreign competition (for example, textiles, shipbuilding, and certain segments of the steel industry in the United States), and exhaustion of inexpensive raw materials. Industrial decline confronts industries—and governments—with a different set of problems, such as excess capacity and inability to generate adequate capital through retained earnings, sale of equity, or borrowing. Without government intervention, a declining industry will undergo substantial shrinkage and restructuring or disappear altogether. Some customers may also suffer losses, particularly if they have been receiving cross-subsidies under the existing price structure. Declining industries are not necessarily dying industries, however. A successful weeding out of weak, inefficient firms may lead to the reestablishment of a self-sufficient, if smaller, industry—that is, a new "mature" phase in the industry's life cycle.

The same three broad policy options can be used to respond to the problems of declining industries. Market-oriented responses rely on market mechanisms and general macroeconomic and social policies to determine the pattern of industrial adjustment. Thus workers who have lost their jobs may receive unemployment insurance and job retraining benefits to cushion that loss, but special programs will not be created for individual industries. A market-oriented response should lead to the survival of the most competitive domestic producers (assuming that demand has not disappeared altogether), but the transition costs may be quite high. This is particularly true if there is substantial excess capacity in the industry: weaker firms may cut prices below the rate at which any firms can survive in the long term in a desperate attempt to win business. The weeding out process may also facilitate the development of monopolies and oligopolies in the industry.

The protectionist response to industrial decline is quite different, involving efforts to preserve existing industry structure and employment levels, often by limiting competition from foreign producers and domestic and foreign substitutes through tariffs and "orderly marketing agreements" (import quotas). Governments may also provide direct assistance for capital and operating purposes, either through subsidy programs or government takeover. In some cases, protectionist responses are defended as temporary measures to help ease financial crises, allowing industries time to make an orderly adjustment instead of being overwhelmed by economic dislocation—for example, the voluntary restrictions imposed in 1981 on Japanese autos imported to the United States.[12] Once in place, however, protectionist programs become difficult to remove, as the groups that benefit from them (especially those likely to suffer most from eventual adjustment) develop a stake in their continuation. Pressure mounts for an expansion of the program's scope, as in the extension of textile agreements to additional fabrics and exporting countries,[13] or for an increase in the severity of restrictions, as in proposals for "domestic content requirements" for foreign auto manufacturers in the United States and Canada.

It is in the declining phase of an industry's life cycle that the differences between protectionist and accelerationist policies are clearest. Whereas protectionist policies seek to preserve the status quo as much as possible, accelerationist policies seek to speed the exit of noncompetitive firms and workers, thus making what remains of the industry more competitive. Japan's Structurally Depressed Industries Law of 1978, for example, allows industries designated "structurally depressed" to be ex-

12. Jose A. Gomez-Ibanez, Robert A. Leone, and Stephen A. O'Connell, "Restraining Auto Imports: Does Anyone Win?" *Journal of Policy Analysis and Management,* vol 2, no. 2 (1983), pp. 196–219.

13. See Vinod K. Aggarwal, "The Politics of Protection in the U.S. Textile and Apparel Industries," in Zysman and Tyson, eds., *American Industry in International Competition,* pp. 249–312.

empted from Japan's antimonopoly law in implementing capacity-scrapping agreements developed and sponsored by the appropriate government ministry; government credit is also available, although it is generally limited to smaller, less diversified firms least able to finance adjustment themselves.[14]

Evaluating Industrial Policy

Because so many different policy options have been labeled industrial policy it is particularly important that any attempt to evaluate them specify clearly what standards are being employed. This study uses three criteria for a successful industrial policy. First, as suggested earlier, it must be *accelerationist*, promoting economic growth through industrial adjustment even where this means "progressively giving away industries to other countries much as a big brother gives his out-grown clothes to his younger brother."[15] This principle does not preclude aid to declining firms or to displaced workers, but it does require that the aid be designed to promote their exit from markets where they are no longer competitive. Excluding protectionist policy from the definition of successful adjustment policy provides a clearer and higher standard for policy success. Virtually all economists agree that protection can be carried out through import quotas, subsidies, tariffs, and entry controls. Most agree that its overall impact on the economy is negative: dollars invested unproductively are not available for investment in emerging industries, and dollars spent subsidizing operating losses are not available for other job-producing consumer purchases.

Second, a successful industrial policy must be *selective*, picking winners and losers. To put it more bluntly, policy must be able to discriminate among industries and firms. Assistance to growing industries will be given only to firms with the best prospects for survival rather than to all applicants that meet preestablished criteria. Investment tax credits, for example, are market-oriented rather than accelerationist policies: they encourage investment and thus may be particularly helpful

14. General Accounting Office, *Industrial Policy: Japan's Flexible Approach*, Report ID-82-32 (GAO, 1982), pp. 66–77.

15. Y. Ojimi, Japan's vice minister of international trade and industry, quoted in Ira C. Magaziner and Thomas M. Hout, *Japanese Industrial Policy* (University of California at Berkeley, Institute for International Studies, 1981), p. 6.

to investment-intensive industries, but they do not direct investment with precision to specific industries that need help or to firms most likely to use capital efficiently.

Targeting assistance successfully requires both expertise and autonomy on the part of program administrators. Even industry-specific programs may be counterproductive if they prolong the life of dying firms, thus weakening the position of others that are more competitive. Moreover, accelerationist policies can easily be subverted into protectionist policies during implementation (for example, by distributing ostensibly selective incentives to all or most of the firms within an industry instead of to those that are most viable).

Finally, a successful industrial policy must be *nimble*—that is, it must be able to change as the life cycle of an industry changes. Government promotional assistance through grants, loans, and tariff assistance may be helpful in an industry's infancy, but it makes little sense as an industry approaches maturity and begins to decline. The goals of financial assistance in a declining industry should be very different from those in the first phase. A successful industrial policy should encourage exit of noncompetitive firms and of employees. Because this life cycle may occur very quickly (less than thirty years in the case of Japanese shipbuilding),[16] government must be able to respond just as quickly.

Industrial policy should also be nimble in anticipating and guiding change rather than merely reacting to it once the financial crisis has occurred. This requires, at a minimum, a permanent and very expert monitoring agency. Moreover, a successful industrial policy must be nimble in yet another sense: able to intervene and not to intervene. When market mechanisms are capable of promoting industrial adjustment without government intervention, or when intervention is no longer required, accelerationist policy would suggest that government withdraw. Although accelerationist policy almost certainly requires a constant planning capability, it definitely does not require constant intervention. Because accelerationist intervention is intermittent rather than constant, adjustment goals are likely to get less attention from policymakers than public needs goals. Adjustment tasks may be assigned to the institutions already administering policies to deal with public needs goals; these institutions may not be well adapted to industrial adjustment

16. Magaziner and Hout, *Japanese Industrial Policy*, pp. 67–71.

tasks and may even be hostile to such policies where they conflict with their current mission.

Constraints on Accelerating Industrial Adjustment

In this section a general analytical framework for examining the politics of industrial adjustment is developed; specific political systems are then considered to see how the constraints on industrial adjustment operate in practice.

The level of involvement by various interests in the formation of sectoral policies is heavily influenced by the *distribution of costs and benefits*. When the impact of a proposed action is substantial and highly concentrated, the affected interests are much more likely to organize successfully than when impacts are relatively small and highly diffused.[17] These groups thus have the incentive and the capability to impose diffused losses on the rest of society. Table 1-2 outlines the probable distribution of costs and benefits under each of the three adjustment policy options outlined in this chapter. Market-oriented policies are likely to have relatively diffuse impacts until an adjustment crisis occurs;

17. James Q. Wilson, *The Politics of Regulation* (Basic Books, 1980), chap. 10. Two additional factors modify the impact of cost-benefit distributions: the certainty and visibility of costs and benefits, and the distribution of resources.

In the sunrise phase of an industry, some competitors will fall by the wayside. Their precise identity is not likely to be clear in the early stages of competition, however. An accelerationist sectoral policy may change that situation: if government chooses to support a single "national champion" as a strong competitor in the international marketplace, anonymous losers may become identifiable ones with a substantial stake in blocking government's choice. In a declining industry, the importance of certainty and visibility is manifested somewhat differently. An accelerationist strategy promotes exit of capital and labor, and a preservationist policy bolsters the status quo. In the short term, an accelerationist strategy produces few visible benefits, while protectionist policy retains production and employment; yet the short-term government outlays for the former strategy may be higher than for the latter. Unless policymakers are capable of taking a long-term perspective, the temptation to produce visible benefits with expenditures is likely to be overwhelming.

Groups may sustain concentrated impacts by an industrial policy decision but have few resources to influence its outcome, and hence be ignored. If a few large and powerful firms have a monopoly on political influence, they may be able to impose all the costs on weaker firms, thus forcing their exit. If political resources are widely distributed among those with a concentrated stake in adjustment decisions, it will be much more difficult to change the status quo; protectionist policies are the likely result.

Table 1-2. *Costs and Benefits of Industrial Adjustment Policies*

Benefits and costs	Policies		
	Market-oriented	Protectionist	Accelerationist
Concentrated benefits	. . .	Firms stay in business; workers retain jobs.	Firms gain selective government assistance.
Diffuse benefits	Consumers benefit through lower costs of more efficient industry.	. . .	Consumers benefit through lower costs of more efficient industry.
Concentrated costs	Firms forced out of market; workers lose jobs.	Customers pay higher prices (if very dependent on product and unable to pass on higher costs to final consumers).	Firms forced out of market; workers lose jobs.
Diffuse costs	. . .	Consumers pay higher prices; taxpayers bear costs of subsidies.	Taxpayers bear costs if transitional assistance is given.

then reliance on market mechanisms will probably result in heavy losses by some firms and workers. Protectionist policies, on the other hand, generally provide something for all firms in an industry, and for their employees, while diffusing costs among consumers, suppliers, and taxpayers. Thus unless one of these latter interests also has a major, concentrated stake (for example, if the customers of the industry are a price-sensitive oligopsony), protectionist coalitions are likely to dominate industrial adjustment decisions.

Clearly, it is easier to build coalitions of support for protectionist policies than for accelerationist ones. Accelerationist policies create both concentrated winners and losers: some firms and workers will have their prospects improved, while others may be forced out of the marketplace. Accelerationist policies may be somewhat easier to achieve in an industry's growth phase than in later phases. In the sunrise phase, the stakes in adjustment disputes are not so high. Those not receiving government assistance (for example, research and development funding) may survive anyway. In an industry's declining phase, government is likely to confront many losers facing significant adjustment costs. Most governments are reluctant to allocate losses directly. Such actions will

Table 1-3. *Industrial Policy Options and the Distribution of Costs and Benefits*

Costs	Benefits	
	Concentrated	Diffuse
Concentrated	STALEMATE:	REJECTION:
	Some protectionist policies (where consumers' interests are concentrated).	Most accelerationist policies.
	Some accelerationist policies (where selective assistance is granted).	Market-oriented policies (during adjustment crisis).
Diffuse	ADOPTION:	GOVERNMENT HAS AUTONOMY
	Most protectionist policies.	IN MAKING CHOICE:
		Market-oriented policies (in the absence of an adjustment crisis).

gain them few friends no matter who the losers turn out to be. Even the Japanese have not proved as adept at promoting adjustment in mature and declining industries as in growing ones. Repeated efforts by Japan's Ministry of International Trade and Industry (MITI) to consolidate Japanese auto and truck manufacturers into a few firms in the late 1960s largely failed.[18] Efforts to promote consolidation and adjustment in declining industries such as aluminum and shipbuilding have also encountered substantial resistance from Japanese firms.[19]

Table 1-3 outlines the probable impact of cost-benefit distributions on the industrial adjustment decisions governments make. Consider first the lower righthand cell. In the absence of an adjustment crisis, both costs and benefits are highly diffused, and pressures for sector-specific solutions are relatively weak. Thus governments are likely to have substantial autonomy in policy choice, and market-oriented policies tend to prevail. Although incentives to seek protectionist policy will still exist for firms and workers within an industry, they may not be able to overcome conflicts within the industry over the distribution of protective benefits or government opposition to protective policies. But an adjustment crisis raises the policy stakes and reduces government autonomy. In which direction will policy move? Both market-oriented and accelerationist policies are likely to be stalemated or rejected outright because

18. Magaziner and Hout, *Japanese Industrial Policy*, pp. 59–63.
19. Ibid., chap. 5.

they impose concentrated costs on part or all of the industry. Protectionist policies, which generally provide concentrated benefits and diffuse costs, are the usual result. Once in place, a protectionist regime is extremely difficult to dismantle, since many elements of a protected industry have a vested interest in the status quo. Renewed competition could force weaker firms out of the market. A return to the lower righthand cell is unlikely once government has undertaken a protectionist response to an adjustment crisis.

Compensation schemes for those interests suffering concentrated losses can lower the barriers to acceptance of acceleration policy, especially in an industry's declining phase when the problems of losers are particularly severe. But such agreements are difficult to negotiate.[20] Successful negotiation is likely to depend upon the number of affected interests. If there are only a few of these groups in a stalemate situation, it will be much easier to develop a satisfactory scheme than when there are many opponents. Thus if a government wishes to create a single national champion in the computer industry where there have been two or three firms, the negotiation and compensation task is a relatively simple one. Attempting to rationalize a textile industry with many firms that differ widely in size, technology, and interests is much more complex.

Even more important in limiting adoption of loss diffusing accelerationist compensation schemes is the possibility of obtaining a "superior"

20. In compensation arrangements, the level of benefits and who will pay are crucial. If compensation is low, the losers will object; if compensation is high, who will pay will become critical. The "winners" (that is, firms remaining in the industry) could pay, but they will object to bearing all the costs, particularly in declining industries where the total gains to winners from exit by weaker competitors are smaller than the losses the losers endure. Governments, too, may object to bearing compensation costs. These problems are less likely for schemes that diffuse compensation costs more broadly, but problems exist nonetheless. A program for collecting and dispensing compensation payments would certainly require government sanction to allow negotiation of an agreement free of antitrust constraints and to compel universal participation (for example, through a tax on sales of remaining firms). Without compulsion, such a program would be doomed by free-rider problems among the winners. Nonparticipating firms could undercut competitors' prices by the amount of the tax and thus expand unit sales. Nor would it be easy to reach agreement on a compensation formula in industries with a variety of firms and workers in different situations, and differing perceptions of their own long-term prospects. Some firms have an interest in strategic bargaining to improve their share of compensation; others might be better off without any agreement, and hence would have no incentive to negotiate in good faith at all. The problem would be particularly severe if near unanimity was required for adoption of the program.

(from the industry's point of view) alternative: protectionist arrangements.[21] Such arrangements—cartelization, for example—try to preserve existing competitive relationships. Most forms of protection do not require complicated compensation arrangements; they are simply reflected in higher prices to consumers. Hence, they are more likely to win broad support among producers.

Political Structures in Policy Choice

The uneven distribution of societal costs and benefits almost always favors adherents of a protectionist policy. Why then don't protectionists win consistently? Part of the answer is to be found in *government preferences* for sectoral policies, a factor often ignored in the literature on U.S. politics. Government institutions are not mere cyphers, registering the balance of societal interests or, even worse, being captured by the most powerful pressure groups among their clientele. Their interests certainly may differ from those of private sector groups. Indeed, they may prevail over societal opposition, particularly when societal interests are stalemated.[22]

Government-industry divergence is particularly likely when firms seek a competitive advantage through government policy or expect government to bear the compensation costs for accelerationist or protectionist policy. Firms seek special tax advantages; government guards the tax base. Industries favor special tariffs or import restrictions; government is wary of retaliatory restrictions by their trading partners. Industries may desire subsidies; government wants to control spending. In each case, industry interests are concentrated, while government interests are relatively small. When viewed cumulatively, however, the interests governments have in preserving their tax base, controlling spending, and maintaining free trade are considerable. Giving in on one set of demands often leads to a rush of further demands. Thus governments develop strategies and procedures that are designed to maintain

21. Protectionist arrangements will not be viewed as superior by all interests. Very marginal producers who are unlikely to survive even with protection would be better off taking whatever compensation they can and exiting. But protectionist solutions are likely to gain approval from a broader array of producers than accelerationist ones.

22. Eric Nordlinger, *On the Autonomy of the Democratic State* (Harvard University Press, 1981); and Steven Krasner, *Defending the National Interest: Raw Materials Investments and U.S. Foreign Policy* (Princeton University Press, 1978), chap. 1.

general rules free from exceptions. Their best response to demands for protection of specific sectors is likely to be a market-oriented response. Groups respond by building broader log-rolling coalitions of individual interests to force their views on governments.

The difficulties in attempting to impose change and pick winners and losers make it unlikely that government will be able to implement, or even attempt, accelerationist policies unless it is able to *compel agreement* when confronted by societal or intragovernmental opposition. Political systems differ in the extent to which consensus is required to arrive at a decision. Systems with multiple veto points may reach a stalemate even when the interests suffering concentrated costs are heavily outweighed by those obtaining concentrated benefits. Other systems offer their government leaders substantial latitude to impose their own wishes, even over concentrated societal opposition. Only in this latter case are accelerationist policies likely.

For a democratic government to be able to carry out policies that impose concentrated costs and diffuse benefits on a regular basis, three attributes must exist concurrently: (1) united government with few veto points, (2) substantial bureaucratic autonomy and expertise, and (3) strong government mechanisms to compel compliance. But these characteristics are in short supply, especially in Canada and the United States, the focus of this study.

United Government

Systems with multiple veto points make it easier for losers to block policy initiatives that would impose costs on them. The U.S. system, for example, offers cost bearers—at least those with some political resources—maximum opportunity to halt such initiatives. Policy can be blocked in a congressional subcommittee, full committee, on the floor of the House or Senate, or in a House-Senate conference committee; it can be vetoed by the president, and it can be challenged by the courts. Moreover, the weakness of legislative parties in Congress requires the construction of separate coalitions for most decisions.[23] Not only does this make passing legislation difficult, but it also increases pressures to

23. See Barbara Sinclair, "Coping with Uncertainty: Building Coalitions in the House and the Senate," in Thomas Mann and Norman Ornstein, eds., *The New Congress* (Washington, D.C.: American Enterprise Institute for Public Policy Research, 1981), pp. 178–220.

distribute benefits widely in order to build winning coalitions. The classic example is the Model Cities program, which was originally intended to pour large sums into a few areas, but ended up promising a much broader dispersal of funds to gain congressional passage in 1966. Multiple veto points may provide a barrier against protectionist outcomes, however: if proponents of such policies cannot assemble a winning coalition at each stage of the policy adoption process, market-oriented policies may survive by default.

Stable parliamentary majorities (either single parties or coalitions) offer fewer veto points to cost bearers and may be able to target benefits more efficiently within individual programs, so long as the benefits provided by all government programs are distributed broadly enough to maintain their support. Although, in theory, parliamentary institutions offer substantial advantages for developing and implementing accelerationist policies, these advantages often go unrealized. Governing parties in parliamentary systems cannot easily escape blame for policy outcomes during their administration, even if those outcomes result from events beyond their control. Thus they will be very reluctant to impose overt concentrated losses. Indeed, one of the most blatant cases of protection in response to sectoral decline can be found in Japan, which has a parliamentary system and is generally considered a paragon of industrial policy. In the Japanese agricultural sector, the ruling Liberal Democratic party has used heavy price supports and import restrictions to protect its rural voting base; consumer prices have risen as a result. Although there has been a rapid shift of workers to other sectors, "government policy has, if anything, served to keep resources in agriculture rather than assisting directly in the long-run process of shifting these resources to more efficient uses elsewhere."[24]

Bureaucratic Autonomy and Expertise

More than a unified government is needed to implement policies that impose concentrated costs and diffuse benefits. Autonomy, a prerequisite for quick and quiet action, and expertise, without which selective targeting is impossible, are also required. Bureaucracies are more likely to have these qualities than are legislatures. Indeed, one of the primary

---

24. Hugh Patrick and Henry Rosovsky, "Japan's Economic Performance: An Overview," in Patrick and Rosovsky, eds., *Asia's New Giant: How the Japanese Economy Works* (Brookings, 1976), p. 46, and also see pp. 40–41.

advantages of parliamentary systems in carrying out industrial policy is that they generally lead to executive dominance in policymaking. For an accelerationist adjustment policy to succeed, bureaucracies must have resources to arrive at positions distinct from those of the weightiest societal actors and to force those decisions upon recalcitrant actors. Intermittent attention to sectoral problems at times of financial crisis is not enough; the goal of industrial policy is to avoid such crises. Thus governments must maintain a highly competent sectoral planning capability, even when intervention is not required. Independent decision-making requires bureaucratic expertise and freedom from constant intervention by other branches of government.

Bureaucrats in the United States are constrained—especially in committing program funds—not only by detailed requirements in authorizing legislation but also by appropriations act language, committee reports, and even legislative "colloquies" that make up part of the program's legislative history and earmark funds for specific (often highly protectionist) purposes. Although Canadian bureaucrats do not face these obstacles, they confront others, notably lobbying by individual ministers and provincial governments or intervention by the cabinet in decisions with strong location-specific consequences. Indeed, the Canadian federal system legitimizes such intervention. In addition to their regular departmental duties, some cabinet members are supposed to serve as the watchdogs of the interests of specific provinces or regions.

In Canada, a federal governmental structure and intense regional conflicts inhibit the bureaucratic autonomy needed to implement accelerationist policies in several other ways. Provincial jurisdiction over key economic sectors (notably natural resources) limits what the federal government can do without negotiating with the provinces, which may have interests very different from Ottawa's and each other's. Moreover, industry locations (for example, grains in the Prairies, autos in Ontario and Quebec, fisheries in the Maritime provinces) have a very strong regional basis, so industrial adjustment decisions are charged with the rhetoric of regional conflict. Governing parties at the federal level are reluctant to undertake adjustment actions that will alienate regional support, even when it is within their jurisdiction to do so. The stronger provincial governments (Ontario and Quebec, for example) may undertake industrial promotion activities directly at variance with Ottawa's.[25]

---

25. On federal-provincial conflict in industrial policy, see Michael Jenkin, *The Challenge of Diversity: Industrial Policy in the Canadian Confederation* (Ottawa:

Conflict over regional inequities has led Ottawa to devote substantial federal resources—through the Department of Regional Economic Expansion (DREE) and its successors—to encouraging firms to locate in underdeveloped areas distant from major markets, despite the fact that such plants are likely to confront substantial competitive disadvantages. In short, where regional impacts are highly concentrated, Canada's federal government, like that of the United States, will have great difficulties imposing costs.

Mechanisms to Compel Compliance

Most policy decisions are not self-implementing. Thus governments are most likely to succeed in enforcing adjustment policies that impose concentrated costs when there are strong penalties for noncompliance. Governments that exercise substantial control over credit through ownership of the banking system, for example, are in a better position to force firms and workers to agree to an adjustment plan. France (through bank ownership) and Japan (through its Fiscal Investment and Loan Program and loans to major banks through the Bank of Japan) have such control; neither the United States nor Canada does. Government ownership of all or part of an industry is an even more obvious form of direct control. But foreign ownership is likely to minimize the ability of government to compel compliance, especially when the subsidiary is expected to conform its plans to that of the multinational parent. This limitation is particularly acute in Canada, where a majority of both the manufacturing and energy sectors are controlled by foreign (mostly U.S.) firms.

The Role of Historical Development

The concurrent development of united government, an autonomous and expert bureaucracy, and strong government mechanisms of control over the economy does not occur overnight; these attributes are the result of a long process of historical development very different from that of either the United States or Canada. They are found primarily in late developing societies where a strong executive and a relatively concentrated group of industrialists have responded to perceived foreign

Science Council of Canada, 1983); and Alan Tupper, *Public Money in the Private Sector: Industrial Assistance Policy and Canadian Federalism* (Kingston, Ont.: Queen's University, Institute of Intergovernmental Relations, 1982).

threats (for example, in Japan and pre–World War II Germany). The dependence of industrialists on the state for capital and permission to enter specific markets leads them to accept more guidance from bureaucrats than would their counterparts in the early developing countries. In the United States, on the other hand, democratic institutions—more specifically, institutions that identified democracy with government limited by a complex system of checks and balances—emerged before the development of a national administrative apparatus and in large measure as a protest against the increasing power of the British imperial state.[26]

It is very doubtful that countries that follow a different development path can ever acquire the institutional characteristics needed to carry out accelerationist policy consistently. Legislatures and businessmen are unlikely to sacrifice their independence. Simply adding new bureaucracies—even extremely competent ones—or new mechanisms of economic control without the other political structures needed to impose concentrated costs usually leads to more costly protectionist outcomes rather than to an acceleration of industrial adjustment.

Comparative Advantage in Industrial Policy Choice

The argument that political system characteristics have a significant and systematic impact on industrial policy choice can be carried another step: political system characteristics may give some governments a comparative advantage in the conduct of some government activities and policies, while putting other governments at a comparative disadvantage. Classical economic theory teaches that when two countries face differing conditions of production for a range of goods, they should specialize in the goods they can produce most efficiently relative to their trading partners and purchase the rest abroad. Clearly, the same is not true for government activities because they generally are not tradable; the U.S. government is not likely to concentrate on space exploration and water projects and contract out social welfare activities to the Swedes. But governments have other alternatives, notably the option of

26. See Steven Skowronek, *Building a New American State: The Expansion of National Administrative Capacities, 1877–1920* (Cambridge: Cambridge University Press, 1982).

refusing to engage in some activities or of developing substitutes that can be produced relatively efficiently.

If, as the argument in the previous section suggests, the United States is an inefficient producer of accelerationist policies and alternative methods of promoting industrial adjustment exist, the United States would be better off specializing in those alternatives. But do alternatives exist? Clearly, protectionist policies are not an acceptable alternative; they delay adjustment rather than encourage it. Market-oriented policies promote adjustment, but in a market-failure situation that adjustment may be slower and more costly than successful accelerationist policies.

The key word here is *successful*. Accelerationist policies are helpful only if they are efficiently applied and are not subverted to become protectionist. Even the proponents of an activist U.S. industrial policy admit that the United States has a long way to go to reach that point. Their argument in favor of trying, however, is analogous to the "infant industry" arguments. An activist industrial policy may lead to short-term inefficiencies, but, they contend, these will disappear as the government develops competence in making industrial policy decisions. In the long run society will be better off having developed this capability. If these barriers cannot be overcome, however, the U.S. comparative disadvantage in pursuing accelerationist policies is likely to be permanent. The argument in this chapter that stable political structures resulting from long historical development are the determinant of industrial policy capability offers little support to the advocates of accelerationist policy in the United States.

The Canadian dilemma is even more unpleasant. The structure of the Canadian economy—high dependence on resource exports, a small domestic market, substantial foreign ownership of industry—makes a market-oriented policy less attractive in Canada than in the United States. But the political barriers to a successful accelerationist policy are, if anything, stronger in Canada. In both countries the economic slowdown following the 1973–74 oil embargo has strengthened demands for sector-specific policies, but in neither country have there been changes in political structure that would promote accelerationist rather than protectionist intervention.

CHAPTER TWO

Adjustment Policy in the North American Rail Industry

SECTORAL policies reflect the difficulties governments have in imposing overt, concentrated losses on domestic groups. Only political structures that allow governments to compel acceptance of those losses are likely to succeed in imposing accelerationist policies. These constraints on industrial adjustment policy described in the previous chapter are clearly present in the North American railroad industry.

The rail sector offers an excellent arena for a comparative examination of industrial adjustment policy and public enterprise in the United States and Canada. Governments in both countries have intervened in their rail industries almost from the beginning of railway development, and the policies have paralleled each other in timing and general direction. Nevertheless, there have been important differences, both in specifics of policy and in instrument choice.

Of course, narrowing the scope of discussion to a single industry has disadvantages as well as advantages. Most notably, the reader must be convinced that the case is not idiosyncratic but generally applicable. Choice of the rail industry case magnifies this problem, for most of the writing on industrial policy focuses on internationally competitive industries such as steel, automobiles, and semiconductors. The U.S. and Canadian rail industries are involved in international competition only to a limited degree, although they face substantial competition from other modes of transportation in most markets. But there is little reason to believe that the difficulties in promoting adaptation are intrinsically different in industries facing international competition from those that do not. Moreover, the same domestic conflicts—those involving competing firms in the industry, suppliers, customers, labor, and communities affected by locational decisions—will arise regardless of international competition. The adjustment crises of the U.S. and Canadian rail industries have posed the central challenge of industrial adjustment policy: if, when, and how to impose the concentrated costs of sectoral change—repeatedly and in very stark form.

Rail policy in both countries has gone through four partially overlapping phases that reflect distinctive adjustment problems in the growth, maturity, and declining stages of the industry. In the first phase, roughly the 1820s to the 1870s in the United States and from the 1840s to 1920 in Canada, the two governments were concerned primarily with providing financial assistance for railway development. Various mechanisms were used to promote industrial growth, including land grants, loans and loan guarantees, subsidies, and (primarily in Canada) public enterprise and public works.[1] Competition among the railways, abetted by insufficiently selective government assistance programs, led to overcapacity problems, particularly in Canada, which in 1917 had more than twice as many railway miles per capita as the United States.[2] Moreover, some of the Canadian lines constructed in response to regional pressures (notably the Hudson Bay Railway) could not be expected to earn a profit in the foreseeable future. In the United States, on the other hand, government aid to the railways was given with the expectation that those carriers would not be indefinitely dependent on the public purse.[3]

As the rail industry in the two countries approached maturity, government policy increasingly was directed at stabilizing the industry. In this second phase, roughly from 1880 to 1930, the major issues in

1. The locus and extent of development assistance differed in the two countries, however. States played the leading role in the United States. Federal aid was concentrated in the period from 1850 to 1873 and was given overwhelmingly in the form of land grants. Total public aid represented roughly 30 percent of railway investment before the Civil War but no more than 15 percent (excluding land grants) between 1861 and 1873, and a negligible share thereafter. See Carter Goodrich, *Government Promotion of American Canals and Railroads, 1800–1890* (Columbia University Press, 1960), pp. 270–71; and Frank Wilner, "History and Evolution of Railroad Land Grants," *ICC Practioners' Journal*, vol. 48 (September–October 1981), pp. 687–99. In Canada, government assistance (including loans and loan guarantees but excluding land grants) totaled more than 40 percent of railway capitalization by 1916. The federal government contributed about three-quarters of promotional assistance, although less for loan guarantees. Government-operated lines comprised about 15 percent of railway capitalization, a figure with no counterpart in the United States. See *Railway Statistics of the Dominion of Canada, 1916* (Ottawa: King's Printer, 1917).

2. Royal Commission to Inquire into Railways and Transportation in Canada, *Report* (Ottawa: King's Printer, 1917), pp. ix–x.

3. Carter Goodrich, "The Revulsion against Internal Improvements," *Journal of Economic History*, vol. 10 (November 1950), pp. 145–69.

railway politics were competition and rates, and the major concern of the U.S. and Canadian governments was mediation of the competing interests of shippers and carriers. Alleged monopoly abuses by carriers concerned shippers, and the railways feared that excessive competition would threaten their earnings. The two governments sought to simultaneously provide competition and reasonable rates to shippers and an adequate rate of return to the railways by regulating railway rates, entry, and exit.[4] In addition, Ottawa responded to rate grievances of developing regions with special statutory arrangements, most notably the "Crow's Nest Pass" rates. This legislation held rates on grain shipped to Pacific and Lakehead ports to the levels prevailing in 1899. As price levels rose, the statutory grain rates required substantial cross-subsidy by the railways.[5]

This chapter focuses on the third and fourth phases of railroad policy. After 1930, the railways faced repeated crises and decline brought on by technological change and increasing competition from other modes of transportation. When confronted by these adjustment crises, both gov-

---

4. In the United States, rate regulation began at the state level. The power of state regulatory commissions was effectively destroyed, however, by the Supreme Court decision in *Wabash* v. *Illinois,* 118 U.S. 557 (1886). This decision removed the state commissions' power to regulate traffic in interstate commerce. The Interstate Commerce Act of 1887 established a federal regulatory presence, but it was ambiguous on how much power the new Interstate Commerce Commission (ICC) should have over rates. Supreme Court decisions in the 1890s limited the ICC's powers. The powers of the commission were strengthened by the Hepburn Act (1906), which gave the ICC authority to set a "just and reasonable" maximum rate, and by the Mann-Elkins Act (1910), which allowed the ICC to suspend rate increases proposed by the railroads pending an investigation. The Transportation Act of 1920 (the Esch-Cummins Act) gave the ICC authority to set minimum rates and limited entry into the rail industry by requiring a certificate of public convenience and necessity for all but the smallest extensions of rail properties. For contrasting views of the origins of federal rail regulation, see Gabriel Kolko, *Railroads and Regulation, 1877–1916* (W.W. Norton, 1965); and Robert W. Harbeson, "Railroads and Regulation, 1887–1916: Conspiracy or Public Interest," *Journal of Economic History,* vol. 27 (June 1967), pp. 230–42.

Rate regulation in Canada began in 1896 in response to shippers' complaints. The task of regulation was first assigned to a cabinet committee, then in 1903 to an independent Board of Railway (later Transport) Commissioners.

5. For a detailed history of the Crow's Nest Pass rates, see A.W. Currie, *Canadian Transportation Economics* (University of Toronto Press, 1967), chap. 4. Canada's Maritime provinces and eastern Quebec benefit from special railway rate arrangements through the Maritime Freight Rates Act of 1927 (MFRA). The Atlantic Region Freight Assistance Act of 1969 (ARFA) extended the subsidy to common carrier truckers. See Howard Darling, *The Politics of Freight Rates* (Toronto: McClelland and Stewart, 1982); and Currie, *Canadian Transportation Economics,* chap. 5.

ernments initially responded with policies designed to preserve the status quo and to diffuse and disguise losses ("protection"). After substantial conflict and debate, however, these policies were partially replaced (beginning in the 1960s in Canada and the 1970s in the United States) by a fourth phase of federal policy that attempts to accommodate change through market mechanisms ("deregulation"). Nevertheless, many protectionist rather than market-oriented policies persist. Neither country has employed accelerationist policies with much success. The concluding section of this chapter attempts to explain why.

The Challenge of Industrial Change

By the mid-1920s, major differences had emerged in the structure of the U.S. and Canadian rail industries. With some modifications, they remain today. The private-sector Canadian Pacific Railway (CP) and federally owned Canadian National Railways (CN) control about 90 percent of the rail market in Canada. Both firms operate on a transcontinental basis and control subsidiaries operating in other transport modes. The U.S. rail industry was and is far more fragmented. Despite several waves of rail mergers, more than twenty large (Class I) railway systems remain.[6] Truly national carriers emerged only in the 1980s. Because about half of all rail shipments in the United States are interlined (carried by two or more railroads before reaching their destination), carriers must simultaneously compete and cooperate.[7] U.S. rail operations were almost entirely in the private sector until the 1970s, except for the Alaska Railroad and a few tiny municipal railways. Until very recently, railways in the United States have been barred from purchasing firms in competing transport modes.[8]

6. There were a total of 32 Class I railways in 1983, but several of them (for example, Union Pacific, Missouri Pacific, and Western Pacific) were under common ownership. In addition to these carriers, there were 26 smaller (Class II) line-haul railways, 270 still smaller (Class III) line-haul railways, and about 142 switching and terminal railways. See American Association of Railroads, *Railroad Facts, 1983 Edition*.

7. On the impact of concurrent railroad interdependence and competition, see Task Force on Railroad Productivity, *Improving Railroad Productivity* (Washington, D.C.: The Task Force, 1973), chap. 8.

8. Railways were, however, allowed to retain trucking operations they held when the ban on further purchases was imposed in 1935.

Sources of Decline

The differences in rail industry structure in the United States and Canada have affected both policy challenges and governmental responses. Nevertheless, the rail industries in the two countries have been buffeted by common economic and political forces, and government policy has exhibited some striking parallels. The first two phases of rail policy in North America reflect the emergence and maturation of railroad dominance in inland transportation. The third, protectionist phase (roughly 1933 to 1967 in Canada and 1933 to 1976 in the United States)[9] developed as a response to the eclipse of this dominance and to the growing influence of rail labor. The traditional conflicts between shippers and carriers continued. Indeed, labor's demands and the growth of intermodal competition made their resolution all the more difficult. Policymakers sought to reconcile the goals of preserving rail service and employment and maintaining the financial health of carriers, while keeping financial assistance to the industry at a minimum.

The development of new transport technologies simply outmoded railways as a carrier for many types of traffic just as rail had outmoded the early canals. Most passengers traveling short distances (including commuters) preferred the more convenient automobile and the lower cost bus; those going long distances, automobiles and airlines. The railways were not able to pass on the rising costs of passenger-train service as the number of riders declined. In freight markets, water carriers cut into the movement of bulk commodities by rail, while increasing reliance on petroleum and natural gas (which move primarily by pipeline) disrupted the railways' market for coal transportation. Trucks generally offered lower costs and superior service for less-than-carload and short-haul traffic.

In both Canada and the United States, the railways grew less able to support the extensive system of cross-subsidies nurtured by government regulation as their highest rated (that is, high value per weight) traffic was diverted to other modes of transportation (primarily trucks). The financial decline of the railways has been furthered by government promotion of rival forms of transportation: airlines through mail contracts, below-cost air traffic control, subsidies for airport construction,

---

9. The end dates represent the first major movement away from protectionist policies. Many of these policies are still in effect.

and research and development spending on military aircraft; barge carriers, through spending on river and canal construction and maintenance by the Army Corps of Engineers; and ocean shipping, through joint Canadian-U.S. assistance for the St. Lawrence Seaway. Highway carriers and automobile owners also benefit from government provision of infrastructure, financed largely through user fees. Moreover, railways must build and maintain their tracks as a fixed cost, subject to property taxation. Other transport modes do not have this obligation for their traffic corridors.

Technological change within the rail industry posed problems on the labor front. The introduction of diesel locomotives and higher capacity freight cars allowed carriers to operate longer and heavier trains and lengthened the distance between stops for servicing. Automation of train-control and clerical operations further reduced manpower requirements, as did rail mergers in the United States. The lines in the conflict were clear: rail management worked to maximize productivity gains; rail labor unions fought to save their members' jobs. Technological improvements also increased the industry's excess capacity problems: more traffic could be carried on fewer lines, and the continued operation of redundant carriers lowered profitability for all. The fragmentation of the U.S. rail industry made the overcapacity problem particularly severe for main-line trackage. By the late 1970s, for example, eight carriers still competed for traffic between Chicago and Kansas City, and five between Chicago and the Twin Cities.

The low level of railway earnings created incentives for railroad companies to diversify into other fields and to disinvest (by not purchasing new track and equipment and deferring maintenance on existing capital stock) in railway operations. Although railroad managers in both countries reinvested more in rail operations than a profit-maximizing strategy would call for, their investments were skewed toward rolling stock (that is, locomotives and cars), which could serve as security for borrowing, over fixed plant. And the routes that individual railroads found most attractive for investment in fixed plant often were those where there was substantial excess capacity when viewed on an industry-wide basis.[10]

10. On railway investment and diversification in Canada and the United States, see Julius Lukasiewicz, *The Railway Game* (Toronto: McClelland and Stewart, 1976), chap. 8; Robert Chodos, *The CPR: A Century of Corporate Welfare* (Toronto: James Lewis and Samuel, 1973), chaps. 7 and 9; Douglas Caves and Laurits Christensen, *Productivity*

Policy Options for Industrial Change

The decline of the rail industry confronted the U.S. and Canadian governments with difficult choices. Preservation of some unprofitable services might have been justified on "public needs" grounds—for example, the costs to society of going without them outweigh the costs of providing them, although users are unable or unwilling to bear the full costs. Commuter rail service in high density markets, which can save fuel, reduce land required for highways and downtown parking, and lower air pollution, is an example. A first task for the two governments, then, was to determine which unprofitable services could be justified as socially necessary and which could not, and to develop a mechanism for financing the former without bankrupting the carriers. Given the weakened capability of the railways to engage in cross-subsidization, this almost inevitably required direct subsidies.

A second and closely related task was deciding how to help the industry adjust its structure to new technology and patterns of consumer demand. Specifically, the choice was among accelerating industrial adjustment, permitting it to occur without interference, or preserving the status quo as much as possible. Table 2-1 outlines the implications of the market-oriented, protectionist, and accelerationist positions for a variety of regulatory and government assistance decisions. The protectionist position recognizes that some operations are profitable and others are not, but it suggests using cross-subsidy within the industry or government operating assistance to preserve existing firms and levels of service and employment. The standard for making such decisions is the status quo rather than a planned industrial structure most consistent with public needs and industrial self-sufficiency. The distinction between public needs and industrial adjustment policies is thus blurred. An obvious danger is inherent in protectionist policy: proponents of service retention will argue that certain services are socially justified when in fact they are not.

The market-oriented and accelerationist positions, on the other hand, call for a clear and conscious distinction between public needs and

in Canadian Railroads, 1956–1975 (Ottawa: Canadian Transport Commission, 1978); Task Force on Railroad Productivity, *Improving Railroad Productivity*, chap. 3; Interstate Commerce Commission, *Railroad Conglomerates and Other Corporate Structures* (Government Printing Office, 1977); and U.S. Department of Transportation, *A Prospectus for Change in the Freight Railroad Industry* (GPO, 1978), chaps. 1–3.

industrial adjustment policies. Neither position would preclude the retention of socially necessary operations, so long as they do not impose a substantial burden on the industry. But where public need has not been clearly demonstrated, both would ease regulation of pricing, exit, and mergers to allow carriers to adjust facilities and services to new patterns of competition and consumer demand. The accelerationist position calls for an active state role in planning and implementing change and, where necessary, the provision of transitional financial assistance to overcome economic and political barriers to industrial change. In the fragmented U.S. rail industry, for example, accelerationist policy might assist in carrier consolidations or shared use arrangements to make greater use of main-line capacity.

Government financial assistance, if it follows accelerationist principles, should not be used to prop up individual firms. Such an approach merely rewards inefficiency. Nor should aid discriminate among transport modes. It makes little sense to subsidize rail shipments of grain, making the price to the shipper lower than truck transport, if the true cost to society of truck shipment is lower. This would distort the incentives to shippers and raise society's overall transportation costs. Instead, government assistance should be selective aid to ease the transition of carriers, communities, and employees to a deregulated environment. Aid might be justified, for example, for transitional equity problems, where some groups, such as furloughed railway workers, must suffer losses in order to develop a more efficient transportation system. In the interest of both fairness and political expediency, temporary aid (for example, job retraining) might be warranted. It also might be justified to correct problems caused by past government policies. Thus capital assistance might be provided to carriers that agree to restructure themselves to concentrate traffic on a few lines.

The Growth of Protectionist Policy

Political pressures were strong in Canada and the United States to preserve the existing industry structure and levels of service even though this might undermine the industry and force reliance on government funding. Policies designed to accelerate industrial adjustment won little support. Although they might produce long-term benefits for society, those benefits were not clear in the short run and were likely to be highly

Table 2-1. *Protectionist, Market-oriented, and Accelerationist Policies toward Railways*

Government regulation and financial aid	Policies		
	Protectionist	*Market-oriented*	*Accelerationist*
Government regulation Of rates and price competition	Cartelize rate-setting to provide adequate rate of return and avoid price competition among carriers with excess capacity; use cross-subsidy to preserve endangered services.	Allow rate-making freedom in markets where competition exists; discourage cross-subsidy and cartelization.	Allow rate-making freedom in markets where competition exists; discourage cross-subsidy and cartelization.
Of exit	Preserve as much service and employment as is consistent with financial stability of the industry.	Allow firms to drop unprofitable services and facilities.	Allow firms to drop unprofitable services and facilities; encourage exit of least competitive firms.
Of mergers and entry	Encourage strong carriers to take over weak carriers; reject mergers that would exacerbate divisions among them; reject intermodal mergers or diversification.	Allow freedom of mergers.	Encourage intramodal and intermodal mergers that will increase efficiency.

Financial aid			
To carriers	Give assistance to preserve existing rail firms and competition among railways.	Avoid financial assistance.	Give assistance only to promote increased efficiency of overall rail network through reorganization of firms, concentration of traffic on most efficient lines, and exit of least efficient firms.
To shippers[a]	Provide operating assistance to carriers and shippers to prevent loss of service to, or competitive position by, shippers.	Avoid financial assistance.	Provide operating assistance only for transitional purposes or where social benefits clearly outweigh costs; avoid discrimination among modes in assistance programs.
To passengers[a]	Provide operating assistance to prevent loss of services.	Avoid financial assistance.	Provide operating assistance only where there are clear externalities or social goals (for example, service to remote communities with no other access).
To rail labor[a]	Provide subsidies (primarily indirectly through carriers) to maintain employment and income of rail workers.	Avoid financial assistance.	Provide transitional assistance only (for example, for retraining).

a. Beneficiaries of government financial assistance. These groups generally benefit indirectly through government aid to carriers.

diffused, while the costs were likely to be clear, concentrated, and short-term to shippers and passengers who lost services, workers who lost jobs, and managers and investors who lost their companies. It is not surprising, therefore, that U.S. and Canadian policymakers adopted a complex set of protectionist policies that tried to simultaneously (1) keep carriers solvent, (2) preserve rail services, and (3) ease the losses in rail employment. Pursuit of one of these goals, however, almost invariably had a negative impact on one or both of the others. Both countries initially attempted to implement protection by tightening regulatory controls already in place. When this response proved inadequate, direct financial assistance was added.

Protecting Carrier Solvency

Threats to railway solvency during the Great Depression were addressed in both countries by easing antitrust restrictions on cooperation among railways. The Emergency Railroad Transportation Act of 1933 in the United States and the Canadian National–Canadian Pacific Act of 1933 both promoted coordination and consolidation of railroad facilities by competing railways. This was seen as a relatively costless means of easing the railroads' plight by cutting their expenses. Coordination efforts failed in both countries, as the railways feared that cooperative actions (for example, trading abandonments of lines or terminals) might lead to a loss of competitive advantage when good times returned.[11] The U.S. measure also sought to encourage rail mergers under the sponsorship of Federal Coordinator of Transportation Joseph Eastman. But Eastman could not compel mergers without new legislation, and consolidation was strongly resisted by shippers (fearing a decline in competition), rail labor (fearing substantial job loss), and railroad managers; only railroad security holders were generally favorable.[12] Eastman's authority lapsed in 1936. Thus tentative federal initiatives to accelerate industrial change fell victim to group opposition.

With the failure of railway coordination as a mechanism to promote carrier solvency, the U.S. government expanded the scope of transport regulation. To prevent destructive competition between railways, truck-

---

11. On the U.S. experience, see Earl Latham, *The Politics of Railroad Coordination, 1933–1936* (Harvard University Press, 1959); on Canada, see Currie, *Canadian Transportation Economics*, pp. 423–25.

12. Latham, *The Politics of Railroad Coordination*, pp. 39–55, 104–10.

ing companies, and barge carriers, the latter two were brought under partial control of the Interstate Commerce Commission by the Motor Carrier Act of 1935 and the Transportation Act of 1940.[13] It would be a mistake, however, to view the commission as a captive of the railroad industry in the postwar period.[14] In fact, widening the commission's regulatory scope simply expanded the number of interests to which it responded. In its rate-setting decisions, the ICC attempted to set rates so that most traffic would be divided among the three modes (so-called *umbrella rate-making*) and to eliminate predatory (that is, below variable cost) rates. Rate competition among railways was further limited by the Reed-Bullwinkle Act of 1948, which legalized collective rate-setting by railroad rate bureaus.[15]

The U.S. government also relied heavily on bankruptcy laws as an instrument of protectionist policy. Section 77 of the federal Bankruptcy Act, added in 1933, clearly subordinated the rights of creditors and stockholders to the public interest in continued operations, so long as there was some hope of profitability after reorganization. Section 77 was so successful in preventing shutdowns that no large railroad was liquidated in the forty-five years it remained in force.

U.S. railway fortunes improved during the war but declined again in the late 1950s as costs and competition from other forms of transportation increased. Financial assistance came only in the face of severe crisis in the industry after regulatory mechanisms failed. In the late 1950s the Interstate Commerce Commission adopted a more permissive policy toward mergers. It hoped to cut carrier costs and reduce excess capacity by eliminating redundant facilities. But mergers had three major draw-

13. On the coalition of forces supporting and opposing these acts, see ibid., chap. 10. Trucking regulation applied only to common carriers (not to companies hauling their own goods in their own trucks), and it excluded unprocessed agricultural commodities. Barge regulation excluded all private carriers and bulk commodities where not more than three commodities were included in the same "tow" (group of barges being towed together).

14. For a view of the ICC as the captive of the rail industry, see Samuel P. Huntington, "The Marasmus of the ICC: The Commission, the Railroads and the Public Interest," *Yale Law Journal*, vol. 61 (April 1952), pp. 467–509.

15. Rate bureaus set rates jointly for all member carriers. Rate bureaus had existed for many years, but their legality was challenged after 1942 by the Department of Justice under antitrust laws. On the history of rate bureaus, see Grant Davis and Charles Sherwood, *Rate Bureaus and Antitrust Conflicts in Transportation: Public Policy Issues* (Praeger Publishers, 1975), chap. 2. On umbrella rate-making, see George Hilton, *The Transportation Act of 1958: A Decade of Experience* (Indiana University Press, 1969), pp. 22–31.

backs as an adjustment mechanism. First, they imposed concentrated costs. As a result of mergers, shippers may lose competition among carriers, competing railways may lose traffic, labor may lose jobs, and the merging carriers themselves may lose profits if they are forced to take in unprofitable carriers in order to win approval for their consolidation. Very reluctant to impose losses, the ICC sought to protect all of these interests in its merger decisions. It imposed labor protection conditions, traffic conditions (requiring merging carriers to maintain a specified level of traffic interchange with their competitors), and in a few cases requirements that merging carriers take in weaker brethren or financially indemnify weaker carriers for traffic losses. Thus in attempting to balance contending interests, the commission undercut the adjustment impact of the mergers, and it took so long in reaching decisions (an average of two and one-half years in the fourteen cases approved between 1955 and 1970)[16] that merger benefits were often weakened further.

A second drawback of the merger process was that it did not allow the commission to restructure the industry effectively. The ICC could respond only to merger proposals submitted to it by carriers and to the competing requests of their competitors (for example, requests for indemnification and for inclusion in or dismissal of the merger). The commission could require railroads to take in other carriers and to sell off lines as a condition of approving a merger, but carriers willing to forgo the merger could escape the attached strings.

Finally, the merger process gave the ICC a way to avoid facing the seriousness of the railway industry's economic decline and its root causes. Because mergers were supposed to produce savings, the commission could put off difficult questions, such as what kind of rail passenger network, if any, was required.

Two of the major merger cases decided by the Interstate Commerce Commission make evident all of these shortcomings. In the Penn Central case, decided in 1966, the commission required inclusion of the bankrupt New Haven to keep the New Haven operating. This regulation-imposed cross-subsidy greatly depleted the already strained resources of the new carrier; it went bankrupt two years after the merger.[17] The second case,

16. U.S. Department of Transportation, *A Prospectus for Change*, p. 51.
17. See *Pennsylvania R. Co.–New York Central R. Co.*, 327 ICC 475,553 (1966) and *Penn-Central Merger and N & W Inclusion Cases*, 389 U.S. 486, 501 (1968). In a related case, the Norfolk and Western was forced to take control of the Delaware and Hudson and the Erie-Lackawanna through a holding company, limiting its liability for the losses of the two weak roads. See ICC Finance Docket 21510, *Norfolk and Western*

the proposed takeover of the Rock Island by the Union Pacific, was the only instance in which the ICC used the opportunity presented by a merger to propose a major restructuring and consolidation of the U.S. rail system. Its decision came in 1974, more than eleven years after the Union Pacific and Rock Island first announced their merger plans. Moreover, the restructuring proposal was made in a preliminary decision by one of the commission's administrative law judges, Nathan Klitenic, rather than by the commission itself, which rapidly backed away from Klitenic's plan when carriers protested. The ICC argued that merger proposals should come from the railways rather than from the commission. It proposed a more modest restructuring, which was also rejected by the Union Pacific.[18] Thus no restructuring occurred—not even the originally proposed Union Pacific–Rock Island merger. In short, even on the rare occasion when the commission took a tentative lead in proposing industrial adjustment, it could do little to compel compliance.

The U.S. industry's earnings remained very low throughout the 1960s and 1970s. Moreover, a number of bankruptcies occurred for which a standard Section 77 reorganization held little hope of returning the firms to solvency. The problems were particularly severe in the northeastern United States. The slow collapse of most of the carriers in the region led to the gradual extension of federal aid. Loan guarantees were given to carriers that could not obtain capital funding in 1958. These were followed in 1970 by loan guarantees and, in 1973, by grants to prevent carrier shutdowns. Rehabilitation assistance was extended by loans in 1973 and then, in 1976, by stock purchases with a mandatory redemption requirement.[19] Participation in these financial assistance programs was generally limited to marginal or bankrupt carriers by requirements that applicants be unable to raise funds elsewhere; therefore, these programs were of little use in promoting industrial restructuring except for combinations

---

Railway Company and New York Chicago and St. Louis Railroad Company–Merger, Etc., 324 ICC 1 (1964), 330 ICC 780 (1967). Delaware and Hudson was sold to Guilford Transportation in 1984; Erie-Lackawanna declared bankruptcy and was included in Conrail in 1976.

18. See *Traffic World,* December 9, 1974, pp. 23–25; and Richard Saunders, *The Railroad Mergers and the Coming of Conrail* (Greenwood Press, 1978), pp. 238–43.

19. Redeemable preference shares are a hybrid between debt and equity, with some characteristics of each. They allow government to advance funds to a firm without immediate payback of interest or principal (a problem for many of the weak carriers). Government gains representation on the board of directors only in case of default. See Albert J. Francese, "Redeemable Preference Shares: Are They a Satisfactory Medium for Deferred Maintenance Assistance?" *ICC Practitioners' Journal,* vol. 44 (September–October 1977), pp. 779–82.

of weak carriers. The loan guarantee program created by the Railroad Revitalization and Regulatory Reform (4R) Act of 1976 did allow profitable carriers to receive funding, but it restricted their ability to increase dividends as long as they had loans under federal guarantee. As a result, profitable carriers did not participate.[20] With each new assistance program, concern over the imminent shutdown of carriers became more evident; the trend was toward indirect subsidy, through subsidized interest and delayed payback and instruments more closely resembling direct equity participation in railroads. Although every effort was made to avoid outright nationalization or even undisguised equity participation, the federal government had become by 1980 the proprietor of both the National Railroad Passenger Corporation (Amtrak) and the Consolidated Rail Corporation (Conrail), and its assistance was keeping several other carriers alive.

In Canada, the effective duopoly of the Canadian Pacific Railway and the state-owned Canadian National Railways as well as precedents for government operating aid to railways led to a different choice of instruments to preserve carrier solvency. Rates were set so that CP was able to meet its fixed charges, while federal loans and later subsidies met CN deficits. Although rate bureaus functioned in Canada, the government's delegation of interprovincial trucking regulation to the provinces made a centralized policy of umbrella rate-making impossible. In the late 1950s, however, competition from other transport modes forced the railways to seek substantial rate increases in markets where they faced less competition. The resulting public outcry led Prime Minister John Diefenbaker to roll back increases in freight rates won by the railways in 1958 and replace them with a general government subsidy to the railways. Although intended as a short-term measure, this subsidy continued until 1967, when it was gradually phased out in favor of subsidies for passenger operations and unprofitable branch lines.

Preserving Rail Services

Policy toward service cutbacks also differed in the two countries. Canada took a more protectionist stance and provided greater financial assistance to retain services.

20. On rail assistance programs, see U.S. Department of Transportation, *A Prospectus for Change*, chap. 7; and General Accounting Office, *Federal Assistance to Rehabilitate Railroads Should Be Reassessed*, Report CED-80-90 (GAO, 1980).

Rail passenger service was one of the most contentious issues in both countries. Regulatory authorities confronted strong political pressures for service retention balanced against enormous losses suffered by the carriers. In the United States, passenger service cuts were deeper just after World War II than in Canada, in part because Canadians were slower to abandon the train for other modes of transportation. More important, however, was Canadian National's reluctance to cut service. While major U.S. railways cut their passenger train miles by 75 percent between 1939 and 1970 and Canadian Pacific cut by 70 percent, Canadian National cut by less than 25 percent (see figure 2-1). This was less a result of government policy than of a corporate strategy that placed little emphasis on profitability. Although both governments adopted laws that eased the restrictions on discontinuance of service (the United States in 1958 and Canada in 1967), passenger deficits continued to mount. Losses reached almost half a billion dollars per year in the United States in the late 1960s, about one-quarter of profits on freight traffic.[21] The Canadian railways were also hard hit by passenger service deficits. Yet until the 1970s, neither government attempted to develop a coherent plan for a national system of service or even a coherent set of criteria for judging requests to cut services.[22] Decisions were made on a route-by-route basis, and regulatory authorities accepted the principle that railways should cross-subsidize passenger service losses with freight profits so long as the exchange did not endanger the carriers' survival. Thus services were cut gradually and unsystematically. Clearly, a cash infusion was necessary if the goals of continued (although reduced) rail passenger service and railway viability were to be kept in balance. Both countries eventually adopted such programs.

In Canada, the National Transportation Act of 1967 gave the new

21. This loss is calculated on a "fully allocated" basis—that is, it includes a share of costs, such as track maintenance and corporate overhead where freight and passenger costs cannot be separated easily. George Hilton, *Amtrak: The National Railroad Passenger Corporation* (American Enterprise Institute for Public Policy Research, 1980), pp. 3–4. Until 1958, authority over passenger train discontinuances was divided among the state regulatory commissions. The Transportation Act of 1958 gave the ICC original jurisdiction over interstate trains and appellate jurisdiction over intrastate service denied discontinuance by state commissions.

22. See Hilton, *The Transportation Act of 1958*, chap. 4; and Canadian Transport Commission, Research Branch, *An Analysis of Railway Transport Committee Decisions, 1967–1980*, Report 1982-06E (Ottawa: Canadian Transport Commission, 1981), chap. 2. Although the CTC report argues that the commission consistently applied the criterion of passenger utilization in its decisions, no clear definition was given to that term.

Figure 2-1. *Passenger Service Train Miles, Selected U.S. and Canadian Railways, 1923–77*[a]

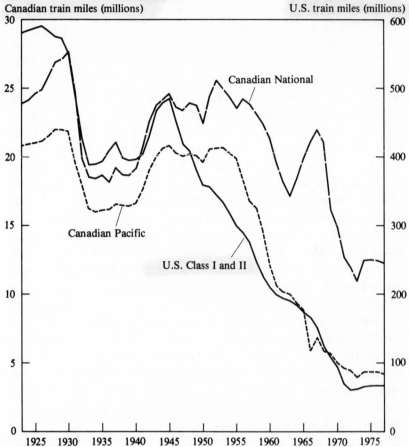

Canadian train miles (millions)   U.S. train miles (millions)

Sources: For Canadian railways: Statistics Canada, *Canadian National Railways, 1923–1971* (Ottawa: Information Canada, 1971); Statistics Canada, *Canadian Pacific Ltd., 1923–1971* (Ottawa: Information Canada, 1973); and Statistics Canada, *Canadian National Railways and Canadian Pacific Ltd.*, catalog 52-213 (Ottawa: Statistics Canada, various years). For U.S. railways: Interstate Commerce Commission, *Transport Statistics in the United States* (Government Printing Office, various years).
a. Includes commuter train mileage.

Canadian Transport Commission (CTC) authority to determine whether individual passenger train services were uneconomic and, if so, whether the service should be continued under subsidy in the public interest. Subsidies were set at 80 percent of estimated losses. The CTC's orders to continue or end service can be reversed, however, by the federal cabinet, and any case in which a railway's request to discontinue service

Table 2-2. *Canadian Transport Commission Passenger-Train-Abandonment Decisions, 1968–75*

Year	Abandonments permitted	Abandonment decisions issued	Cumulative abandonments permitted	Cumulative abandonment decisions issued
1968	1	1	1	1
1969	0	0	1	1
1970	6	9	7	10
1971	4	10	11	20
1972	0	41	11	61
1973	0	9	11	70
1974	1	1	12	71
1975	2	2	14	73

Source: Canadian Transport Commission, *Annual Report*, 1968–76.

is refused is automatically reheard after five years.[23] The broad criteria in the National Transportation Act for retaining unprofitable passenger trains gave substantial discretion to program implementors.[24] As table 2-2 makes clear, the CTC used this discretion primarily to preserve uneconomic services: by 1973 only eleven of seventy decisions by the CTC had allowed discontinuance.

There is a striking coincidence between the pattern of CTC decisions and the electoral cycle. Most of the decisions favoring discontinuance were made in 1970; they slowed tremendously as the 1972 election approached. This pattern continued throughout the period of Liberal minority government following the 1972 election. In fact, the CTC ordered a service added in the Toronto area just prior to the 1974 election.[25] Not until the Liberal party won a safe majority in the 1974 election did discontinuances resume, and then on a much reduced schedule, for decisions on most routes had already been made.

Political pressures contributed to the Canadian Transport Commis-

23. Railway Act, *Revised Statutes of Canada*, 1970, chap. R-2, sec. 260(5); and National Transportation Act, *Revised Statutes of Canada*, 1970, chap. N-17, sec. 64(1).

24. The CTC has broadly defined *uneconomic* to mean not simply currently unprofitable, but "incapable of being rendered profitable to the railway under any feasible alterations in railway operating practices, equipment assignment, scheduling, pricing, or other aspects of passenger service under railway control." See Canadian Transport Commission, *Railway Transport Committee Decisions, 1967–1980*, p. 12.

25. Canadian Transport Commission, Railway Transport Committee, Decision and Order No. R-18042, February 1, 1974. Several persons interviewed for this study stated that this decision came as a direct result of pressure from Department of Transport (later Transport Canada) officials to assuage commuter groups in that area.

sion's adoption of a protectionist position. Public hearings in areas threatened with discontinuances have usually been dominated by proponents of service retention, and both the Railway Transport Committee of the CTC and commission staff have been deeply affected by the sheer volume of protest. In addition, successive Liberal governments appointed politically sensitive individuals to the CTC as a reward for service rendered, and each of the commission's presidents has previously served in Liberal cabinets. Even without direct government interference, commissioners are likely to be conscious of the political consequences of the CTC's actions on the party in power and of their own dependence on the government for reappointment.

If the federal cabinet had used its authority under the National Transportation Act to reverse or alter CTC decisions preserving uneconomic passenger train services, the commission almost certainly would have received the signal that more discontinuances were in order. But the cabinet never forced cuts prior to 1981; it was less concerned with rising passenger train subsidies than it was with avoiding public wrath. In fact, the cabinet's veto power was used only to block a cutback in service. Rather than end the problem of unprofitable passenger train services, the National Transportation Act merely shifted the financial burden.

The subsidy program failed to control passenger deficits or improve service. Thus in 1977 Ottawa created a new government-owned corporation, VIA Rail Canada, to take over intercity passenger services under full federal subsidy. In so doing, the Canadians followed the example of the United States, which in 1970 had established Amtrak, a quasi-public corporation, to take over unprofitable passenger train services with the mandate of making them self-supporting. This rapidly proved impossible, and Amtrak also began to require growing federal subsidies.

Uneconomic branch lines were another problem confronting the U.S. and Canadian governments.[26] The greatest costs of light density lines come not from their fixed costs (for example, maintenance and taxes), but from the continued crew and equipment costs of operating very short, slow trains on often poorly maintained lines where a small amount

26. Canada's Board of Railroad Commissioners gained authority over all rail line abandonments in 1933. Previously, it had authority only when the railway had committed itself through its act of incorporation or other agreement to maintain the line; Canadian National Railways lines had required cabinet approval. See Canadian Transport Commission, *Railway Transport Committee Decisions, 1967–1980*, p. 61.

of traffic remains.[27] Abandonment of completely unused or "shipper abandoned" lines generally provokes the least public opposition, but it does little to help the carrier's financial problems. Clearly, some group is going to have to bear losses for the other lines: either the shippers who lose service or the carriers who must continue it at a loss.

In Canada, the fate of branch lines has been intertwined with the Crow's Nest Pass rates on export grain. These artificially low rates give grain elevator companies an incentive to retain small, inefficient elevators on underutilized branch lines. Prairie farmers view the "Crow rate" and the local branch line as their birthright. The branch-line system itself is hopelessly overbuilt, designed for an era when hauls of twenty miles or more by truck to grain elevators were not economically feasible for most farmers. Canadian governments have wanted to change the rates and allow branch lines to be abandoned, but until 1983 none had the political courage to push through a reform. Fewer than 500 of the more than 19,000 miles in the three Prairie provinces (Alberta, Saskatchewan, and Manitoba) were abandoned between 1945 and 1965, when nearly all of the lines were frozen until 1975 by federal cabinet order; subsequently, more than 80 percent were frozen until after the year 2000.[28] But imposing protectionist solutions through regulation worsened the railways' financial problems. The National Transportation Act of 1967 created a subsidy program that compensates railways for traffic that originates on branch lines declared by the Canadian Transport Commission to be uneconomic, but not for grain traffic that does not originate on such lines. Branch-line subsidies exceeded $170 million by 1980. These subsidies and similar ones for unprofitable passenger trains were intended to be temporary, but potential losers from adjustment argued successfully before the CTC or pressured the cabinet for their continuation. Moreover, the branch-line subsidies covered only operating costs; they did nothing to solve the growing problem of branch-line deterioration and grain car shortages,

27. See the Task Force on Railroad Productivity, *Improving Railroad Productivity*, chap. 5.
28. See Harold Purdy, *Transport Competition and Public Policy in Canada* (Vancouver: University of British Columbia Press, 1972), chap. 15. The abandonment figure for the U.S. "bread-basket" states (Illinois, Indiana, Iowa, Kansas, Minnesota, Missouri, Montana, Nebraska, North Dakota, and South Dakota) is somewhat higher: a 6.5 percent decline in railway mileage owned between 1945 and 1970. ICC, Bureau of Transport Economics and Statistics, *Statistics of Railways in the United States*, year ending December 31, 1945; and ICC, Bureau of Accounts, *Transport Statistics in the United States*, year ending December 31, 1970.

for the railways were unwilling to invest in lines and rolling stock that lose money. By the mid-1970s, many lines had to be taken out of service or limited to slowly moving traffic.

The resulting federal investment in the Prairie rail system did not develop as part of a preconceived master plan; in fact, each government initiative was undertaken with a general election expected in the near future. Nevertheless, a series of incremental steps has removed much of the grain transportation investment burden from the railways. In 1977 the federal government announced a program to rehabilitate Prairie branch lines; by the time it is completed about 4,000 miles of line will have been upgraded at a cost of more than $1 billion. And by 1981 the government had purchased or leased 12,000 grain hopper cars to replace the aging boxcar fleets.[29] Most of the hopper cars purchased by Ottawa clearly state "Government of Canada" on their sides to remind Western voters of Ottawa's benefaction.

Although railways in the United States did not have the problem of statutory grain rates and were allowed larger cutbacks in mileage by the Interstate Commerce Commission, they, too, had uneconomic branch lines.[30] When the Northeast rail crisis threatened to lead to massive abandonments, Congress passed a formula grant program to states in the region. The program, begun in 1974, was expanded to cover the rest of the nation by the Railroad Revitalization and Regulatory Reform Act of 1976. The original intent of the program, like those under the National Transportation Act in Canada, was to extend services *temporarily* so that shippers would not face a sudden cutoff of service; individual lines were eligible for only two or three years of subsidy. As in Canada, however, those standards were later relaxed, and subsidies were continued. The 4R act also made rehabilitation funding available to the states on a formula-grant basis.[31] As originally implemented, these provisions were almost purely protectionist, and very inefficiently so: only lines

29. An additional 1,000 hopper cars each have been purchased by the provinces of Alberta and Saskatchewan, while Manitoba leased 400 cars. See J. C. Gilson, *Western Grain Transportation: Report on Consultations and Recommendations* (Ottawa: Supply and Services, 1982), pt. 2, p. 9. In addition, Ottawa and the railways agreed in 1974 to share the cost of a boxcar rehabilitation program, with Ottawa contributing $3.43 million, Canadian National $2 million, and Canadian Pacific $1.43 million.

30. The ICC granted abandonments totaling 18,943 miles between 1946 and 1963. Michael Conant, *Railroad Mergers and Abandonments* (University of California Press, 1964), p. 114.

31. *Railroad Revitalization and Regulatory Reform Act of 1976*, sec. 803, 90 Stat. 31, 130, February 5, 1976.

that had previously been authorized for abandonment—generally the most hopeless lines, long since abandoned by most shippers—were eligible for assistance, while lines with better prospects but not enough traffic to justify additional carrier investment were not.[32]

The Local Rail Services Assistance Act of 1978 (LRSA) attempted to overcome these problems by widening eligibility for light density lines while preserving the format of a fixed-sum matching grant to the states.[33] As a result, the burden of making sensitive abandonment decisions shifted away from federal agencies; state and local governments became the last resort for shippers desperate to keep branch lines open.[34] Federal spending on light density rail lines has been substantially less than in Canada, peaking at just under $100 million in 1978. The states quickly put most LRSA spending into rehabilitation projects rather than into service continuation subsidies. The Omnibus Reconciliation Act of 1981 ended continuation subsidies altogether,[35] and the Reagan administration is phasing out remaining LRSA rehabilitation funding. States have also taken efforts to preserve rail services abandoned by major carriers. A number of states have used federal funds and their own resources to purchase abandoned lines or to help local authorities and private groups purchase them.[36]

Shipper interests in Canada's Prairie and Maritime provinces, and consignees in the Maritimes, have had more success in obtaining permanent subsidies than their U.S. counterparts, in part because regional cleavages are more intense. But an explanation of policy differences must also include the allies that regional subsidies are able to enlist. In Canada, provincial governments have actively supported regional subsidies and lower freight rates and have bargained on behalf

---

32. On the shortcomings of the 3R and 4R act programs, see *Local Rail Services Assistance Act of 1978*, S. Rept. 95-1159, 95 Cong. 2 sess. (GPO, 1978).

33. Local Rail Services Assistance Act of 1978, 92 Stat. 3059, November 8, 1978. LRSA roughly quintupled rail mileage eligible for assistance, from about 14,000 miles in 1978 to 70,000 miles in 1979. U.S. Department of Transportation, *13th Annual Report, Fiscal Year 1979*, p. 25.

34. *Railway Age*, September 8, 1980, pp. 82–83. On LRSA, see also *Railway Age*, July 14, 1980, pp. 30–32.

35. Sec. 1192(b).

36. Operations in states that take a direct ownership role—for example, Vermont, Michigan, and South Dakota—have generally been contracted out to private sector carriers. See Benjamin J. Allen and David B. Vellenga, "Public Financing of Railroads under the New Federalism: The Progress and Problems of Selected State Programs," *Transportation Journal*, vol. 23 (Winter 1983), pp. 5–19.

of their constituents in federal-provincial negotiations for maintenance of those concessions. With only ten provinces rather than fifty states to listen to, the provincial voices are relatively much stronger, and the Canadian government can ignore them only at significant political cost.

The nature of the federal Parliament also reinforces incentives for regional subsidies. Because parties are "disciplined" (all caucus members are expected to support the party's position in floor votes), legislators often cannot vote their local constituency interests. The party in power therefore must use other mechanisms to show responsiveness to Canada's diverse regional interests. Programs of direct region-specific aid are a common solution. Incentives to provide such programs are particularly strong when a party lacks representatives from a region (as the governing Liberals did in the 1970s and early 1980s), for if such a party hopes to make a comeback in that region, it must make extraordinary efforts to show that it can address that area's needs. Passage of regional subsidies is also made easier by party discipline within Parliament, which allows party leaders to enact these programs without the need to "log roll" (that is, combine unrelated programs that could not win majority support individually but can do so as a package) or construct winning coalitions for each program.

In the United States, however, political parties are too weak to provide ready-made majority coalitions in Congress. Hence, most programs provide benefits *across* regions. Construction of coalitions in the railway arena has proved to be difficult because few regional claims for special treatment are perceived to be legitimate, and persistent and united carrier support is lacking. Moreover, the executive branch has consistently opposed subsidies except during severe crises in the rail industry. Passage of subsidies has depended upon their ambiguity of purpose. Protectionists generally see aid programs as providing continued service, while deregulationists tend to see them as transitional. The unstable support coalitions of these compromise programs have kept subsidies small and intermittent.

Preserving Rail Employment

The third goal of protectionist rail policy in the United States and Canada was to cushion the impact of industry decline on rail workers. The loss of jobs has been particularly severe in the United States, as figure 2-2 shows, because freight traffic grew more slowly than in Canada

Figure 2-2. *Rail Employment, Selected U.S. and Canadian Railways, 1926–80*[a]

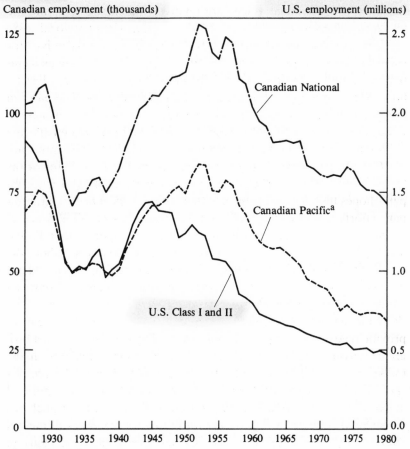

Canadian employment (thousands)   U.S. employment (millions)

Canadian National

Canadian Pacific[a]

U.S. Class I and II

Sources: Same as figure 2-1.

a. Includes railway, express, and telecommunications employees; excludes hotels and subsidiary companies.

b. Includes railway, express (until 1972), news, commercial communications, and highway transport-rail (1956–64 only) employees; excludes hotels and other operations.

while passenger traffic dropped off more quickly. Mergers and abandonments created additional opportunities for labor cutbacks. Labor gained protection against cutbacks in 1933, when a ban on layoffs due to coordination was adopted as part of the Emergency Railroad Transportation Act. In 1936, these conditions were replaced by a negotiated compensation agreement (the "Washington Conditions") that the ICC later imposed in a variety of job-threatening situations, including mergers, facility coordinations, abandonments, and bankruptcies.[37] Employees were not guaranteed compensation, however, for job losses due to technological change, business downturns, or discontinuance of individual operations (for example, passenger trains). The compensations awarded by the ICC were paid for by the carriers until 1974, when legislation establishing Conrail transferred the costs of protecting displaced Conrail workers to the federal government. It was felt that the new carrier could not bear the costs of standard labor protection arrangements.

Unable to win statutory protection against, or compensation for, work force reductions, rail employees in Canada have been forced to rely on collective bargaining to protect their jobs. But the strong duopoly of Canadian Pacific and Canadian National at the bargaining table has not helped them. Rail labor in Canada has been unable to win the same degree of protection against cutbacks as their U.S. counterparts.

The Shift toward Deregulation

Dissatisfaction with preservationist rail policies was already widespread in both the United States and Canada by the late 1950s. Palliative measures, such as Canada's Freight Rate Reduction Act and the loan guarantee provisions of the United States' Transportation Act of 1958, promised no solutions, critics claimed, but only deeper, inadequately planned government involvement with no end in sight. Proponents of deregulation based their views on the need to rely on the marketplace to allocate traffic between modes of transportation and to determine levels of service and employment. They argued that the railway industry was not senescent, but was being killed by government-imposed burdens, while shippers suffered from collusive rate-making. Their proposed solution: make the railways self-sufficient again by allowing them to specialize in those segments of the transportation market where they can compete effectively.

This philosophy was clearly presented in the 1961 report of Canada's Royal Commission on Transportation (the MacPherson Commission).

37. The Transportation Act of 1940 included slightly different minimum protections, giving employees statutory as well as agreement protection. The conditions imposed by the ICC in its decisions, however, were usually modifications of the "Washington Conditions."

The commission's report did not urge complete reliance on the market; it recognized that a few shippers were effectively "captive" to the railways because of their location and commodity characteristics and that a residual rate-making power might be necessary to protect them. But the report recommended that this power be applied only in exceptional cases. It also suggested that the Canadian government might wish to continue some uneconomic services where social benefits outweigh the costs (for example, passenger service to communities with no road access). In such cases Ottawa rather than the railways should pick up the tab.[38]

It was not the power of the deregulationists' arguments that led the Canadian and U.S. governments to change their policies, but the breakdown of regulation as a policy instrument. Confronted with rapidly rising subsidies, executive branch policymakers saw deregulation as an alternative to a spending "black hole." Differences between the two countries in the timing and scope of rail deregulation reflect variations in the timing of rail industry financial crises, the distribution of costs and benefits of a policy shift, and the capability of governmental institutions to compel change.

In Canada, rapidly rising subsidies under the Freight Rates Reduction Act forced the federal government to act. Both major railways supported deregulation. Moreover, the domination of the rail market by these two nationwide carriers meant that traffic interchange, and the collective rate-making bodies designed to facilitate that interchange, provoked much less political conflict than in the United States.

Controversy over the MacPherson Commission's recommendations, despite carrier and government support, made the minority governments under Conservative John Diefenbaker (1962–63) and Liberal Lester Pearson (1963–68) reluctant to press for change. By 1967, when the National Transportation Act was finally passed, subsidy payments under the Freight Rates Reduction Act had climbed over the $100 million per annum mark. As already noted, some of the act's provisions were subverted to become precisely the sort of palliative programs for

38. Bowing to political reality, the MacPherson Commission did not recommend changes in the Crow's Nest Pass grain rates, although it strongly urged that the federal government compensate railways for their losses. This recommendation was never acted upon because of opposition in western Canada. See Royal Commission on Transportation, *Report,* vol. 1 (Ottawa: Queen's Printer, 1961); and Darling, *The Politics of Freight Rates,* chap. 10.

uneconomic services (notably branch-line subsidies and passenger-train subsidies) that the MacPherson Commission sought to avoid. Nevertheless, the act did give the railways the power to set rates within a broad range without government interference.[39] The most intransigent opponents of rate-making freedom—grain farmers in the Prairies—were partially bought off with "side payments" from the federal government: the highly favorable Crow's Nest Pass rates remained unchanged. The freight rate issue continues to be very sensitive, however. In 1973 the government once again froze freight rates for a two-year period; a federal subsidy compensated the railways for lost revenue.

The grain rates dispute was not resolved until 1983. After a long attempt to build consensus among the railways, producers, and grain elevator companies, the government under Pierre Trudeau (1968–79, 1980–84) finally won passage of a measure that gave the railways compensatory rates while it gradually shifted an increasing share of the cost of grain transport to the producers. But the government's plan did not attempt to impose losses on farmers; instead it limited future gains through inflation. The federal government agreed to assume in perpetuity the railways' 1981–82 crop-year revenue shortfall (more than $600 million), while sharing future cost increases with shippers.[40] In short, the agreement constitutes a rescue and reentrenchment of government-assisted protection for grain shippers rather than rate deregulation.[41]

Deregulation of the transportation market began much later in the United States than in Canada, in part because the larger number of

39. The National Transportation Act required that all rates at least cover variable costs and removed from commission jurisdiction rates no higher than 250 percent of variable costs. Canadian railways already had authority to negotiate agreed charges with shippers. See Railway Act, *Revised Statutes of Canada*, 1970, chap. R-2, sec. 276–78. The commission could also suspend rates or conditions for carriage that "prejudicially affect the public interest," notably by creating "an unfair disadvantage beyond any disadvantage that may be deemed to be inherent in the location or volume of traffic, the scale of operation connected therewith or the type of traffic or service involved," or "an undue obstacle to the interchange of commodities between points in Canada." National Transportation Act, *Revised Statutes of Canada*, 1970, chap. N-17, sec. 23. The National Transportation Act also eliminated the long- and short-haul clauses of the Railway Act, which had fallen into disuse in any case.

40. Part of the ensuing subsidy payment to the railways is tied to railroad investment in expanding western rail capacity.

41. House of Commons of Canada, *Western Grain Transportation Act*, 32 Parl. 1 sess., 1980–81–82–83, chap. 168. See Kenneth Norrie, "Not Much to Crow About: A Primer on the Statutory Grain Freight Rate Issue," *Canadian Public Policy*, vol. 9, no. 4 (1983), pp. 434–45.

carriers, with widely differing interests and financial constraints, made it more difficult to reach a common industry position.[42] U.S. carriers were more divided on the issue of rate deregulation because they would have to pay a higher price for it. Shipper interests as well as the administrations of both Gerald Ford and Jimmy Carter demanded that the antitrust immunity granted to railroad rate bureaus be substantially weakened in any move toward deregulating rates. As in Canada, much of the debate revolved around the question of how to protect captive shippers.

Preliminary steps toward deregulation were taken by the Railroad Revitalization and Regulatory Reform Act of 1976.[43] Congressional support for rail reform was grudging at best: the act passed only because President Ford made regulatory reform a quid pro quo for his support for assistance to Conrail. Under the 4R act, the ICC would lose power over maximum rail rates unless a railway exercised "market dominance" over a shipper, and the ICC was required to consider the adequacy of carrier revenue in its decisions. However, the commission's broad interpretation of market dominance, combined with the railroads' reticence to propose innovative rates, scuttled most regulatory rate reform under the act.[44]

Pressure for rail deregulation in the United States continued to grow after 1976, especially as federal financial aid to Conrail grew beyond initial projections. Supporters of rail deregulation repeatedly stated that Conrail could not become self-sufficient without additional flexibility to set rates and close unprofitable routings.[45] The policy impasse began to break in 1979, when President Carter appointed two very strong proponents of deregulation to the Interstate Commerce Commission. Under

42. On the carriers' proposals for deregulation and their difficulty in arriving at a common position, see *Traffic World,* March 5, 1979, p. 18; April 30, 1979, pp. 20–21; and November 12, 1979, pp. 15–16.

43. 90 Stat. 41.

44. According to a report by the House Interstate and Foreign Commerce Committee, "From 45 to 97 percent of the representative commodities making up the bulk of railroad business fell within the area of [market dominance] regulation." See *Rail Act of 1980,* H. Rept. 96-1035, 96 Cong. 2 sess. (GPO, 1980). See also the statements of William Dempsey, Brock Adams, and Daniel O'Neal in *Implementation of the 4R Act,* Hearings before the Subcommittee on Surface Transportation of the Senate Committee on Commerce, Science and Transportation, 96 Cong. 1 sess. (GPO, 1979), serial 96-5.

45. See, for example, the statement by the chairman of Conrail, Edward Jordan, in *Railroad Deregulation Act of 1979,* pt. 2, Hearings before the Subcommittee on Surface Transportation of the Senate Committee on Commerce, Science and Transportation, 96 Cong. 1 sess. (GPO, 1979), serial 96-41, pp. 704–12.

the aggressive leadership of the new chairman, Darius Gaskins, the commission permitted carriers and shippers to negotiate contract rates, challenged the antitrust immunity of railroad rate bureaus, and exempted some traffic (fresh fruits and vegetables) from ICC rate control.[46]

Passage by Congress of the Staggers Rail Act of 1980 legitimized and extended most of the changes made by the ICC over the previous two years. The act provides increased rate-making freedom for the railways, although less than exists in Canada.[47] It also explicitly legalizes contract rates between shippers and carriers, limits the activities of railroad rate bureaus, and expedites abandonment proceedings. States are required to regulate intrastate rates in a manner consistent with the principles of the Staggers act—that is, they must not require railroads to carry traffic at less than variable cost. Although a number of concessions to specific shipper interests were included in the act in order to win passage,[48] the commission has implemented the act in a manner strongly oriented toward deregulation.[49] The most dramatic deregulating changes in the United States resulted from ICC administrative actions rather than from legislation. Once the ICC adopted change, the same institutional characteristics (for example, multiple veto points) that earlier had served to block change made it difficult to alter the new status quo.

Substantial restructuring is also occurring in the U.S. rail industry, although with minimal government leadership. The 4R act of 1976 gave the secretary of transportation authority to convene special conferences

46. Interstate Commerce Commission, *Annual Report*, 1979, pp. 36–43.

47. Rates below variable cost were declared illegal. Rates above an upper ceiling (160 percent of variable costs, rising to 180 percent in 1984) could be regulated, but carriers were granted a "zone of flexibility" within which rate increases could not be challenged. Staggers Rail Act of 1980, 94 Stat. 1985, October 14, 1980. On the Staggers Act, see Theodore E. Keeler, *Railroads, Freight, and Public Policy* (Brookings, 1983).

48. High-cost eastern ports retain standing to request rate parity among Atlantic ports; agricultural shippers won repeal of "demand-sensitive" (seasonal) rates; environmentalists won rate restrictions on recyclables; a single municipal utility in San Antonio even managed to win a special legislative provision giving it temporary relief from rate increases on coal shipments.

49. The ICC has exempted major categories of traffic (containers and trailers on flatcars, boxcar traffic, and export coal movements) from regulation and has weakened both the market dominance test for captive shippers and the restrictions on railroad ownership of other transport modes. The commission also allowed railways (notably Conrail) to close routings that did not offer them an adequate rate of return. On ICC promotion of deregulation before and after passage of the Staggers act, see Thomas Gale Moore, "Rail and Truck Reform—The Record So Far," *Regulation*, vol. 7 (November–December 1983), pp. 33–41. Moore estimates (p. 34) that close to two-thirds of rail rates have been freed from maximum-rate regulation.

of carriers (under an exemption from antitrust laws) to seek consolidation of rail facilities; once again, however, the U.S. Department of Transportation saw government's role as a facilitator rather than as an active planner and implementor.[50] The Milwaukee Railroad Restructuring Act, passed in 1979, widened eligibility for government assistance to railroads engaging in restructuring projects designed to consolidate traffic on fewer lines of higher average traffic density.[51] But these provisions have largely gone unused. Rather than following the government's lead in restructuring, carriers have planned mergers themselves that exclude weak carriers. Since 1980, the ICC has approved a series of huge (primarily end-to-end) rail mergers. A major realignment of U.S. railways has resulted.[52] Further evidence of a shift toward market-oriented policy can be seen in changes in federal bankruptcy laws enacted in 1978 that have weakened the role of the ICC (making liquidation of failed carriers in the United States easier). In addition, labor protection requirements have been eased for carriers currently engaged in bankruptcy proceedings.

Although both Canada and the United States have moved away from entrenched protectionist principles in recent years, the shift to a market orientation is far from complete. Neither government has developed a market test or a clear set of public interest criteria for deciding the level of rail passenger service. Most of Canada's rail system in the Prairies remains frozen until the year 2000. And while rate regulation has been eased in both countries, government financial assistance remains, much of it with a decidedly protectionist cast. This is particularly true of Canada, as a comparison of federal government rail expenditures in the two countries shows. In the United States, federal rail spending began from a tiny base in 1970 (figure 2-3). Rapid spending growth in the 1970s was fueled primarily by the Northeast rail crisis and federal support for Amtrak. Expenditures peaked in 1981, with payment of more than $2 billion to the estates of Conrail's bankrupt predecessors for the company. With the resolution of the Northeast rail crisis and the completion of Amtrak's modernization program, federal rail expenditures in the United States declined substantially in the following years. Subsidies to Amtrak compose the bulk of remaining outlays.

50. See U.S. Department of Transportation, *A Prospectus for Change*, pp. 80, 86–87.
51. Sect. 24, 93 Stat. 736, 747, November 4, 1979.
52. The commission has also decided to end routine imposition of traffic protective conditions in rail consolidations. *Traffic Protective Conditions*, 366 ICC 112 (1982).

56   POLITICS OF INDUSTRIAL CHANGE

Figure 2-3. *Federal Rail Expenditures in the United States,*
Fiscal Years 1969–85[a]

Billions of 1982 dollars

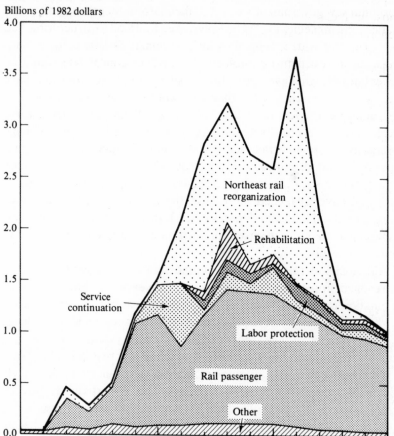

Sources: *Budget of the United States Government, Appendix,* various years; U.S. Department of Transportation, Federal Railroad Administration, Office of Federal Assistance, *Annual Report on Railroad Financial Assistance Under Title V of the Railroad Revitalization and Regulatory Reform Act of 1976 and Section 3 of the Emergency Rail Services Act of 1970, Fiscal Year 1982* (Government Printing Office, January 1983); and U.S. General Accounting Office, *The Federal Investment in Amtrak's Assets Should Be Secured,* Report PAD-81-32 (GAO, March 1983). Data for 1985 are projected.

a. *Northeast rail reorganization* includes administrative costs of the United States Railway Association; loans made under the Regional Rail Reorganization Act of 1973 (loan repayments are treated as negative outlays); purchase of Conrail securities; settlement of the litigation brought by the estates of Conrail's bankrupt predecessors; payments made as a result of defaults on loan guarantees granted by the Interstate Commerce Commission under the Transportation Act of 1958; loans made under the Emergency Rail Facilities Restoration Act; and transitional assistance related to the transfer of Conrail commuter rail services to local authorities. Excludes administrative expenses of the U.S. Department of Transportation and Interstate Commerce Commission in planning the reorganization of the Northeast rail system. *Rehabilitation* includes the purchase of redeemable preference shares under Title V of the Railroad Revitalization and Regulatory Reform Act of 1976. *Labor protection* includes payments made to the Railroad Retirement Board for protection of Conrail employees under the Regional Rail Reorganization Act of 1973, as amended, and under the Northeast Rail Service Act of 1981; to Rock Island Employees under the Rail Safety and Service Improvement Act of 1982; and payments under the Milwaukee Railroad Restructuring Act and Rock Island Railroad Transition and Employee Assistance Act. *Service continuation* includes rail service

The Canadian pattern is very different (figure 2-4). Federal rail expenditures in Canada began the 1970s from a much higher base than those in the United States. The form of these outlays has changed: general subsidies have been ended, and the recurrent financial crises at Canadian National Railways have been eliminated. But rather than following the peak-and-decline pattern of the United States, federal rail expenditures in Canada have increased fairly constantly, driven by grain transportation and passenger service subsidies. Growth in grain subsidies has been particularly explosive and shows no sign of abating in the near future. By 1985 federal rail expenditures were about the same in Canada as in the United States, although the economy is only one-tenth as large. In short, railway politics and policies in the United States and Canada retain many elements of the protectionist accommodation of group and regional interests that have been dominant since the Great Depression.

The Failure of Accelerationist Policy

Over the past half century, the Canadian and U.S. governments have attempted accelerationist policies only during periods of severe crisis in the rail industry, and then largely without success. Neither country has developed and implemented a long-term plan to guide the course and pace of rail industry change. But is it realistic to expect a successful accelerationist rail policy from these two governments? After all, the United States and Canada have market economies in which private enterprise enjoys substantial decisionmaking autonomy. Nevertheless, both governments have been able to exercise strong control over industry decisions—notably control over exit, rates, and consolidations—with enormous consequences for the adjustment of the industry to changing technology and consumer demand. The Canadian and U.S. governments have not been unaware of the need for adjustment in their rail industries,

---

subsidies under the Regional Rail Reorganization Act of 1973 and later acts; payments for loan guarantee defaults; and Interstate Commerce Commission payments for directed service. *Rail passenger* includes federal grants to Amtrak for operations, capital projects, and labor protection; and expenditures for acquisition and improvements under the Northeast Corridor Improvement Project. Loan guarantee commitments to Amtrak, which were paid off by the federal government in fiscal 1984 after the company defaulted, are included in the fiscal year in which the original obligation of funds took place. Expenditures exclude federal grants for commuter rail services channeled through the Urban Mass Transportation Administration. *Other* includes expenditures on railroad research and development (including the High-Speed Ground Transportation program) and railroad safety by the U.S. Department of Transportation, and payments to the Alaska Railroad Revolving Fund. Totals exclude administrative expenses of the Federal Railroad Administration and Interstate Commerce Commission.

Figure 2-4. *Federal Rail Expenditures in Canada, 1970–85*[a]

Millions of 1982 Canadian dollars

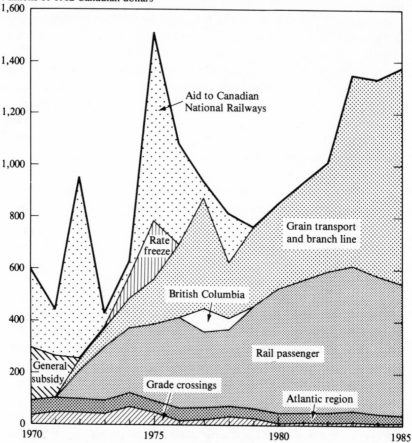

Sources: *Public Accounts of Canada,* various years; Government of Canada, *Estimates* and *Supplementary Estimates,* 1985–86; Canadian National Railways, *Annual Report,* various years; and Canadian Transport Commission, *Annual Report,* various years. All data are for federal fiscal years ending on March 31. Canadian National Railways loan and stock purchase data have been converted from nearest calendar year.

a. *Aid to Canadian National Railways* includes purchase of 4 percent preferred shares in the company and changes in the principal on loans and advances to the company from the Government of Canada. Also includes federal payments to meet CN deficits and payments compensating CN for termination of tolls on the Victoria Bridge in Montreal. Dividends paid by CN to the government are treated as negative outlays. Excludes interest paid on debt and effects of the 1978 recapitalization on debt principal. Excludes payments to CN Marine for ferry services and Gulf railway interface. *General subsidy* includes "normal payments" under Section 413 of the National Transportation Act. *Rate freeze* subsidy includes payments to railways in 1973 and 1974 for revenues forgone as a result of a rate freeze. *Grain transport and branch line* subsidies include payments to the railways for traffic originating on unprofitable branch lines pursuant to the National Transportation Act; payments to the railways under the Western Grain Transportation Act; contributions toward rehabilitation of Prairie branch lines; and payments to the Canadian Wheat Board and to the railways for acquisition, rehabilitation, maintenance, leasing, and operation of hopper cars and boxcars for transportation of grain in Western Canada. *British Columbia* subsidy includes payments to the province of British Columbia and to Canadian National Railways in 1977 and 1978 for rail projects in that province. Excludes port development expenditures related to northeast British Columbia coal development. *Rail passenger* includes subsidies to railway companies under the National Transportation Act for continuing unprofitable passenger services and stock purchases in and grants to VIA Rail Canada. Excludes grants to the provinces for commuter rail programs. *Atlantic region* subsidies include payments under the Maritime Freight Rates Act and the Atlantic Region

but because of the complex political pressures confronting them they have viewed industrial adjustment goals as something to be minimally satisfied rather than maximized. For the most part, concern with "public needs" goals has dominated.

These priorities stem both from the underlying structure of costs and benefits and from the way decisions are made. The Interstate Commerce Commission's and Canadian Transport Commission's quasi-judicial decisionmaking process for individual line abandonments and passenger train discontinuances is antithetical to an adjustment planning approach: services are considered only when the railways bring a case, and individual services are considered on their own merits rather than as part of a national system.[53] The case approach also reinforces the emphasis of the ICC and CTC on the public needs aspects of their responsibilities: the negative service and employment consequences of cutbacks are concentrated and highly visible, while individual abandonment and discontinuance decisions can make only modest contributions to solving the carriers' financial woes. Thus shippers' interests have tended to be favored in abandonment cases. The railroads adapted by bringing cases only for lines with little or no traffic (hence little or no opposition), which are not the greatest money losers. The ICC also attempted to avoid imposing losses in merger cases, and thus often took years to make decisions. Nevertheless, aggrieved parties frequently challenged commission decisions in the courts, further delaying final decisions.

Executive and regulatory agencies in the United States and Canada have rarely been given explicit restructuring authority, and the limited powers they have had they have not used. U.S. Transportation Coordinator Eastman did not press for consolidations between 1933 and 1936, and the secretaries of transportation have made little use of their authority to propose and guide consolidations granted by the 4R act. Significant government-directed restructuring of the North American rail industry has occurred only during times of industrial crisis—notably with the

53. The ICC does not have jurisdiction over discontinuance of intercity passenger trains operated by Amtrak.

Freight Assistance Act and payments to Canadian National Railways for the TerraTransport containerization program. Includes also payments to Canadian National Railways to supplement pensions to former employees of Newfoundland railway, steamship, and telecommunication services and to the Intercolonial and Prince Edward Island Employee's Provident Fund. *Grade crossings* includes payments by Transport Canada and the Canadian Transport Commission, except for those listed under "Urban Transport" in the Public Accounts.

b. Total expenditures are slightly overstated because aid to Canadian National Railways (except programs included in other sections of this figure) becomes negative after 1978.

creation of Canadian National Railways early in this century, and of Amtrak, Conrail, and VIA Rail in the 1970s. Equally important, government-directed restructuring has been limited to those segments of the industry where carriers were either least able to resist or least interested in doing so. Moreover, the short-term consequences of those changes, whatever the government's original intent, were generally more protective than accelerationist.

Why has restructuring authority been granted so seldom and exercised so weakly? The railways have opposed government-planned restructuring because it may impose losses on them—possibly forcing a few out of business, splitting up others, and adversely affecting the competitive position of still others. Even those companies that are not injured view government-planned restructuring with caution: it sets a dangerous precedent, and they might not fare so well in a second round. Nor have efforts to develop a basic network of unprofitable but socially or politically necessary rail operations held any appeal for carriers, for once government has given its imprimatur to a set of services, it is very difficult to remove it. Canada's Prairie rail network is the classic example. What begins as an accelerationist initiative is likely to end as a protectionist one.

Users of rail services have also been wary of restructuring and planning efforts. Ending unprofitable operations may improve service for some shippers and passengers, but others lose service altogether. Rail industry employees have perhaps the least to gain from government-planned restructuring, which would accelerate the already precipitous drop in rail employment since World War II. In the United States, railway-paid labor protection agreements offered them most of the benefits that any government plan would offer. Thus until carriers proved incapable of making these payments, rail labor was better off under the status quo.

The U.S. and Canadian governments lack the capabilities needed to counteract societal opposition or indifference to accelerationist policy. Elected officials were particularly reluctant to take the blame for cuts in service that would inevitably come with restructuring or designation of a network of essential operations. Moreover, the recent history of the North American rail industry has been characterized by conflict between bureaucracies and by the overruling of bureaucratic decisions by elected officials. The Canadian cabinet responded to political concerns by placing most Prairie branch lines outside the purview of the Canadian Transport Commission. In the United States, Congress has been reluctant to give any discretion to the executive branch, fearing that it would pay insufficient attention to service needs. After the U.S. Department of Transportation used its power to designate the routes of the newly formed Amtrak to make substantial cuts in the U.S. rail passenger network, Congress feared that it would do so again in the case of Conrail. Thus an independent agency (the U.S. Railway Association) was set up to do Conrail planning.

Protectionist policy, with its incremental cutbacks in service and substandard financial performance for carriers, pleased none of the major societal or governmental actors involved in rail policymaking. Nevertheless, it was more palatable to all concerned than an accelerationist policy that threatened carriers with a further loss of autonomy (and, for some in the United States, possible extinction), users with loss of services, and employees with a loss of jobs. For governments reluctant to take the blame for service cutbacks and unwilling to create additional precedents for rail industry financial dependence on government, a protectionist policy was the path of least resistance.

When the costs of protectionist policy became intolerable, Ottawa and Washington turned primarily toward market-oriented policies rather than accelerationist ones. These market-oriented policies had a substantial political advantage over accelerationist policies: instead of having to choose concentrated cost bearers among carriers, communities, and employees, the two governments merely had to acquiesce as market forces did the choosing for them.

CHAPTER THREE

The Politics of Policy Instrument Choice

CITIZENS are primarily concerned with the outcomes produced by government action: adequate transportation and housing, clean air and water, and safe streets, for example. Similarly, the important clashes in industrial policy decisions are likely to concern outcomes, whether they be protectionist, market-oriented, or accelerationist. But conflicts may also arise over how the benefits are provided—over the instruments used to deliver policy. Policy choices do not determine instrument choices, although the two decisions are often made concurrently. Nor are conflicts over instrument choice simply reflections of an underlying conflict over policy goals.

Instrument choices are controversial because of the costs and benefits they impose on those responsible for implementing the policy, on their clientele, and on competitors. Consider the auto industry. If a government wants to protect domestic producers from foreign competition, it has several instruments it can use. Tariffs, a form of taxation, are one obvious response. A government can also require a substantial domestic content in automobiles or negotiate "voluntary" import quotas with foreign governments—two forms of regulation. A third option is to provide low-cost loans or loan guarantees to domestic automakers to make them more competitive. A government can also subsidize the operating costs and modernization efforts of domestic automakers or take them over and operate them as a public enterprise.

The level of domestic auto sales and employment might be the same regardless of the instrument chosen, but the costs imposed on automakers, employees, and consumers vary. Stockholders of firms subject to nationalization may not wish to lose control of their holdings. Consumers may resist the higher prices, decreased options, and long delivery times resulting from import quotas. Central budgetary agencies are likely to oppose subsidies to the private sector unless they are accompanied by cost controls.

62

Instrument choice also has important implications for industrial adjustment policy. First, instrument choice decisions offer an opportunity to change industry structure and government goals by creating new actors and mechanisms of influence over the industry. Thus instrument choices are likely to have policy implications as well, whether intended or not. Second, instruments have differing capabilities for accelerating industrial change. While instruments can be substituted for one another to some extent, individual policy instruments have distinctive advantages and disadvantages. Regulation, for example, can help prohibit certain types of behavior by firms or industries, but it may be inadequate when additional resources need to be injected into an industry, and it is a clumsy mechanism when government wants to induce (rather than foreclose) specific types of behavior by individual firms. Thus if a government relies very heavily on regulation and eschews public enterprise and subsidies, it may be at a disadvantage in dealing with many types of industrial adjustment tasks.

Governments choose policy instruments for reasons in addition to their industrial adjustment capabilities, however. This chapter examines a broad range of instrument capabilities and institutional constraints that influence those choices. It begins by outlining the major instrument options open to governments and some of the capabilities and weaknesses of each instrument, giving particular attention to public enterprise. A discussion of differences between the United States and Canada in their use of public enterprise follows. Possible explanations for the selection or rejection of public enterprise are then considered. The chapter argues that the choice of policy instruments is not simply the byproduct of economic conditions and government policy objectives; rather, U.S.-Canadian differences in the use of public enterprise can best be explained in terms of the cost-benefit distributions and political structures outlined in chapter 1. Political structures, in particular, exercise a decisive influence on the instrument preferences of policymakers and on their ability to win approval for those preferences.

Options for Instrument Choice

The policy instruments available to governments can be divided into three main categories: administrative (for example, state enterprise and direct delivery by government agencies), financial incentive (for example, tax policy, loans and debt guarantees, and various types of purchase arrangements), and regulatory. Each has distinctive strengths and weaknesses. Although each instrument may not be equally applicable in every instance (regulatory and incentive approaches would not be acceptable in providing for national defense, for example), in most cases governments have several options for delivering policy.

The probability of a particular instrument being chosen is determined by a number of factors. First, instruments have what may be called *economic attributes*. Some instruments offer—in theory at least—more direct control by policymakers than others. Instruments may also differ in their ability to take advantage of private sector production efficiencies, in their cost to government, and in the precision with which their benefits can be targeted. Second, policy instruments have differing *political attributes*. Some policy instruments are easier to use because they do not show up in budget totals or do not require immediate government outlays. Obviously, the line between economic and political attributes is not precise because economic attributes can have political implications, and vice versa. Finally, the advantages and disadvantages of a policy instrument will not necessarily be the same in all cases in all countries. Thus *political system constraints*—attributes not of the instrument itself but of its environment—will be considered later in this chapter. Table 3-1 presents six major policy instruments and the economic and political attributes (characterized as advantages and disadvantages) that are likely to be associated with each of them.[1] No attempt is made here to be exhaustive in relating each attribute to each instrument; rather, the focus is on the most distinctive attributes associated with each instrument.

Administrative Instruments

Maximum government control over policy delivery is generally offered by administrative policy instruments such as government agencies and public enterprise. (The terms *public enterprise, state-owned enterprise,* and *government corporation* will be used interchangeably here.) In general, public enterprises have the following attributes: (1) they are

1. In the jargon of political science, these are "ideal typical" attributes of the instruments, just as the instrument categories are themselves ideal type simplifications of a diverse set of instruments. Whether the attributes actually are present depends in large measure on political system constraints.

organized as corporations, (2) they sell rather than give away their products, (3) they are expected to be self-supporting, and (4) government or one of its state enterprises plays a dominant proprietary role in their management through equity ownership or appointment to the board of directors. But exceptions can be found to each of these rules. Some government corporations (for example, the Federal Financing Bank in the United States) operate essentially as parts of their sponsoring departments, and some unincorporated entities that formally are parts of departments (for example, the Alaska Railroad while it was federally owned) operate with autonomy more characteristic of public enterprise. Other enterprises, such as Amtrak, have some equity participation by the private sector but may operate in ways indistinguishable from their wholly owned kin. Still others (for example, the Legal Services Corporation and the Canada Council) are not primarily engaged in commercial activity. For many government corporations, financial self-sufficiency is a far-off dream at best. Thus these characteristics should be thought of as guidelines to a very complex reality rather than as necessary defining characteristics.

Public enterprise has several characteristics that make it attractive to policymakers. It offers a middle road between the flexibility and efficiency thought to inhere in private enterprise and the control possible with direct management by a government agency. Public enterprise is free of many of the restrictions—civil service hiring and firing, salary limitations, public access to information—that would hinder a government agency trying to function in a market environment. It can also reduce the administrative burden on government and keep political influence out of certain government functions. At the same time, state enterprises may incorporate noncommercial goals without government intervention in the day-to-day affairs of the firm.[2] If a serious dispute arises between government and enterprise, the prerogatives of ownership are likely to lead more quickly and surely to an outcome satisfactory to government than the prerogatives of a regulator or giver of contracts.

Public enterprise can also provide government with information and expertise that it might not be able to obtain using financial incentive or regulatory mechanisms. This expertise can be particularly helpful in extractive industries dominated by foreign multinational corporations

2. See the discussion in Government of Canada, Privy Council Office, *Crown Corporations: Direction, Control, Accountability* (Ottawa: Supply and Services, 1977), pp. 16–22.

Table 3-1. *Instrument Options for Government*

Basic approach	Instrument	Advantages of instrument	Disadvantages of instrument
Administrative	Public enterprise	—Flexibility and efficiency. —More direct control than with incentive instruments. —Information and expertise.[a] —Stable commitment.[a]	—May be difficult to control. —Difficult to dismantle. —Likely to provoke strong societal opposition.[a]
	Government agency	—Maximum financial and political control.	—May be inflexible and unable to innovate. —Long-term planning difficult because of close supervision (yearly appropriations).
Financial incentive	Loan guarantees	—No initial government expenditure.	—High contingent liability. —Inappropriate where long-term financial assistance required.
	Tax policy	—Less administrative burden on government. —Budget totals lowered.[a]	—Ineffective in aiding nontaxpayers. —Difficult to target effectively. —Budgetary priorities obscured.
	Purchase (subsidies, grants, and contracts)	—Effective targeting. —Uses private sector efficiencies. —Flexibility for short-term programs. —Accurate identification of costs.	—Direct demand on budget.[a] —May create dependence relationships. —May lead to oversupply.
Regulatory	Regulation	—Low direct cost to government.	—Inappropriate where financial assistance needed. —Hides costs of government action. —Inefficient allocation of resources. —Difficult to encourage "positive" acts.

a. Instrument attributes that are primarily political rather than economic.

(that may use intrafirm transactions to minimize their payment of economic rents) and in industries heavily dependent upon government subsidies.

Finally, the establishment of a public enterprise in a particular sector generally implies a long-term commitment by the government to action in that industry even though the government may not desire such a commitment. Creation of a public enterprise greatly complicates the problem of "exit" from an industry, for that firm and its employees have a strong interest in resisting efforts to dismantle it. Public enterprises may become quite adept at building grass-roots support among clientele groups.[3]

These attributes of public enterprise also give it certain advantages as an instrument of accelerationist industrial policy. Nationalization of several private sector firms to form a single public enterprise can serve as a vehicle for substantial sectoral restructuring. State enterprise managers are likely to have a more thorough knowledge of market conditions than bureaucrats do; this information can be extremely helpful to government officials in formulating sectoral policy. And public enterprise managers are presumably more responsive to government policy initiatives than their private sector counterparts, although part III of this study will show that this is not always so.

The disadvantages of public enterprise are closely related to its advantages. As noted earlier, government-owned firms are difficult to dismantle. Because they have more autonomy than government agencies, they may be more difficult to control. They may stress financial returns to the exclusion of noncommercial goals or pay insufficient attention to costs due to their access to the public purse.[4] Indeed, the conflict between the two attributes of control and flexibility is perhaps the central dilemma of public enterprise. State-owned firms must follow legitimate direction by government and must be shielded from illegitimate influence, but there is little agreement on which interventions are legitimate and which are not. Some trade-offs between flexibility and control must be made, but there are no easy guidelines to follow.

3. On the problem of exit, see Albert O. Hirschman, *Exit, Voice and Loyalty* (Harvard University Press, 1970). For an application to public enterprise, see John Baldwin, *The Regulatory Agency and the Public Corporation: The Canadian Air Transport Industry* (Ballinger, 1975). On enterprise-clientele relations, see Philip Selznick, *TVA and the Grass Roots* (University of California Press, 1949; Harper and Row, 1966).
4. Annmarie Hauck Walsh, *The Public's Business* (MIT Press, 1978), p. 6.

Finally, public enterprise has an important political disadvantage. If production of a good or service by a public enterprise preempts or competes with private sector producers, it is likely to spark more societal opposition than would financial incentives to the private sector.

Government agencies are a second form of administrative instrument. They offer, in theory at least, the advantages of maximum financial and political control in policy selection and implementation. Program managers are directly responsible to political executives, and financing occurs through the normal budgetary process. Government agencies also have disadvantages as policy instruments, as table 3-1 shows. They may be inflexible and lack the ability to innovate. Close supervision (including, in the United States, annual appropriations for most agencies) makes long-range planning difficult.[5]

Financial Incentive Instruments

Financial instruments offer governments a variety of alternatives to state enterprise and direct administration. *Loan guarantees* (for example, to the Lockheed and Chrysler corporations) steer private credit to sectors where government has an interest. They have the advantage of requiring no immediate expenditure of government funds, but they also have serious limitations: they are inappropriate for funding the long-term operating losses of dying industries because they create a growing government obligation with no hope that the loans can be paid back. In addition, loan guarantees create contingent liabilities that seriously complicate budgetary planning.[6] Thus loan guarantees are likely to be more useful in promoting adjustment in the sunrise and mature phases of an industry than in its declining stage.

Tax policy allows governments to influence the private sector, not through direct government expenditure, but by providing incentives through the tax code. Tax incentives help hold down government spending, allowing officeholders to proclaim their fiscal restraint.[7] Of

5. Harold Seidman, *Politics, Position and Power,* 2d ed. (New York: Oxford University Press, 1975), p. 5.

6. U.S. Congressional Budget Office, *Loan Guarantees: Current Concerns and Alternatives for Control, A Compilation of Staff Working Papers* (Government Printing Office, 1979).

7. See Stanley Surrey, "Tax Subsidies as a Device for Implementing Government Policy: A Comparison with Direct Government Expenditures," in U.S. Congress, Joint

course, government revenues are reduced, so savings are illusory. But voters generally do not perceive this. Tax incentives also have serious problems and limitations: individuals and organizations that do not pay taxes cannot benefit. Moreover, tax incentives are likely to obscure budgetary priorities because they are not generally regarded as government expenditures. As a mechanism for industrial adjustment, tax incentives have the disadvantage of being difficult to target at specific firms. Tax credits for research and development expenditures in growing industries, for example, may lead to duplication of efforts by many firms at government expense, with little assurance that any of the firms will have the financial strength to bring their discoveries to market.

Purchase in all its variants (for example, procurement, subsidies, grants, outside contracts) provides incentives through direct government expenditures.[8] Through purchase arrangements, governments can take advantage of efficiencies of private sector operation and, for programs of short or indeterminate duration, provide goods or services without adding permanent employees or facilities. Purchase can also target assistance to individual firms more effectively than regulation and tax incentives. These attributes may be particularly helpful in the short-term, carefully targeted interventions characteristic of accelerationist policy. But there are parallel disadvantages to purchase arrangements. Unlike tax incentives, purchases show up in the budget. And unless subsidies are carefully targeted, they may simply provide unneeded revenues for groups that would have acted in the desired fashion without subsidy or create an oversupply of a desired good or service.[9] As chapter 2 noted, poor targeting of subsidies led to excess railway construction, especially in Canada. Purchase arrangements may also lead to such strong relations of mutual dependence between government agencies and their major contractors that the government becomes obligated to back a contractor in difficulty while lacking effective control over

Economic Committee, *The Economics of Federal Subsidy Programs: A Compendium of Papers* (GPO, 1972), pp. 74–105; Ken Woodside, "Tax Incentives vs. Subsidies: Political Considerations in Governmental Choice," *Canadian Public Policy*, vol. 5 (Spring 1979), pp. 248–56; and Charles Schultze, *The Public Use of Private Interest* (Brookings, 1977).

8. For a general discussion of contracting, see Murray Weidenbaum, *The Modern Public Sector* (Basic Books, 1969); and Ira Sharkansky, *Whither the State?* (Chatham House, 1979).

9. See George Break, "Subsidies as an Instrument for Achieving Public Economy Goals," in U.S. Congress, Joint Economic Committee, *The Economics of Federal Subsidy Programs* (GPO, 1972), pp. 1–6.

management. For example, when the Lockheed Corporation, a major defense contractor, was threatened with bankruptcy in 1971, the U.S. government felt compelled to provide loan guarantees to the company.

Regulatory Instruments

Regulation uses commands rather than incentives to gain compliance, maintaining both funding responsibility and ownership in the private sector. Thus, considering its tremendous economic impact, regulation has a relatively low direct cost to government.[10] Regulation also has disadvantages, however. If firms are unable to pass on the costs of regulation to consumers they will fail or become dependent upon direct government aid. Some economists argue that regulation promotes inefficient allocation of resources and hides the true costs of government decisions.[11] Perhaps most important, regulation is likely to be inadequate when a positive rather than a negative response is sought—for example, when government wants a firm to produce a specific product rather than end a proscribed practice. This is a strong handicap in carrying out an accelerationist industrial policy.

Patterns of Instrument Choice in North America

Nations differ markedly in their instrument choices—for example, in their use of public enterprise. Cross-national data on public enterprise activity are subject to particularly severe problems of data comparability, but table 3-2 gives fairly realistic rankings of a number of Western industrial countries. Canada is near the middle of these rankings, while the United States is at the bottom.[12] There are additional differences

10. The administrative expenditures of federal regulatory agencies total about $3 billion per year, while the "costs" of regulation to the U.S. economy in the mid-1970s were variously estimated at between $66 billion and $130 billion per year. See Paul MacAvoy, *The Regulated Industries and the Economy* (W. W. Norton, 1979), pp. 21, 130–31.

11. Richard Posner, "Taxation by Regulation," *Bell Journal of Economics and Management Science,* vol. 2 (Spring 1971), pp. 26–27, 41–43.

12. For overviews of public enterprise in the two countries, see Lloyd Musolf, "Public Enterprise and Public Interest in the United States," in André Gelinas, ed., *Public Enterprise and the Public Interest* (Toronto: Institute of Public Administration of Canada, 1978); Ronald C. Moe, *Administering Public Functions at the Margin of Government: The Case of Federal Corporations,* Congressional Research Service Report 83-236GOV (CSR, 1983); and Allan Tupper and G. Bruce Doern, eds., *Public Corporations and Public Policy in Canada* (Montreal: Institute for Research on Public Policy, 1981).

Table 3-2. *Public Enterprise Shares of Selected Western Economies*

Country	Percent of gross fixed capital formation	Employment as percent of labor force
Austria	19.2	13.7
Belgium	13.1	5.2
Canada	14.8	3.0
Denmark	8.3	3.4
France	14.0	7.3
Germany, Federal Republic of	10.8	7.2
Ireland	11.8	7.3
Italy	15.2	6.6
Japan	11.2	2.8
Netherlands	12.6	3.6
Spain	15.6	2.9
Sweden	15.3	8.2
United Kingdom	16.8	8.1
United States	4.4	1.5

Sources: All data on gross fixed capital formation are for various years in the late 1970s and are from R. P. Short, "The Role of Public Enterprises: An International Statistical Comparison," table 1, in Robert H. Floyd, Clive S. Gray, and R. P. Short, *Public Enterprise in Mixed Economies: Some Macroeconomic Aspects* (Washington, D.C.: International Monetary Fund, 1984). Employment data, except for Canada, are from "The State in the Market," *The Economist*, December 30, 1978, p. 40. These data are for various years in the 1970s and were derived from data from Organization for Economic Cooperation and Development (OECD), European Centre for Public Enterprise, and national sources. Canadian employment is for 1975 and is from Richard M. Bird, *Financing Canadian Government: A Quantitative Overview* (Toronto: Canadian Tax Foundation, 1979), p. 4.

between the two countries in their sectoral distribution of public enterprises. Table 3-3 gives a partial listing of U.S. and Canadian public enterprises (both federal and state or provincial), divided into four broad sectors: infrastructure, manufacturing, energy and natural resources, and financial services. There are some similarities between the two countries in infrastructure-type industries. But even here, Canadian Crown corporations have no U.S. counterparts in many industries (for example, airlines, telecommunications), while in others (railways, radio and television, electricity) their share of their respective national markets is far greater than in the United States.

National differences are much more evident in the manufacturing and energy and natural resources sectors. Public enterprise plays virtually no role in these sectors in the United States, but it is quite active at the federal and provincial levels in Canada. Canadian state ownership is particularly interesting because government-owned firms—Canadian National Railways, Petro-Canada, the Canadian Broadcasting Corporation (CBC), and Air Canada, for example—often operate alongside private corporations rather than function as monopolies.

Table 3-3. *Selected Public Enterprises in Canada and the United States*

Industry	Canada	United States
Manufacturing		
Steel	Sydney Steel Corporation	None
	Sidbec	
Aerospace	Canadair	None
	DeHavilland of Canada	
Nuclear power plants	Atomic Energy of Canada, Ltd.	None
Transportation equipment	Flyer Industries	None
	Urban Transportation Development Corporation	
Energy and Natural Resources		
Petroleum and petrochemicals	Petro-Canada	U.S. Synthetic Fuels Corporation[a]
	Alberta Energy Corporation[b]	
	Ontario Energy Corporation	
	Saskatchewan Oil and Gas Corporation	
	Société Québécoise d'Initiatives Pétrolières	
Mining	Cape Breton Development Corporation	None
	Canada Development Corporation[b]	
	Eldorado Nuclear, Ltd.	
	National Asbestos Corporation of Quebec	
	Potash Corporation of Saskatchewan	
Infrastructure		
Airlines	Air Canada	None
	Nordair (1979–84)	
	Pacific Western Airlines (1974–84)	
	NorOntAir	
	Quebecair	
Railways	Canadian National Railways	Consolidated Rail Corporation
	VIA Rail Canada	Amtrak
	Alberta Resources Railway	Alaska Railroad
	British Columbia Railway	
	Ontario Northland	
Trucking	CN Route	None
	Northern Transportation Company, Ltd.	
Waterways and harbors	St. Lawrence Seaway Authority	St. Lawrence Seaway Development Corporation
	Canada Ports Corporation	

Table 3-3. *Selected Public Enterprises in Canada and the United States (continued)*

Industry	Canada	United States
Waterways and harbors (continued)		Port Authority of New York and New Jersey and others
Broadcasting	Canadian Broadcasting Corporation	Corporation for Public Broadcasting
Telecommunications	CN Communications Teleglobe Canada Provincial telephone companies	None
Postal services	Canada Post Corporation	U.S. Postal Service
Electricity	Hydro-Quebec, Ontario Hydro, B.C. Hydro, and other provincial companies	Tennessee Valley Authority and municipal companies
Financial Services		
Banking	Alberta Treasury Branches Province of Ontario Savings Office	None
Commercial credit	Federal Business Development Bank	None
Housing credit	Central Mortgage and Housing Corporation	Government National Mortgage Association
Agricultural credit and insurance	Farm Credit Corporation Provincial crop insurance companies	Commodity Credit Corporation Federal Crop Insurance Corporation
Export development	Export Development Corporation	Export-Import Bank Overseas Private Investment Corporation
Deposit insurance	Canada Deposit Insurance Corporation	Federal Deposit Insurance Corporation Federal Savings and Loan Insurance Corporation
General insurance	Saskatchewan Government Insurance and other provincial companies	None
Pension insurance	None	Pension Benefit Guaranty Corporation

a. Financing of private sector projects only; no direct production role.
b. Partial ownership.

The operation of public enterprises in more sectors in Canada than in the United States does not mean that U.S. governments forgo intervention entirely in those sectors. Rather, the differences reflect the willingness of Canadian governments to employ public enterprise in addition to regulatory and incentive instruments used in both countries. Telephones, oil, broadcasting, and airlines are four prominent sectors in which U.S. governments have implemented their policies primarily through regulation, while Canadian governments have used public enterprise as well.

The higher barriers to use of public enterprise in the United States appear to be to their operation in specific sectors and by the federal government rather than to public enterprise per se. There are few public enterprises engaged in manufacturing and resource extraction in the United States. But government corporations are quite common at the state and municipal levels, where thousands of such firms operate hospitals, transit systems, ports, and housing projects.[13]

Why has the choice of policy instruments differed so greatly in the United States and Canada? The next section addresses this question.

Explaining Instrument Choice

Earlier in this chapter, three broad hypotheses were suggested to explain why governments differ in their selection of policy instruments: the economic attributes of the instruments, the political attributes of the instruments, and the constraints resulting from the broader political system. This section rejects the economic attributes of instruments as a sufficient explanation of instrument choice. A superior explanation can be found in the interaction of the political variables.

Economic Variables

Policy instruments have different economic advantages and disadvantages, as outlined in table 3-1. Thus governments with different economic circumstances or policy goals may choose policy instruments with attributes tailored to their own particular needs.

13. Walsh, *The Public's Business*.

DIFFERENCES IN NATIONAL ECONOMIES. Differences in national economic circumstances, such as the size of national markets and adequacy of private capital, can have an important influence on instrument choice even when governments pursue similar goals (for example, balanced regional development). Table 3-4 presents some of the economic conditions that may lead to the establishment of public enterprise, the instrument characteristics needed for an adequate response to these conditions, and the instruments from table 3-1 that are most appropriate under the circumstances.

Differences in national economic circumstances offer plausible explanations for much of the variation in instrument choice between Canada and the United States. Throughout its history, Canada has needed to make substantial infrastructure investments to facilitate export of its raw materials and to create a unified national economy distinct from that of the United States.[14] The size and risk of such investments and the relative underdevelopment of Canadian capital markets encouraged permanent commitment in the form of public enterprise, particularly where the alternatives were "the state or the United States."[15] The role of U.S.-based multinational corporations in Canada's economy has led the Canadian government to establish government-owned firms as "national champions" and as sources of expertise in markets dominated by multinationals (Petro-Canada in the oil industry, for example).

Differences in national economies cannot sufficiently explain instrument choice, however. For each of the economic conditions listed in table 3-4, the righthand column of the table lists several policy instruments that can be used to respond. Economic circumstances are likely to be more helpful in explaining *whether* a government will intervene than *how* it will intervene. Economic conditions may create a propensity for state intervention in some form and perhaps narrow the range of applicable instruments. For example, most governments would not employ debt guarantees to sustain a clearly senescent industry because firms could not repay the loans. Rarely, however, will economic conditions dictate the choice of public enterprise or any other single policy

14. Hugh G. H. Aitken, "Defensive Expansionism: The State and Economic Growth in Canada," in W. T. Easterbrook and M. H. Watkins, eds., *Approaches to Canadian Economic History* (Toronto: McClelland and Stewart, 1967), pp. 182–221.

15. This was the choice posed by proponents of the Canadian Broadcasting Corporation. See Frank Peers, *The Politics of Canadian Broadcasting, 1920–1951* (Toronto: University of Toronto Press, 1969), p. 441.

Table 3-4. *Industrial Problems and Instrument Responses*

Economic circumstances	*Nature of problem*	*Requirements for adequate response*	*Possible instruments*
Collective goods	Benefit cannot be restricted to those who pay for it, so firms cannot provide the goods (for example, street lighting) profitably.	Permanent subsidy or cross-subsidy.	Public enterprise; government agency; subsidy.
Natural monopoly	Economies of scale make competition costly and lead to a market monopoly; pricing abuses (for example, in electricity and local phone services) may result.	Stabilization of competition or regulation of monopoly rates.	Public enterprise; regulation.
Infant industries	Owing to their small scale and lack of advanced technology, industries cannot compete with imports.	Protection of markets, capital assistance, or restructuring of industry to create larger firms.	Public enterprise: regulation (import restrictions); tax policy (tariffs); subsidy; loan or loan guarantee.
Premature enterprise	Sufficient market to provide commercial return does not yet exist (for example, railway through unsettled area).	Capital assistance or sharing of risk.	Public enterprise; subsidy; loan or loan guarantee.
Senescent industry	Commercial return is no longer possible due to product obsolescence (for example, buggy whips) or international competition (for example, shipbuilding).	Long-term operating and capital assistance or phase-out of industry.	State enterprise; subsidy.
Collection of economic rent	Government seeks to maximize revenue from fixed-supply good without making that good uncompetitive in price (for example, mineral lease).	Information, expertise, and control.	Public enterprise; tax policy.

instrument. Many of the economic conditions cited in table 3-4 do not require administrative instruments. Natural monopolies can be stabilized through regulation; premature enterprises can be aided through loans, loan guarantees, or subsidies; and senescent industries can be bailed out through subsidies.

The distinctive advantages of public enterprise—commitment, information, flexibility, control—make it particularly appropriate for rescuing senescent industries (which require a long-term commitment of funds) and for collecting economic rent (which requires detailed information). Increasing management flexibility may be helpful in both situations. But even in these cases, other instruments can be substituted for public enterprise. Neither situation requires economic attributes unique to a single instrument for an adequate response. Thus national differences in those conditions cannot provide a sufficient explanation of variations in use of public enterprise. Economic circumstances, however, do play a critical role in governments' instrument choice by making intervention probable, by limiting the number of applicable instruments, and by placing nationalization on the agenda.

DIFFERENCES IN POLICY GOALS. Governments may also vary in their use of public enterprise because they make different policy decisions that require different instrument attributes. Country A might decide to pursue protectionist policies, for example, while Country B chooses to accelerate industrial adjustment. The means differ because the ends differ.

Explanations of instrument choice based on policy goals have the same problem as those based on economic circumstances. Although policy goals limit the number of applicable policy instruments, they do not pinpoint a single instrument of choice. For example, the economic attributes of public enterprise can be used either to hasten or to delay industrial adjustment. Thus policy choice is not a sufficient explanation of why public enterprise is selected.

Political Constraints

The economic attributes of policy instruments leave decisionmakers considerable discretion in instrument choice. For a more complete explanation of the greater use of public enterprise in Canada than in the United States, the political attributes of instruments and societies must be considered. These political constraints may influence (1) the extent to which an instrument's economic attributes are likely to be present in particular cases—for example, policymakers' perceptions of whether they will really be able to control a specific public enterprise; (2) what instrument attributes governmental and nongovernmental actors value; and (3) the obstacles opponents of a particular instrument choice are able to place in the way of its adoption.

PAST CHOICE. Several political factors can influence instrument choice. A first is past choice. Because decisionmakers often lack the time and information to evaluate fully the relative merits of various policy instruments, they may base their decisions largely upon precedent.[16] The more familiar an instrument, the more likely it is to gain acceptance. (Familiarity can also breed contempt, of course, and if a policy instrument has been a spectacular failure, it is unlikely to be used again.) Thus instruments already in place in a given policy arena will continue to be favored over new ones even if changes in policy or in economic conditions make them less efficacious. Moreover, techniques that have proved satisfactory in one policy arena will be borrowed for application in other contexts even if they are not suitable.

Reference to past choice has obvious appeal in explaining recent U.S. and Canadian instrument choices. Canada is clearly beginning from a larger base of state enterprise activity. Yet a repetition of past choices does not necessarily indicate that they determined present choices. More important, reference to past choice offers little insight into how the existing base of state enterprise activity was achieved. Nor is it consistent with the widespread diffusion of knowledge about public enterprise operations and performance; the reluctance of federal policymakers in the United States to use state-owned firms can hardly be attributed to ignorance. Past choice may accurately predict short-term changes, but it neither explains the origins of long-term differences in policy instruments in the United States and Canada nor the institutional prejudices that underlie those differences.

IDEOLOGY. An alternative approach is to examine political ideology. In this view, national variations in the use of policy instruments are caused by differing popular beliefs, presumably reflected in the countries' party systems. Thus socialist governments, and governments where socialist parties represent a substantial, accepted minority, will tend to use administrative instruments, while free enterprise–oriented govern-

16. The classic statement of this approach is Charles Lindblom, "The Science of Muddling Through," *Public Administration Review*, vol. 19 (Spring 1959), pp. 79–88.

ments will tend to use incentive or regulatory instruments.[17] More generally, administrative instruments will be selected only where the public accepts the notion of the state as an active participant in molding society as well as an impartial mediator.

Numerous scholars have stressed the ideological differences between Canada and the United States. Anthony King, for example, asserts that "the state plays a more limited role in America than elsewhere because Americans, more than other people, want it to play a more limited role."[18] The alleged dominance of classical liberalism in the United States (which is seen to reject all state action that does not have as its goal protection of individual rights) is often contrasted with more diverse ideologies north of the Forty-ninth Parallel.[19] As a result, Canada has, and the United States lacks, a viable socialist tradition and party and a popular belief that the state must play an active role in society in addition to an arbitrating one. Both of these attributes ostensibly make selection of state enterprise more likely.

Clearly, socialism has a stronger electoral pull in Canada than in the United States. The New Democratic party (NDP) has formed the governments of three Canadian provinces.[20] The NDP draws more than 17 percent of the popular vote in federal elections and wins an average of 9 percent of the seats in the House of Commons. Although explicit coalition governments are not used in the House of Commons, the NDP has supported several Liberal minority governments in exchange for legislative concessions, most recently from 1972 to 1974. The NDP is clearly a permanent actor in the Canadian political system, and NDP governments have been very active in using public enterprise.

The strength of socialist beliefs and parties is not in itself adequate to explain use of public enterprise in Canada, however. Each of Canada's three major parties has established state-owned enterprises while in

17. For an explanation of the extent and performance of public enterprise that focuses on ideological factors, see Walsh, *The Public's Business,* chaps. 1 and 2.

18. Anthony King, "Ideas, Institutions and the Policies of Governments, Part III," *British Journal of Political Science,* vol. 3 (1973), p. 416.

19. See Gad Horowitz, *Canadian Labour in Politics* (Toronto: University of Toronto Press, 1968), chap. 1; Louis Hartz, *The Liberal Tradition in America* (Harcourt, Brace and World, 1955); and Kenneth McRae, "The Structure of Canadian History," in Louis Hartz, ed., *The Founding of New Societies* (Harcourt, Brace and World, 1964), pp. 219–74.

20. The provinces and the years the NDP was in power are Saskatchewan (1944–64, 1971–82); British Columbia (1972–75); and Manitoba (1972–75, 1981–present). Prior to 1961, the NDP was called the Cooperative Commonwealth Foundation.

power.[21] As H.V. Nelles points out, the existence in Canada of the "concept of the positive, interventionist state" legitimizes government ownership.[22]

Even in this broader formulation, the ideological hypothesis cannot explain patterns of public enterprise activity in Canada and the United States. In particular, it does not account for within-nation differences in public enterprise activity. Presumably, ideological opposition to public enterprise should be reasonably consistent in all sectors and at all governmental levels. This is not the case, however. There is more public enterprise activity at subnational levels in the United States than at the federal level, and there is federal activity in a few sectors.

COSTS AND BENEFITS. A more promising explanation of instrument choice—and one that is able to differentiate among economic sectors—focuses on the way political coalitions are built and conflicts adjudicated in specific choice situations. An important political attribute of public enterprise—the high probability that its use will spark societal opposition—has already been noted. The discussion of concentrated versus diffuse costs and benefits developed in chapter 1 provides a helpful framework for explaining why this is so.[23] Many interests—owners, suppliers, customers, competitors, and employees—are likely to be affected by nationalization and by the distinctive attributes of public enterprise—most notably, commitment, information, flexibility, and control. It is impossible to generalize about either the interests (that is, costs borne or benefits gained) or the structure of those groups (concen-

21. Examples include Canadian National Railways, Ontario Hydro, and the Canadian Broadcasting Corporation (the Progressive Conservative party); Trans-Canada Airlines and Petro-Canada (the Liberal party); and Saskatchewan Potash and B.C. Resources (the New Democratic party). However, left-of-center political parties (the NDP and the Parti Québécois) create public enterprises more frequently than other political parties. See Aidan R. Vining and Robert Botterell, "An Overview of the Origins, Growth, Size and Functions of Provincial Crown Corporations," in J. Robert S. Prichard, ed., *Crown Corporations in Canada: The Calculus of Instrument Choice* (Toronto: Butterworths, 1983), pp. 320–24.

22. H. Vivian Nelles, *The Politics of Development: Forests, Mines and Hydro-Electric Power in Ontario, 1849–1941* (Toronto: MacMillan of Canada, 1974), p. 1. See more generally chaps. 1 and 12. Nelles believes that these values continue to exist because they serve the needs of the Canadian business community.

23. For an alternative view—instrument choice as a result of politicians' efforts at vote maximization—see M. J. Trebilcock and others, *The Choice of Governing Instrument* (Ottawa: Supply and Services, 1982), chap. 1. While such an approach is not inconsistent with the view taken here, it seems more fruitful to this author to focus on the interests most directly affected by instrument choice decisions.

trated or diffuse) across all possible nationalization decisions. Even in specific cases, the interests of each group may differ depending on the specific policy choices associated with the choice of instruments (for example, whether all segments of an industry are to be nationalized or only parts of it). It is possible, however, to indicate likely alignments and important exceptions to those alignments.

Owners of a firm that is proposed for nationalization presumably will represent a concentrated interest opposed to nationalization since they will lose the earning power of their assets. But if the earning power of those assets is low or negative and the government's offer of compensation is generous, owners might change their minds. (Of course, if a new firm is to be started, rather than an existing one taken over, opposition from existing owners will not be a problem.) Competitors are also likely to oppose nationalization, fearing that public enterprise will gain unfair access to investment opportunities and government funding or be used to keep their prices down.

Suppliers and customers, on the other hand, may support nationalization, but they are unlikely to be strong proponents since they generally have little to gain or lose from it. Public enterprise implies a stable commitment (and thus a continuing demand for suppliers' products), but most suppliers sell to many firms and so have little stake in instrument choice decisions. Customers in most cases are a large group whose individual members similarly have little stake in instrument choice. Employees may favor public enterprise because of the implied government commitment to maintaining the firm (and hence their jobs), but that view may be tempered if nationalization brings with it a loss of collective bargaining rights—notably the right to strike. In short, those interests most likely to have a *concentrated* stake in instrument choice—existing owners and competitors—probably will oppose use of public enterprise. Thus public enterprise is likely to be rejected for most interventions, if it is even considered at all.

The distribution of costs and benefits helps to explain why federal public enterprise activity in the United States is concentrated in the credit and insurance sectors. Public enterprise is concentrated in areas where beneficiaries are well organized and where there are no potential competitors. The Federal Deposit Insurance Corporation (FDIC), for example, serves the interests of banks that want to be able to assure depositors that the federal government, not some consortium of insurance companies, is insuring their deposits. The Overseas Private Investment Corporation and Pension Benefit Guaranty Corporation offer risk-reducing services to corporations and workers, respectively, that have generally been unable to attract private sector insurers because of their high risk or size. The creation of the Government National Mortgage Association (Ginnie Mae) in 1968 relieved the private sector (formerly mixed ownership) Federal National Mortgage Association of much of the burden of supporting housing for low-income groups.[24] The absence of private sector competitors also helps to explain the sectors in which public enterprise is active at the subnational level (urban mass transit and public housing, for example).

GOVERNMENT INSTITUTIONS. Support by government officials for public enterprise may overcome societal opposition or tip the balance in favor of that instrument. This is particularly true when societal interests are stalemated or when costs and benefits of nationalization are highly diffused.[25] Because nationalization generally imposes concentrated losses on at least some groups, a government's ability to compel agreement is also important. The system of decentralized power and strong checks and balances in the United States offers opponents of any proposal numerous veto points where they can attempt to block it. Moreover, the requirement under the Government Corporation Control Act that all federal public enterprises be created by statute has institutionalized limitations on the power of the executive to create them.[26] In Canada's parliamentary system, by contrast, the tight linkage between the cabinet and the governing party in the House of Commons, party discipline in the Commons, and dominance by a single house within the legislature allow the executive much more freedom to obtain measures it desires and block those it opposes. Indeed, the federal executive in Canada has at its disposal several devices that allow it to establish Crown corporations with little or no consultation with Parliament. The most complicated and time-consuming method is to have a special act passed by Parliament. In addition, a minister can establish Crown corporations without parliamentary approval under the Canada Business Corporations Act, or as a

24. Lloyd Musolf, *Uncle Sam's Private, Profit-Seeking Corporations* (Lexington Books, 1983), pp. 114–15, and chap. 3.
25. Of course, differences of opinion within government are likely—for example, among line agencies that believe they can control a public enterprise more effectively than subsidy recipients, budgetary agencies that are concerned about the difficulty of terminating a public enterprise, and legislators who are worried about excessive enterprise independence.
26. Musolf, "Public Enterprise."

subsidiary of an existing Crown corporation under the statutes governing that firm. In two cases (VIA Rail Canada and Loto-Canada), federal Crown corporations were established through "$1 appropriations" in appropriations acts.[27]

Equally important, concentration of power in the executive branch in Canada shapes government preferences. Canadian government leaders are more likely than U.S. leaders to feel that they can control public enterprises once they have established them. Committees in the Canadian House of Commons lack the expertise, independence, staff support, and prestige of their U.S. counterparts and are therefore incapable of issuing rival commands to the enterprise once it is in place. Because power in the U.S. federal government is highly fragmented, leaders in both the executive and legislature might fear that a public enterprise will inevitably succumb to political intervention by the other branch and to interest group claims that neither government nor the enterprise will have the autonomy to resist. Thus one of the major economic advantages of public enterprise, control, may not hold in practice.

Although fragmentation of power within a single level of government (for example, the national government of the United States) makes adoption of state enterprise more difficult and less attractive to political leaders, conflict between national and subnational governments may have the opposite effect. In Canada, leaders at both the federal and provincial levels of government may use public enterprise to advance their own economic development objectives at the expense of the goals of the other level of government. The relatively small number of provincial governments (ten) increases their legitimacy and visibility as defenders of distinctive regional economic interests. And regional conflict is exacerbated by party discipline in a parliamentary system: to keep the government from falling, federal legislators in the governing party must vote their party's position even when it goes against the wishes of their constituents. Thus provincial governments rather than federal legislators have come to be seen as the primary defenders of provincial interests. Ottawa and the provinces compete for citizen support in areas such as job creation and job saving. In this competition, public enterprise offers substantial advantages over subsidizing private sector firms— namely, more control and higher visibility. In the case of infrastructure industries (for example, telephones, electricity, and railways), provincial

27. Royal Commission on Financial Management and Accountability (Lambert Commission), *Final Report* (Ottawa: Supply and Services, 1979), pp. 333–35.

ownership guarantees that control of a sector essential to regional development will not fall into "outside" hands.[28] It is not surprising that government preferences are very different in the United States, where the states are more numerous and the level of federal-state conflict is lower.

The greater ability of Canadian governments to compel agreement (at least when consensus between Ottawa and the provinces is not required) affects the strategies that societal interests adopt toward instrument choice. Because they know that a determined government can compel adoption of its proposals, they are likely to view obstinance and obstruction as unprofitable strategies. Interest groups and firms are not powerless in Canada, especially if they can paint their grievances in regional terms and make settlement of the dispute subject to federal-provincial negotiations. But in many industry-specific disputes, that strategy simply is not possible. Owners and competitors of a firm proposed for nationalization usually seek the best possible arrangement of "side payments" rather than oppose nationalization on principle.

Canada's economic structure also creates a somewhat different pattern of interests than exists in the United States. Foreign firms, primarily from the United States, play an important role in many Canadian industries. Firms subject to nationalization are more likely than in the United States to be foreign-based, and hence they have relatively weak leverage in the Canadian political system. Domestic support for "patriation" of a firm may be high, and Canadian-owned firms are not likely to view nationalization of foreign-based firms as a precedent to be extended to them. In certain sectors, such as aircraft and nuclear power plant manufacturing, there probably would be no Canadian presence without government intervention of some kind. In these cases there are neither concentrated beneficiaries nor cost-bearers, so government has substantial autonomy in choosing instruments. In most instrument choice decisions, the relatively oligopolistic character of many Canadian industries makes it easier to negotiate a system of side payments to firms remaining in the market, with nonnationalized

28. Moreover, public enterprise allows the federal and provincial governments to intervene in sectors where they would be constitutionally barred from doing so through taxing or regulatory powers—for example, Alberta's and Ontario's ownership of airlines. On rival state-building in Canada, see Larry Pratt, "The State and Province-Building: Alberta's Development Strategy," in Leo Panitch, ed., *The Canadian State: Political Economy and Political Power* (Toronto: University of Toronto Press, 1977), pp. 133–62.

enterprises receiving specified benefits (for example, subsidy, protected market share, or guaranteed rate of return) in exchange for acquiescence in government plans.

The incentives for public ownership in infrastructure sectors are different. Canadian industry faces constant threats from U.S. competitors that have the permanent advantage of a large domestic market. Tariff protections are limited by international agreements. The state can help Canadian businesses to survive by providing infrastructure at low cost.[29]

In short, even where economic differences between the United States and Canada contribute to greater use of public enterprise in the latter, it is because of the way that they affect the strategies of societal and governmental interests. In Canada, strong regional conflict and a dependent economy create societal support for public enterprise, while concentrated governmental power makes public enterprise both more attainable and more desirable to political executives.

Instrument Choice and Industrial Adjustment

As noted at the beginning of this chapter, governments usually do not have industrial adjustment objectives in mind when they choose policy instruments. But because instruments have different capabilities, governments that exclude specific instrument choices may thereby limit their adjustment policy choices as well. Accelerationist policy requires instruments that are selective, "nimble," and capable of promoting change. Regulation is an awkward mechanism for accelerating industrial change because of problems in making the instrument selective and in promoting specific desired actions rather than simply preventing undesirable ones. Tax policy is also difficult to target effectively to specific firms if they are not in a tax-paying situation. Loan guarantees are most effective during the growth phase of an industry, when loss allocation and compensation of losers are least required. Direct provision by a

29. Regarding the establishment of Ontario Hydro, Nelles argues that "from the outset the crusade for public power was a businessmen's movement: they initiated it, formed its devoted, hard-core membership and, most important, they provided it with brilliant leadership. By the phrase 'the people's power,' the businessmen meant cheap electricity for the manufacturer, and it was assumed that the entire community would benefit as a result." Nelles, *The Politics of Development*, pp. 248–49.

government agency is rarely considered for most industries, which leaves *purchase* (in the form of selective subsidies) and *public enterprise* as the most suitable instruments for accelerating adjustment. Both have the potential to promote positive actions, are highly selective, and offer policymakers substantial control to change the instrument's use as an industry moves through its life cycles. Of course, these instruments can also be used for protectionist policies and often are—a subject to be addressed in part III. The high barriers to use of public enterprise in the United States nevertheless exclude from the U.S. government's repertoire an instrument with many of the attributes needed to implement accelerationist goals.

CHAPTER FOUR

Rail Nationalization in the United States: The Politics of Impasse

RAILROADS in the United States remained almost entirely under private ownership until financial crisis in the 1960s and 1970s threatened the industry. This chapter examines the U.S. government's response to three key episodes in that adjustment crisis: the near collapse of rail passenger service in 1970, the failure of the Penn Central Railroad and other northeastern carriers in 1970 and following years, and the bankruptcy of the Milwaukee Road and the Rock Island railroads in the latter half of the 1970s. The political constraints on instrument choice discussed in chapter 3 are used to explain rail nationalization decisions and the resulting pattern of government ownership. This chapter will also assess whether nationalization decisions in the United States promoted significant adjustment in the industry or merely preserved the existing rail industry structure and patterns of service and employment. The next chapter will examine rail nationalization decisions in Canada and draw comparisons between the two countries.

Protectionist federal rail policies in effect through the late 1970s attempted to maintain carrier solvency, preserve service, and ease rail unemployment, while minimizing government expenditures. In striving to balance these conflicting goals, the federal government relied primarily on regulation of rates, mergers, and exit from the industry. Only when regulation proved incapable of reaching these goals were the first tentative steps toward public ownership made with the establishment of Amtrak in 1970 and Conrail in 1973. Innovation in policy instruments served as a substitute for innovation in policy—that is, for a shift toward deregulation.

It was never the government's intent to take over ownership of the railroads, however. Amtrak and Conrail were established with the stated intention of avoiding nationalization, and both retained elements of

private ownership for several years. The Nixon administration reluc-
tantly supported the creation of Amtrak and Conrail because it believed
that "quasi-private" corporations offered the minimum financial involvement that would be politically viable, while providing sufficient
executive control to minimize future demands. Congressional opponents
of cutbacks in service, on the other hand, saw "quasi-public" corporations as a means of ensuring that rail policy would not be dominated by
a budget-conscious executive. The federal government's refusal to
choose between the fundamental goals of continued passenger and freight
service and the financial viability of the railroads doomed any hope of a
private sector solution. Public enterprise thus emerged, unplanned, in
the struggle over implementation of these goals.

The multiple veto points within the federal government contributed
greatly to this impasse. Implementing an accelerationist industrial policy
requires united government, bureaucratic autonomy and expertise, and
mechanisms to compel compliance. The U.S. process is the antithesis
of these conditions. It makes a workable consensus imperative because
groups can use veto points to avoid having losses imposed on them,
places a premium on postponing conflict as a means of preserving
consensus, and thus ensures that the solution reached will not differ
radically from the status quo.

Some features of accelerationist policy were evident in the creation
of Amtrak and Conrail (for example, system-wide planning, cutbacks in
unprofitable operations, government-funded transitional assistance for
labor), but protectionist goals—and policy impasse—were dominant.
During the 1970s, recognition of the need for rail industry adjustment
grew, and it became clear that Amtrak and Conrail had not been effective
vehicles for promoting substantial and continuing change. This perceived
failing led later administrations to reject the public or quasi-public
corporation approach in dealing with the Rock Island and Milwaukee
Road bankruptcies.

Preserving Passenger Service: Amtrak

The National Railroad Passenger Corporation, commonly known as
Amtrak, grew out of the spectacular decline of intercity rail passenger
service in North America after World War II. As table 4-1 indicates, the
number of passenger train miles operated in the United States dropped

Table 4-1. *Decline of U.S. Rail Passenger Service, 1949–69*

Year	Passenger-train miles, or PTM (thousands)	PTM decline over previous year (thousands)	PTM decline as percent of previous year	Rail passenger net revenue (thousands of dollars)	Passenger deficit as percent of freight net revenue
1949	382,313	27,058	6.61	−649,627	48.6
1950	359,055	23,258	6.08	−508,508	32.9
1951	356,391	2,664	0.74	−680,822	41.9
1952	345,533	10,858	3.05	−642,390	37.3
1953	333,919	11,614	3.36	−705,538	38.9
1954	317,672	16,247	4.87	−669,553	43.4
1955	299,235	18,439	5.80	−636,693	36.1
1956	290,358	8,877	2.97	−696,938	39.5
1957	275,286	15,072	5.19	−723,483	44.0
1958	246,828	28,458	10.34	−591,543	35.7
1959	225,461	21,367	8.66	−523,692	32.8
1960	209,677	15,784	7.00	−466,289	32.9
1961	198,699	10,978	5.24	−390,495	29.7
1962	193,457	5,242	2.63	−374,993	25.2
1963	189,568	3,889	2.01	−378,618	23.7
1964	183,825	5,743	3.03	−389,008	23.7
1965	173,579	10,246	5.57	−398,029	21.6
1966	165,439	8,140	4.69	−379,744	19.5
1967	150,762	14,677	8.87	−460,414	26.9
1968	123,458	27,304	18.11	−462,129	25.8
1969	107,982	15,476	12.53	−437,498	24.4

Source: For passenger-train mileage, Interstate Commerce Commission, *Transport Statistics in the United States, 1969*, pt. 1: *Railroads*, p. 49; for passenger deficit data, George Hilton, *Amtrak: The National Railroad Passenger Corporation* (Washington, D.C.: American Enterprise Institute for Public Policy Research, 1980), pp. 3–4. All data include both intercity and commuter passenger service for Class I and Class II railroads.

from 382 million in 1949 to 108 million in 1969. The Interstate Commerce Commission (ICC) used its authority over passenger train discontinuances to slow this decline, but it did not attempt to stop it. ICC permission for train discontinuances accelerated beginning in 1967, as passenger deficits began to rise again. Yet most of the remaining trains were unprofitable. Passenger service losses drained off about one-quarter of the industry's freight generated profits during the late 1960s. The Penn Central Railroad suffered the greatest losses, an estimated "fully allocated" deficit of $90 million in 1969.[1]

1. This deficit includes a share of common costs (for example, track maintenance and headquarters expenses) that cannot be easily separated from freight operations. The "solely related" deficit was closer to $60 million. See Interstate Commerce

The financial crisis of the U.S. rail industry necessitated some new initiative, but the choice of a public enterprise approach was by no means inevitable. Indeed, Amtrak's "nationalization" was ambiguous, incremental, and unintended by most of its creators. Because the choice of policy instrument was closely linked to a highly contentious policy choice, congressional and executive leaders sought to avoid a precise definition of Amtrak's status as long as possible. Public enterprise evolved from disjointed and often inconsistent decisions rather than from a single planned process.

Amtrak originated as an attempt by the U.S. Department of Transportation to solve a specific political problem: how to continue gradual elimination of unprofitable passenger trains in the face of rising public and congressional opposition while trying to salvage a core of services from those that remained. Three very different approaches to the rail passenger problem emerged in 1969. Congressional proposals centered on a subsidy program for a core of "essential" services; in addition, the Department of Transportation would acquire passenger equipment and lease it to those railroads that could not afford to modernize rolling stock themselves. The railroad industry, while preferring to get rid of unprofitable services, backed subsidies as the most likely route to immediate relief from passenger deficits.[2] But subsidies (especially permanent ones) were anathema to the Nixon White House and the Bureau of the Budget. They favored allowing the railroads to cut out unprofitable passenger trains without restriction.

Commission, Bureau of Accounts, *Transport Statistics in the United States, 1969*, pt. 1: *Railroads* (ICC, 1969), p. 217. On the decline of rail passenger service and the response by Congress and the ICC, see George Hilton, *The Transportation Act of 1958: A Decade of Experience* (Indiana University Press, 1969), chap. 4; and Hilton, *Amtrak: The National Railroad Passenger Corporation* (Washington, D.C.: American Enterprise Institute for Public Policy Research, 1980), chap. 1. Hilton argues that Amtrak grew out of policymakers' mistaken belief that railroad passenger service had declined because carriers discouraged passenger traffic with bad service, whereas the real cause of the decline was competition from other modes. However, this chapter will show that most executive policymakers were aware (although many legislators probably were not) that establishment of a new organization would not be sufficient to make rail passenger service profitable again. They nevertheless supported Amtrak as a means to further their own policy goals.

2. *Passenger Train Service*, Hearings before the Subcommittee on Transportation and Aeronautics of the House Committee on Interstate and Foreign Commerce, 91 Cong. 1 sess. (Government Printing Office, 1969). The railroad industry's views were developed in a bill introduced on their behalf by Senator Vance Hartke, S. 2750. See *Congressional Record*, July 31, 1969, pp. 21593–94.

The U.S. Department of Transportation took a middle position. Secretary John Volpe and the assistant secretary for policy and international affairs, Paul Cherington, suggested the establishment of a National Railroad Passenger Corporation modeled after the successful Communications Satellite Corporation (Comsat). Railpax, as it was first called, was to be a hybrid of public and private features.[3] The president of the United States would appoint a majority of its board, and the secretary of transportation would designate a system of route end points. Railpax would choose the routes to run and take over marketing and scheduling functions, while contracting with the railroads for operation of the trains.

Despite the important federal role in establishing Railpax, the corporation was to be a "for profit" enterprise and was not to be an "agency or establishment of the U.S. government." It was to be owned, at least initially, by private sector railroads that would pay an entry fee roughly equal to one year's avoidable losses on passenger service in exchange for stock in the corporation.[4] There was also a provision for sale of preferred stock to the general public if the company ever became profitable. Federal financial assistance was to be limited to a grant of $40 million for organizational costs, research, and improvements in equipment and reservations and $60 million (later $100 million) in loan guarantees for purchasing rolling stock. Direct operating subsidies were to be avoided. Federal assistance was viewed as a limited, one-time-only expense; only the $40 million grant would be "on budget"—an important consideration for the budget-conscious Nixon administration.

DOT officials saw Railpax as an answer to the railroads' preoccupation with profitable freight operations and their negligible recent investments in passenger equipment. More important, Railpax was the only politically viable alternative to congressional proposals for operating subsidies for passenger trains.[5] The department's proposal contained a contradiction,

3. The Railpax idea was first suggested in a 1961 study (the "Doyle Report") commissioned by the Senate Commerce Committee. The analogy between Amtrak and Comsat, while apparently taken seriously by some participants in the formation of Amtrak, is inappropriate. Government sponsorship of a single communications satellite company was justified by arguments that the industry was a natural monopoly, an infant industry, or laden with foreign policy considerations. Rail passenger service, on the other hand, was a senescent industry with virtually no possibility of becoming profitable.

4. DOT's proposal encouraged railroad participation by a "blackmail" provision: any railroad that did not join Railpax would not be allowed to drop any passenger service in the basic system until January 1, 1974 (changed in the Rail Passenger Service Act to "any intercity passenger train whatsoever," and January 1, 1975, respectively).

5. Cherington discussed the political problem in a memo to Volpe: "Unless we can

however. If Railpax was to consist solely of the few remaining profitable routes, there was little need to set up a new corporation. If, on the other hand, it was to provide a revitalized passenger service over a substantial route structure, it would need a very large investment in rolling stock, roadbed, and stations. But Railpax's modest initial capitalization was likely to be used up rapidly in operating losses before improvements could be made. Thus there was a close link between the size of Railpax and its "publicness:" a large Railpax would almost certainly require additional government funding.

Aware that DOT's Railpax proposal could not possibly succeed with the funding levels proposed, White House and Bureau of Budget officials refused to clear it for presentation to Congress.[6] Nevertheless, department officials did discuss the proposal informally with Senate Commerce Committee members and staff, promising that the Railpax proposal would be cleared imminently to delay committee action on subsidy legislation. Then early in 1970, two developments—the increasingly desperate financial plight of the Penn Central and ICC action on discontinuance petitions for some of the most important remaining rail passenger services—forced the committee to act. Fearing that if it did not move quickly no services would be left to preserve, the committee reported a subsidy bill on March 14 that authorized $435 million over four years for rolling stock acquisition and operating subsidies. The committee's report also contained correspondence between DOT officials and Committee Chairman Warren Magnuson and Subcommittee Chairman Vance Hartke concerning the Railpax proposal still being held up by the White House

---

outline our program to the Senate Committee not later than Monday, the Committee will adopt what we regard as a clearly inadequate and fiscally wasteful program. What is more, the Republican members of the Committee, having no program of their own and no program of the administration to support, will vote, in large numbers, for the Magnuson-Hartke [subsidy] bill. This reduces even more the probability that the President, at some future date, might veto the Senate bill on budgetary grounds since it would require repudiation of Congressional Republicans." Memorandum from Assistant Secretary Paul W. Cherington to Secretary John Volpe, December 5, 1969, p. 1.

6. See interview with Budget Director Robert Mayo, "Who Poxed Railpax? Not I, Says Mayo," in *Railway Age*, February 23, 1970, p. 12. On the Department of Transportation's dispute with the White House, see "Will an Acceptable Passenger Train Formula Emerge?" *Railway Age*, January 19, 1970, p. 53; "White House Delays Decision on DOT 'Railpax' Rail Passenger Service Plan," *Traffic World*, January 24, 1970, pp. 72–73; "A Helluva Way to Run a Transportation Policy," *Railway Age*, January 26, 1970, p. 46; and "Money Is Roadblock to Revival of Passenger Trains," *Congressional Quarterly Weekly Report*, February 6, 1970, p. 352.

and Budget Bureau. It also included a revised version of the Railpax plan (in the form of an individual opinion by Senator Winston Prouty), a minority opinion by three Republican senators attacking the committee bill and tacitly endorsing Senator Prouty's approach, and the ICC's comments to the Bureau of the Budget on an earlier draft of the DOT proposal.[7] In short, the committee report constituted an invitation to the White House to release DOT's Railpax bill and a threat to pass the more costly Magnuson-Hartke subsidy bill if it did not.

In the face of this threat, the White House finally decided to support the Railpax proposal, and it was introduced as a substitute to the Senate subsidy bill with the backing of the committee leadership. Support was also obtained from the three interest groups most concerned with rail passenger service: carriers, labor, and passengers. The Association of American Railroads (AAR) and its members backed Railpax as the only politically feasible means of gaining immediate relief from passenger service losses. They did not see Railpax as a threatening precedent for further government control over the railways because passenger service was a fairly compartmentalized segment of their business. Moreover, the bill required that as many Railpax operations as possible be carried out by contract with the railroads, allowing them to retain control over operations on their tracks. And since Railpax was avowedly experimental, many of the trains could be expected to disappear after 1973.

Rail labor and the National Association of Rail Passengers (NARP), a small but effective consumer lobby, had very different reasons for backing the Railpax proposal. Rail labor groups were primarily concerned with jobs, and Railpax offered the best prospect for preserving passenger trains as well as a government-guaranteed labor protection arrangement for employees laid off due to later cuts in the Railpax system. NARP supported Railpax because it took passenger service out of the hands of the railroads, which the association believed had deliberately downgraded service to win discontinuances from the ICC.

The Railpax compromise did not reflect an agreement either on policy objectives or on the nature of the instrument chosen to resolve the problem. For one side it represented the best method of cutting service, for the other the most effective way of preserving and improving service. Congressional debate did not resolve these fundamental conflicts among

---

7. *Rail Passenger Service Act of 1970*, S. Rept. 91-765, 91 Cong. 2 sess. (GPO, 1970), pp. 36–41, 72–88. See also "Senate Commerce Committee Backs Passenger Train Aid," *Congressional Quarterly Weekly Report*, March 20, 1970, p. 796.

Railpax's supporters. Four major features of the new corporation remained unclear in the Rail Passenger Service Act of 1970 passed by Congress: (1) the degree of government control, (2) the size of the system, (3) the adequacy of funding, and (4) whether the corporation was to be permanent or temporary.

As noted earlier, Railpax was a curious hybrid of public and private features. The act defined Railpax as a for profit corporation, but it did not allow the corporation to make cuts in its basic system of routes for twenty-six months. Moreover, a majority of the board of directors— including a consumer representative and the secretary of transportation ex officio—were to be designated by the president. Even the terminology of congressional debate was unclear: House sponsors generally referred to Railpax as private or quasi-private; its Senate sponsors viewed it as quasi-public.

The size of the system to be operated by Railpax was also left unresolved by Congress. DOT sought maximum discretion for the secretary to cut unprofitable operations. The act required that the secretary of transportation designate a basic system, taking "into account the need for expeditious intercity rail passenger service within and between all regions of the continental United States."[8] The act did not allow review of the secretary's system by either Congress or the courts. Thus DOT could eliminate trains without congressional pressure to preserve specific routes and trains, but the requirement for a national system forced it to retain many long-distance trains that could not possibly be profitable. Completely conflicting predictions about the size of the system to be designated were made by the bill's managers in the Senate and the House; as a result, many legislators were unprepared for the magnitude of the cuts that followed.[9]

---

8. Rail Passenger Service Act of 1970, 84 Stat. 1329, sec. 201, October 30, 1970.

9. Senate proponents of Railpax assured their colleagues that cuts in service would be minor. Senator Prouty stated, "Every indication is that most of the major routes would continue to have service, and service with increased frequency. . ." and "I am told . . . that such a basic system would include approximately 80 percent of the intercity rail passenger trains now operating." *Congressional Record,* May 5, 1970, pp. 14172, 14174. See also Senator Hartke's statement, *Congressional Record,* May 6, 1970, p. 14281. But in the House debate four months later, Congressman William L. Springer, one of the bill's managers, claimed that Railpax would not operate "a nationwide network as we have known it in the past. It will necessarily concentrate upon corridors of high density travel. . . . I would expect that it would be a small proportion of the remaining 500 passenger trains now operating across the land." *Congressional Record,*

Underfunding was another unresolved problem. On this matter there appears to have been a conspiracy of silence between rail passenger proponents in Congress and within DOT. Both groups feared that President Nixon would veto the bill if Congress increased funding levels, and both wanted to ensure that the program got off the ground. When Railpax began operating, it would be easier, they felt, to return for an additional authorization.[10]

The question of Railpax's permanence was also unresolved; the act required the corporation to run its designated system only until July 1973. Railpax had powerful enemies within the executive branch, and proponents of rail passenger service had little commitment to Railpax per se. In sum, the public record of legislative intent is very ambiguous, a not surprising reflection of the incompatible interests of Railpax supporters.

This ambiguity was more difficult to maintain after DOT announced Railpax's route end points. (The board of directors chose the actual routes between those cities.) In fact, the Department of Transportation plan, in an attempt to develop a compromise acceptable to the Congress (on route structure) and to the Bureau of the Budget (on costs) seriously overstated the number of trains that could be maintained. One former DOT official summarized the process this way in an interview:

> Volpe's people were not technicians. They would hack something out of capital expenditures, and then someone would take some more out, without realizing that it would increase operating expenditures. It got to be a flat-assed lie. It had really blown the whole analytical effort, but by this time we were so committed to the program that we wouldn't let them [the Office of Management and Budget] win.

In transmitting the department's route recommendations to President Nixon, Secretary Volpe warned that the system was "the minimum which has a chance to be acceptable to the public and the Congress. It is our judgment that any further reduction is likely to cause Congress to

October 13, 1970, p. 36595. This view is also clearly presented in H. Rept. 91-1580 on the bill.

10. Senator Hartke stated, "The members of this committee were quite concerned last year when the original money limitations were put in [the 1970 Rail Passenger Service Act]. We did that at the request of the administration when they balked at the bill that the committee had approved which would have authorized $435 million for this program. This committee was not unaware of the fact that the program was being underfunded." *Administration's Request for Additional Funding for Amtrak,* Hearings before the Subcommittee on Surface Transportation of the Senate Commerce Committee, 92 Cong. 1 sess. (GPO, 1971), p. 5.

seize the initiative in designating the system."[11] The Railpax system, rechristened Amtrak and inaugurated on May 1, 1971, eliminated more than half of the remaining mileage of intercity passenger trains. These cutbacks were almost entirely outside the Northeast (Boston to Washington) Corridor, primarily in highly unprofitable long-haul operations.

Within four months of beginning operations, Amtrak had used up its original appropriation and was beginning to use its owner railroads' entry fees to meet operating expenses. By October 1971, it estimated that it would soon have to use its guaranteed loan authority for operating costs. To avoid bankruptcy, Amtrak applied for additional federal funding. In 1972 Congress authorized an additional $225 million in grants and $100 million in guaranteed loan authority. It also increased its control over Amtrak.[12] The corporation was required to make monthly reports to Congress on its operations and was made subject to the Freedom of Information Act. The salaries of its executives were limited to the level of cabinet officers. In addition, Congress extended Amtrak's route structure, mandating three new services and encouraging additional "experimental" routes. The corporation was directed to take over control and operation of rail service as much as possible rather than contracting with the railways. This was an important step by Congress toward ensuring Amtrak's permanence. Although this action was taken to improve managerial control over employees, and hence to improve service, its political effect was to make it more difficult to dismantle the corporation; the railway brotherhoods gained a stake not only in the services Amtrak provided but also in the corporation itself.[13]

Legislative developments after 1972 followed a similar pattern. Congress passed legislation to "improve" Amtrak almost every year, giving

11. Volpe memorandum to President Nixon, November 24, 1970, p. 5. Even so, the system was cut back further at White House insistence. After review by the ICC and state regulatory agencies, the secretary's final plan added back a number of routes cut by the White House and Bureau of the Budget.

12. Amtrak Financial Assistance, 86 Stat. 227, June 22, 1972.

13. These changes were not made without conflict, however. Even within Congress there were significant differences. House sponsors emphasized Amtrak's experimental, potentially temporary nature. Senate sponsors insisted that the only alternative to the existing arrangement was a more clear-cut nationalization of Amtrak, and they denied that Congress had intended profitability to be the primary goal for the corporation. See in particular the statements of Congressmen Staggers, Springer, and Adams in the *Congressional Record*, March 15, 1972, pp. 8488–89, 8505, 8508–09; June 13, 1972, p. 20636; and of Senators Hartke and Weicker, *Congressional Record*, April 27, 1972, p. 14773; June 8, 1972, pp. 20234–36. See also *Amendments to the Rail Passenger Service Act of 1970*, S. Rept. 92-756, 92 Cong. 2 sess. (GPO, 1972), pp. 6–7.

particular attention to increasing congressional control over Amtrak vis-à-vis the executive. The Amtrak Improvement Act of 1978 formally recognized that Amtrak would probably never be profitable.[14] Instead the company had become a ward of the federal government, highly dependent for both direction and financing. The Omnibus Reconciliation Act of 1981 eliminated most of the vestiges of Amtrak's quasi-private status by issuing preferred stock to the secretary of transportation in recognition of DOT investment in the company and by eliminating railway (common stock) representatives from Amtrak's board of directors.[15]

It is impossible, however, to pinpoint when a decision to nationalize Amtrak was made. There was no such decision. Congress and the executive failed to *point* Amtrak in a definite direction with a clear and consistent mandate; instead, they *pushed* Amtrak through a series of incremental, compromise measures.

One outcome of the establishment of Amtrak is clear: it halted the decline in intercity rail passenger operations. Amtrak's initial (May 1971) system represented a substantial cut over prior operation by the railways. But Amtrak grew from 26 million train-miles in 1972, its first full year of operations, to 30 million in 1975. The corporation's deficits grew even more rapidly, as its role as an experimental vehicle for promoting industrial adjustment was rapidly replaced by that of a preserver and rehabilitator of rail services.

Rescuing Regional Services: Conrail

At the same time that the federal government was trying to define a proper role for Amtrak, it faced an even greater crisis: the threatened collapse of most of the major railroads based in the Northeast. Penn Central was by far the largest of these carriers. In attempting to solve the regional rail crisis, the federal government was forced once again to consider various forms of government ownership. Yet no clear directions in policy or policy instruments emerged, and decisions were often delayed until shutdown was imminent. Even then, movement toward public enterprise was incremental and disjointed, as policymakers sought

14. 92 Stat. 923, sec. 11, October 5, 1978.
15. 95 Stat. 357, 689, sec. 1174(a), 1175.

Figure 4-1. *U.S. Revenue Freight Ton-Miles, by District, 1929–83*[a]

Billions of ton-miles

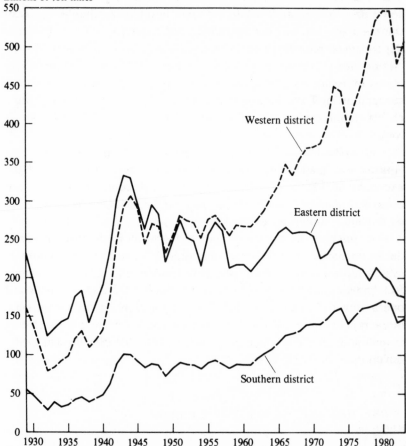

Sources: For 1929–61, unpublished data from the Association of American Railroads; for 1962–67, Association of American Railroads, *Railroad Facts, 1968 Edition;* for 1968–82, *Railroad Facts, 1983 Edition.*
a. Class I railroads.

to employ less direct policy instruments. Failure to resolve the impasse between proponents of market-oriented solutions in the executive branch and those concerned with retention of services in Congress, the ICC, and elsewhere led to simultaneous pursuit of conflicting goals and to the creation of two hybrid corporations, the United States Railway Association (USRA) and the Consolidated Rail Corporation (Conrail).

Changes in the U.S. transportation market after World War II hit the northeastern railroads particularly hard (see figure 4-1). Industry in the region was not growing as rapidly as elsewhere, and much of the growth that did occur was in high value goods, which are particularly susceptible to diversion to trucks. Coal traffic, the largest single commodity movement in the Northeast, fell 8 percent in the latter half of the 1960s.[16] The passenger outlook was equally bleak; northeastern railroads had not only a disproportionate share of unprofitable intercity passenger service but also costly commuter operations in several cities. The impact of these developments on railway finances was disastrous. Net railway operating income for carriers based in the northeastern United States fell from $196.6 million in 1962 to a deficit of $101.6 million in 1970 and net return on rail investment from 1.8 percent to a negative 0.93 percent.[17] The railroads responded by diversifying their investments and deferring maintenance. Standards of service to shippers slipped, which led, of course, to further loss of traffic.

During the 1960s, many northeastern railroads turned to mergers to cut labor costs and consolidate facilities and services. Two mergers outside the industrial heartland of the United States (roughly north and east of Pittsburgh) created large, relatively affluent lines with a strong traffic base in hauling coal.[18] But the mergers in "trunk line territory" (the Erie Railroad and the Delaware, Lackawanna and Western Railroad to form Erie Lackawanna in 1960; the Pennsylvania Railroad, the New York Central Railroad, and the bankrupt New York, New Haven and Hartford Railroad to form the massive Penn Central in 1968) proved only that joining sick companies together makes a larger sick company.[19] These mergers did not eliminate the "strong carrier-weak carrier" division in the Northeast. Instead, a number of Northeast carriers sought protection under Section 77 of the Bankruptcy Act, beginning with the Jersey Central in 1967, followed by the Boston and Maine in March 1970, Penn Central in June 1970, Lehigh Valley in July 1970, Reading in November 1971, and Erie Lackawanna in June 1972. All except Boston and Maine would eventually end up as part of Conrail.

16. *The Penn Central and Other Railroads: Report to the Senate Committee on Commerce,* Committee Print, Senate Committee on Commerce, 92 Cong. 2 sess. (GPO, 1972), pp. 26–27, 124.
17. United States Railway Association, *Preliminary System Plan,* 1975, vol. 1, pp. 244–45. This is for Class I railroads in the Eastern District only.
18. Norfolk and Western merged with the Virginian in 1959 and with the Nickel Plate and Wabash in 1964; Chesapeake and Ohio combined with the Baltimore and Ohio and Western Maryland to form the Chessie System in the mid-1960s.
19. See Richard Saunders, *The Railroad Mergers and the Coming of Conrail* (Greenwood Press, 1978), chaps. 12–14; and Joseph Daughen and Peter Binzen, *The Wreck of the Penn Central* (Little, Brown, 1971).

By the end of 1974, only the Delaware and Hudson, a small "bridge" carrier, was still precariously afloat in the old industrial heartland of the Northeast.[20]

The existing regulatory framework failed to achieve the protectionist goal of giving Northeast railroads a sufficient return on investment; rail employment and service to shippers were under severe pressure. The traditional railroad bankruptcy process under Section 77—which assumed a return to profitability was possible if creditors' claims were temporarily suspended and then adjusted—seemed of dubious applicability given the region's traffic trends. Some reorganization of the Northeast carriers was clearly necessary, but a federally imposed plan would almost inevitably involve picking winners and losers among railways, communities served, and employees. This is precisely what protectionist policy sought to avoid. Nor would such a plan solve the enormous problem of deferred maintenance; only an infusion of capital could do that. Any infusion of federal funds, however, ran the risk of increasing pressure to preserve the status quo in service and employment.

Constitutional Obstacles to Policy Choice

Proposals to resolve the Northeast rail crisis faced constitutional problems as well as political ones. The first problem was the erosion of assets. Continued deficit operations in the public interest after a carrier seeks protection of the courts create new claims against the estate that have priority over prebankruptcy interests.[21] This clearly violates the creditors' and shareholders' Fifth Amendment rights against taking private property without just compensation. Section 77 of the Bankruptcy Act allows suspension of those rights, but only so long as reorganization into a profit-making corporation is possible within a reasonable period of time.[22] The time at which reorganization becomes

20. A "bridge" carrier originates and terminates little traffic of its own; it is therefore highly dependent on interchanges with other carriers.

21. In their interim report of January 1, 1973, the Penn Central trustees estimated that at least $300 million in priority claims had been added by the end of 1972.

22. *Brooks-Scanlon Co.* v. *Railroad Commission of Louisiana,* 252 U.S. 396 (1920); *Railroad Commission of Texas* v. *Eastern Texas Railroad,* 262 U.S. 79 (1924); and *New Haven Inclusion Cases,* 399 U.S. 392 (1970). The Supreme Court addressed these issues in the Northeast rail crisis in *Regional Rail Reorganization Act Cases,* 419 U.S. 102 (1974).

sufficiently unlikely to permit further erosion is by no means clear and must be decided by the judge presiding over the bankruptcy.

The second constitutional issue in the Northeast crisis also related to "taking." Section 77 allows the bankruptcy court to force creditors to accept stock in a reorganizing railroad in place of their original claims. This would be the lowest cost option for the government, but it could be imposed only where there was a reasonable possibility of a profitable entity emerging—a dubious proposition for the Northeast bankrupts. At the other extreme, outright nationalization would constitute an exercise of eminent domain powers (that is, condemnation) rather than a reorganization. Condemnation would require payment in cash, or in a cash equivalent such as government bonds, rather than in stock in the new corporation as Section 77 allows. Department of Transportation officials also feared that mandatory conveyance would be more costly than a negotiated settlement.[23] A negotiated settlement, on the other hand, might drag on indefinitely or fail altogether and could be criticized as a bailout to stockholders.

Although the prospects for successful reorganization under Section 77 seemed remote, the high cost of outright nationalization (estimated at up to $13 billion) made it an option of last resort, regardless of its operational advantages or disadvantages. Policymakers thus sought a middle course that ensured conveyance but with minimum government expenditure. The Amtrak-style, government-sponsored corporation thus seemed a likely prospect. Designing such a quasi-public entity would be difficult, however. If the bankrupt railroads were forced into a mandatory conveyance with no chance of making a profit, the courts might rule that the government had exercised its eminent domain powers.[24]

23. See the letter of November 14, 1973, from Transportation Secretary Claude Brinegar to Senators Warren Magnuson and Norris Cotton of the Senate Commerce Committee, printed in *Rail Services Act of 1973*, S. Rept. 93-601, 93 Cong. 1 sess. (GPO, 1973), pp. 130–33.

DOT feared that the requirement for payment in cash or bonds would also prevent a new corporation from being profitable unless that cost was absorbed by the federal government. On the search for middle ground solutions, see Vera Hirschberg, "Penn Central's Continuing Crisis Provokes First Serious Nationalization Studies," *National Journal*, September 25, 1971, pp. 1946–55.

24. For a further discussion of the "taking" issue, see Michael J. Malbin, "Court Action Spurs Congressional Action to Save Northeast Rail Services," *National Journal*, December 8, 1973, pp. 1821–26; and John Harr, *The Great Railway Crisis: An Administrative History of the United States Railway Association* (Washington, D.C.: National Academy of Public Administration, 1978), pp. 132–38. A third option would

Pressure and Procrastination

Congress initially responded to the Northeast rail crisis by passing the Emergency Rail Services Act of 1970 (ERSA), which attempted to minimize direct federal outlays by authorizing loan guarantees up to $125 million for operating expenses of the Northeast bankrupts.[25] The act was explicitly billed as a time-buying measure. Its congressional sponsors promised a long-term legislative solution within three months. But there was no such bill, only three years of what Congressman Brock Adams (who later became secretary of transportation) called "patchwork solutions." As long as the trains were still running, both Congress and the executive preferred "planning" to decisionmaking.[26]

It was the constitutional issue of asset erosion that finally prompted definitive congressional action. Judge John Fullam, presiding over the Penn Central reorganization, ruled in March 1973 that the constitutionally acceptable limits to erosion of the estate were fast approaching. Fullam ordered the trustees to develop an acceptable reorganization plan or prepare to liquidate by July. Only congressional action, he warned, could prevent a complete shutdown of the Penn Central by October.[27]

Although Judge Fullam's ruling forced Congress and the Nixon administration to make a policy choice, it did not determine whether that choice would be protectionist, market-oriented, or accelerationist. The direction of policy would be determined by how the following questions were resolved: Who would plan the restructuring of the

---

be to wait for court-ordered liquidation and purchase desired properties then. The problem with liquidation, in addition to potential disruption of service, is that properties would no longer be encumbered by a requirement to provide common carrier service. The value of many rail properties, notably in urban areas, would be substantially higher without such restrictions on use.

25. 84 Stat. 2137, January 8, 1971.

26. Some decisions were made quickly, however. When Penn Central's trustees unilaterally changed crew size in February 1973 to cut operating expenses, the United Transportation Union struck. Congress passed back-to-work legislation (also rescinding the work rule changes) in less than sixteen *hours,* but once again failed to come up with a permanent plan for the Northeast railroads. Railway Labor-Management Disputes-Settlement, 87 Stat. 5, February 9, 1973. Changes in work rules was one of the three conditions the trustees had listed in a report to Judge Fullam as necessary for making the Penn Central viable. The other two conditions were full compensation for Amtrak and commuter operations, and substantial cuts in the Penn Central route structure.

27. U.S. District Court for the Eastern District of Pennsylvania, Memorandum and Order No. 1137 Re: Reorganization Planning, March 6, 1973.

Northeast bankrupts that seemed inevitable to all parties? Who would own the facilities in the restructured system, and how would they be conveyed? How could rail labor be protected? How much money would the federal government put into the system and would it be in the form of loans, grants, or stock purchases?

The Nixon administration, acting primarily through the Department of Transportation, pursued a mixture of accelerationist and market-oriented policies. It supported three goals throughout the crisis: streamline the rail network as much as possible, keep the railroads in the private sector, and keep federal expenditures to an absolute minimum. Early DOT proposals followed the Amtrak approach: the secretary of transportation would designate a core system of lines to be served and create a new private sector corporation to operate the most promising lines of the Northeast bankrupts. Labor expenses would be cut by offering older workers incentives for early retirement and by firing workers with least seniority. Federal funding was to be limited to $40 million for start-up costs.[28]

The Interstate Commerce Commission and congressional leaders emphasized preservation of rail service and employment. The commission proposed that it, rather than the Department of Transportation, plan the restructuring of the Northeast railroads, with the carriers leasing their roadbeds to the federal government during a three-year period of planning and capital improvements. Changes in work rules and cuts in rail employment would be delayed during this period, and a branch line preservation subsidy was to be instituted. Total costs of the ICC plan were estimated to be as high as $630 million per year.[29] As House and Senate committees began intensive consideration of these and other proposals in the latter half of 1973, outright nationalization fell by the wayside: the high acquisition cost made it unacceptable to Congress as

28. Although most DOT officials did not believe that restructuring could take place without substantial federal funding, there was, as in the case of Amtrak, severe pressure from the White House, OMB, and Treasury to take a "hard line on money." See Harr, *The Great Railway Crisis*, pp. 85–87, 108. See also *Northeast Rail Transportation*, pt. 1, Hearings before the Subcommittee on Transportation and Aeronautics of the House Committee on Interstate and Foreign Commerce, 93 Cong. 1 sess. (GPO, 1973), p. 234. See more generally pp. 217–44 and Brinegar's statement in *Northeastern Railroad Transportation Crisis*, Hearings before the Subcommittee on Surface Transportation of the Senate Committee on Commerce, 93 Cong. 1 sess. (GPO, 1973), p. 259.

29. See H.R. 6591, and ICC Chairman George M. Stafford's explanation in *Northeast Rail Transportation*, pp. 173–76. For DOT's view of the bill, see *Northeastern Railroad Transportation Crisis*, pp. 265–66.

well as to the administration. In an elaborate process of interest group consultation, Congress sought to develop a bill that would meet Judge Fullam's deadline (by protecting the estates) and would avoid a presidential veto (by limiting expenditures). The resulting series of compromises were embodied in the Regional Rail Reorganization (3R) Act of 1973.[30]

The act created a new nonprofit government corporation, the United States Railway Association (USRA), to plan the restructuring of the Northeast bankrupts over a fifteen-month period (later extended). Congressional leaders hoped that USRA would give more attention to service goals than either DOT or a private corporation was likely to provide, but less than the preservation-oriented ICC. USRA was instructed to develop a preliminary restructuring plan. The Rail Services Planning Office, a new branch of the ICC, would then hold public hearings on this proposal. Finally, USRA would issue a final plan specifying the lines that would be conveyed to a new private sector Consolidated Rail Corporation (Conrail), sold to profitable rail companies or to Amtrak or local transportation authorities, or abandoned. Congress retained the right to a one-house veto over the final plan. In addition to its planning role, the USRA was to serve as the conduit for federal aid to Conrail, monitor that assistance, and act as litigant for the government in court suits over valuation of properties conveyed to Conrail.

The compromise character of the 3R act was evident both in the goals mandated by Congress and in the makeup of the USRA board of directors. In developing its plans, the United States Railway Association was directed to consider a variety of incompatible goals, including creation of a "financially self-sustaining rail service system," "establishment of improved high-speed rail passenger service," "retention and promotion of competition," and "minimization of job losses."[31] Clearly, trade-offs would have to be made, but the act's inclusion of many protectionist

30. 87 Stat. 985, January 2, 1974. For a detailed discussion of the bargaining process, see Harr, *The Great Railway Crisis*, chaps. 3–5. House Transportation and Aeronautics Subcommittee Chairman John Jarman estimated the cost of nationalizing the Northeast bankrupts at more than $10 billion. *Congressional Record*, November 8, 1973, p. 36352. On the change in congressional thinking about nationalization, see Congressman Brock Adams's testimony in *Northeastern and Midwestern Railroad Transportation Crisis*, Hearings before the Subcommittee on Surface Transportation of the Senate Committee on Commerce, 93 Cong. 1 sess. (GPO, 1973), pp. 870–87.

31. 87 Stat. 985, sec. 206(a).

goals made it virtually impossible for USRA to reject these objectives completely. The association's board was composed of three representatives of the federal government (the secretaries of transportation and treasury and the chairman of the ICC, or their representatives), a chairman designated by the president, and representatives selected by the president from lists provided by organizations of profitable railroads, labor, governors, mayors, large and small shippers, and financial institutions. All nongovernment members of the board were subject to Senate confirmation. Congress thus avoided DOT control of the planning process and ensured that service goals would be well represented in USRA's deliberations.

The issues of ownership and conveyance were also resolved through compromise. The 3R act tried to avoid the appearance of mandatory conveyance in order to prevent a presidential veto. It gave some discretion to the judges presiding over the Northeast bankrupts to order liquidation rather than inclusion into Conrail, but that discretion was intentionally quite limited.[32] Stock in Conrail compensated the creditors and shareholders of the Northeast bankrupts, but provision was made for transfer of additional USRA obligations if necessary to be "fair and equitable" to the estates.[33]

Like Amtrak, Conrail was a for profit corporation and not a government agency or instrumentality. As in the case of Amtrak, however, there were some unusual restrictions. Conrail was required to operate all of the properties conveyed to it by the *Final System Plan* for at least two years. So long as more than half of the corporation's debt was owed to or guaranteed by USRA or the federal government, Conrail was

32. The 3R act required in sec. 207(b) that the Northeast bankrupts be reorganized pursuant to the act unless (1) they could be reorganized on an income basis in a reasonable period *and* separate reorganization would better serve the public interest, or (2) the act did not provide a process fair and equitable to the estate. Yet the decision whether an individual railroad would be included in Conrail had to be made 180 days before the USRA released its *Preliminary System Plan*. Thus the courts would be making their decisions with little knowledge of the financial structure of the new corporation. The act also established a Special Court with power to review District Court decisions and to consolidate eventually all rail reorganization proceedings for companies reorganizing under the act. A final "fairness and equity" judgment would be made by the Special Court after conveyance, with provision for direct appeal to the Supreme Court. For DOT's criticism of earlier drafts of the act, see Secretary Brinegar's letter of November 14, 1973, to Senator Magnuson, reprinted in *Rail Services Act of 1973*, S. Rept. 93-601, 93 Cong. 1 sess. (GPO, 1973), especially pp. 132–33.

33. *Regional Rail Reorganization Act of 1973*, H. Rept. 93-744, 93 Cong. 1 sess. (GPO, 1973), pp. 58–60.

prohibited from engaging in nontransportation activities, and a majority of its board of directors were to be government appointees.[34]

Institutionalized involvement of interest groups was most clearly evident in the development of labor protection agreements. Cutting labor costs was crucial to the establishment of a self-sufficient Conrail, but overly generous protective arrangements for laid-off employees could also bankrupt the new carrier before it began operations. Nor could rail labor be made to bear the full costs of cutbacks: its power in Congress would ensure that.[35]

In September 1973, Transportation Secretary Claude Brinegar encouraged the establishment of a committee of labor leaders and presidents of profitable railroads from outside the Northeast; their mission: to search for a compromise that would win labor support for the restructuring process without bankrupting Conrail. The resulting labor protection agreement essentially guaranteed workers with five years of service their current income (escalated with general wage increases) until age sixty-five. Lifetime earning guarantees went far beyond the standard conditions imposed by the ICC in line closings, passenger train discontinuances, and other rail industry cutbacks. (Those guarantees generally lasted six years.) Lifetime earning guarantees were not new to the rail industry: they had been agreed to by the managers of ostensibly solvent railways, including Penn Central, to gain labor support for carrier mergers.[36] Thus most of Conrail's unionized workers (those from Penn Central) were not gaining terms more favorable than they had under existing arrangements.

The Conrail case was different from previous agreements, however. First, the costs were shifted to the federal government, up to a maximum of $250 million, because Conrail could not hope to carry the burden on its own. Second, Conrail was expected to be a financially marginal carrier

34. Under the Regional Rail Reorganization Act of 1973 (87 Stat. 985, sec. 301[a]), the secretary of transportation, the chairman and president of the United States Railway Association, and five other presidential nominees were to serve on a fifteen-member Conrail board. The Railroad Revitalization and Regulatory Reform Act of 1976 (91 Stat. 31, sec. 611) changed the Conrail board to thirteen members, with USRA appointing five. Direct government representatives were eliminated from the board.

35. Harr states, "Chairman Staggers of the House Commerce Committee let it be known that he would not support the [Northeast rail] bill unless labor backed it." *The Great Railway Crisis*, p. 148.

36. For background on the development of rail industry protective arrangements, see United States Railway Association, *Conrail at the Crossroads: The Future of Rail Service in the Northeast*, April 1981, chap. 7.

at best, not a highly profitable carrier. For both of these reasons, the administration and congressional Republicans initially rejected the labor protection agreement as too costly and not representative of the needs of Conrail (which did not yet exist) or the federal government. But unified support from rail management and labor, combined with the fear that the entire bill would be wrecked without a protection agreement, caused the labor provisions to be adopted virtually unchanged as Title V of the 3R act.

The money issue was also resolved through compromise. Most of the funding under the 3R act was to be in the form of loans from the United States Railway Association (guaranteed by the federal government) of up to $1.5 billion, with a maximum of $1 billion for Conrail.[37] The association would raise the money in private markets and reloan it to the railroads. This method kept spending out of federal budget totals, which pleased the Nixon administration, and avoided the intense political wrangling of annual appropriations. But it also could create problems: unlike equity investment, it would require sufficient cash flow from Conrail to start repayment immediately. And if there were no profits, as in the case of Amtrak, it simply delayed an inevitable accounting. The 3R act also provided $558.5 million in grants for specific tasks for which repayment would be economically or politically impractical.[38]

Although the Regional Rail Reorganization Act of 1973 did address the issues pressed upon it by Judge Fullam's order, it did not make a decisive choice in either policy or policy instruments. Whether protectionist policies would be rescued or replaced would depend on how USRA weighed the act's conflicting goals (notably economic viability, adequacy of service, and intramodal competition) in its plans. And, as in the case of Amtrak, the scope and structure of operations would be more important than the ambiguous wording of the act in determining whether Conrail was to be a private or public sector corporation.

37. Most of the remaining $500 million was expected to be used for improvement of Amtrak's Boston-Washington Northeast Corridor.

38. A total of $43.5 million was given to the United States Railway Association, the Department of Transportation, and the Interstate Commerce Commission for planning; $85 million to the bankrupt railroads to prevent a shutdown of operations (and erosion of estates); $250 million for labor protection; and $180 million to preserve rail service for up to two years on lines scheduled for abandonment by the *Final System Plan* or to acquire and modernize such lines. The branch line program required a matching state contribution of at least 30 percent of total funding. Funding for acquisition was to be in the form of loans or loan guarantees, but use of federal grant funds was allowed with approval of the secretary.

The Planning Process and Beyond

The financial provisions of the 3R act were not adequate to solve the Northeast rail crisis. This became evident early in the USRA planning process. Additional grants were appropriated for USRA planning ($14 million) and for operating the bankrupts until conveyance ($197 million). The big problem, however, was providing capital for Conrail. Additional funding to improve Conrail's roadbed would be necessary unless there were massive cuts in the system—cuts that would be politically impossible to implement. In any case, a substantially smaller system would require increased funding for branch line and labor protection payments.[39] More loans were out of the question: Conrail's predicted level of earnings was so low and so uncertain that additional fixed interest charges would almost certainly bankrupt it as soon as it began operating. Grants were unacceptable to the Nixon and Ford administrations.

The Republican-dominated USRA board was determined to find a funding device that would keep Conrail a private enterprise. It rejected, at one extreme, proposals for nationalizing the roadbed (at least temporarily) while retaining a private sector Conrail to operate the trains; that option might make it more difficult to cut fixed plant in the future and constituted a major break with private sector solutions. At the other extreme, USRA turned down the approach favored by the new secretary of transportation, William Coleman: a controlled transfer of properties to solvent carriers with minimal federal aid. This approach foundered on the unwillingness of the solvents to take over important portions of the bankrupts, particularly along the eastern seaboard, where high-cost terminal operations are concentrated.

The board's compromise solution was for Conrail to sell USRA a mixture of debentures and preferred shares, both having seniority over other (estate-held) securities and both with mandatory redemption requirements. Interest or dividends on the two types of securities could be paid in additional preferred shares if necessary. This would cut demands on Conrail's cash flow during the period of intense rehabilitation, but it raised the possibility of a gradual, "backdoor" nationalization. Ford administration representatives on the USRA board insisted that they hold a majority voice in decisions to cut off aid to Conrail if it

39. Harr, *The Great Railway Crisis*, pp. 316–28, 370–71. Only so-called "Conrail ¼," which would cut the reorganizing carriers' 23,000 miles down to about 6,000 miles, had a chance of being funded within the $1 billion limitation.

failed to meet business targets, and in return they agreed to raise rehabilitation aid for Conrail from $1 billion to $2.1 billion.

To increase the financial viability of the Northeast rail industry, the United States Railway Association cut lines with light traffic—about 23 percent of the mileage operated by the carriers being reorganized.[40] In addition, USRA opposed cross-subsidizing unprofitable passenger and freight operations within Conrail. Other decisions of the board reinforced protectionist policies. To continue competition in the Northeast, the board decided to sell portions of the insolvent carriers to profitable companies (primarily the Chessie System), even though this would require more federal aid, permit elimination of fewer facilities, and lower the probability of creating a profitable Conrail. The USRA also tried to protect solvent carriers in the region by offering them track ownership or operating rights. These decisions were also intended to protect Conrail: the USRA feared that if Conrail appeared to be a monopoly, it would be excessively regulated, and political interference could prevent it from achieving the goals of the *Final System Plan*.[41]

The USRA tended to seek compromise solutions rather than substantial innovation largely because of the conflicting goals forced on it by the 3R act. But board members also felt that near consensus was necessary to prevent endless revisions of its plan by Congress or sabotage by the executive branch.[42] The board united around positions supported by a majority and rejected highly divisive proposals such as a DOT recom-

40. These lines carried only about 2.2 percent of traffic on the reorganizing carriers. The *Final System Plan* also authorized the abandonment of 1,158 miles already out of service and transferred ownership of the Boston-Washington Northeast Corridor to Amtrak. Lines eliminated by the plan were not immediately abandoned, but made "available for subsidy" under the federal-state shared cost program established by the 3R act. These lines represented about 58 percent of light density lines studied by the USRA, but carried only 12 percent of traffic on those lines. United States Railway Association, *Final System Plan*, vol. 2, pp. 2–3.

41. *Final System Plan*, vol. 1, pp. 16–17; *Final System Plan Supplementary Report*, September 1975, p. 110; See also Harr, *The Great Railway Crisis*, pp. 350–53, 363–65, 506–07, 520–21. The USRA had originally favored a "Three Systems East," with both Chessie and Norfolk and Western receiving major portions of the reorganizing carriers. However, Norfolk and Western refused to enter what it saw as an inevitably money-draining operation. The USRA rejected a proposal that would have split the bankrupts into two competing systems—basically Penn Central plus Ann Arbor versus a combined Lehigh Valley-Erie-Lackawanna-Reading-Jersey Central (known as MARC-EL)—because it would have led to increased funding requirements and perhaps would have created two carriers dependent on the federal government rather than one.

42. On the pattern of consensus-building within the USRA board, see Harr, *The Great Railway Crisis*, pp. 394–95, 531–33.

mendation that the USRA press for major changes in work rules to improve labor productivity. Board members felt that such a stand could cost labor support for the *Final System Plan*.[43] Nongovernment members also coalesced in opposition to the Department of Transportation's "controlled transfer" of the reorganizing carriers' properties to solvent railroads. In this way the board defined a middle ground between the department's hard line in favor of deep cuts in service and communities' efforts to preserve all service.

In reviewing the final plan and implementing legislation proposed by the United States Railway Association, Congress reopened many of the issues considered during the planning process. Congressional leaders (notably Vance Hartke, the chairman of the Senate Surface Transportation Subcommittee) pushed for increased funding and service for Conrail and Amtrak and attempted to transfer responsibility for rail planning outside the Northeast from the Department of Transportation to USRA. The department, on the other hand, tried to hold the line on funding (it resisted congressional efforts to ease interest requirements on USRA-held securities) and to maintain the possibility of controlled transfer if Conrail did not meet its financial targets. In addition, Secretary William Coleman tried to link approval of the final plan to regulatory reforms easing the ICC's control over rates and abandonments while giving his department increased powers to push rail mergers. When both houses passed a bill not to his liking, Coleman recommended that President Ford veto it.

Again a shutdown of the Northeast carriers appeared possible. Shippers and rail labor pressured DOT and Congress to reach a compromise. Direct negotiations between the department and congressional staff finally led to an agreement that followed USRA's final plan on major points relating to Conrail but cut funding by about $1.5 billion. These compromises were incorporated in the Railroad Revitalization and Regulatory Reform (4R) Act of 1976, approved with overwhelming majorities in the House and Senate.[44]

---

43. Ibid., pp. 420–23.
44. 91 Stat. 31. The 4R act differed from the *Final System Plan* and 3R act in several important respects. It temporarily increased the federal share of funding to continue service on lines suggested for abandonment by the *Final System Plan*. It reduced government appointees on the thirteen-member Conrail board to six; the USRA rather than the president would appoint these members. (The secretary of transportation was no longer included on the board.) The 4R act also eliminated payment of additional

Conrail began operating on April 1, 1976, but its problems were not over. Indeed, difficulties began even before the conveyance date. The planned transfer of substantial amounts of track and equipment to the solvent Chessie System and the Southern Railway fell through when the two companies and labor failed to agree on wages and working conditions. The 3R act's labor protection agreement (unaltered by the 4R act) was the major stumbling block: Chessie and Southern did not want to take on employees operating under more generous agreements than their own, fearing that current employees would demand similar protections. Union leaders could not agree to proposals that would leave transferred employees worse off than those remaining with Conrail. As Jack Harr put it in his study of USRA, "The job protection and labor benefits in Title V of the 1973 Act deprived the unions of any incentive to agree to anything less in the Chessie and Southern negotiations. They had nothing to gain, and possibly something to lose."[45] Most of those lines were transferred to Conrail, and trackage rights were given to the tiny Delaware and Hudson Railway in order to provide limited rail competition to major Northeast markets and connections for the D and H.

Problems continued to mount after conveyance. The increases in traffic and improvements in service forecast for the new corporation failed to materialize, and Conrail began suffering heavier than expected losses in 1977.[46] Congress authorized the issuance of additional preferred shares in 1978 and again in 1980, raising the total rehabilitation and working fund assistance to more than $3.6 billion.[47] The USRA began to accumulate Conrail stock in lieu of the interest Conrail could not afford to pay on debentures. Conrail remained nominally a private sector

---

stock as interest on preferred shares, although not on debentures, and added a one-House veto over any cutoff of funding to Conrail. Interest on preferred shares was to be paid in cash, but only when Conrail had cash available. Interest would not be cumulative. The conferees were explicit on the reasons for adopting the veto provision on a cutoff of funds to Conrail: "This review is designed to negate any possibility of executive branch control over corporate management decisions." *Railroad Revitalization and Regulatory Reform Act of 1976*, S. Rept. 94-595, 94 Cong. 1 sess. (GPO, 1976), pp. 191–92.

45. Harr, *The Great Railway Crisis*, p. 673. See more generally pp. 663–74.

46. Through the end of 1980, Conrail suffered a cash loss from operations of $800 million rather than the positive cash flow of $535 million projected by the *Final System Plan*. United States Railway Association, *Federal Funding of Conrail: Rail Service Objectives and Economic Realities*, December 1980, p. 10.

47. The Staggers Rail Act of 1980 (secs. 504, 703) also authorized an additional $235 million for labor protection payments, for a total of $485 million. See also the United States Railway Association Amendments Act of 1978, 92 Stat. 2397, secs. 2–3.

corporation until settlement of the Penn Central estate's conveyance-taking suit against the federal government in November 1980. That settlement gave the Department of Transportation control of the estate's Conrail shares and consequently a direct ownership role in Conrail. DOT also gained the right to appoint five of the corporation's thirteen directors and thus increased leverage to press for a controlled transfer of Conrail properties to solvent private sector railroads.

As in the case of Amtrak, the gradual evolution of Conrail from federal ward to public enterprise reflects the importance of policy impasse. In the Northeast rail crisis, a stalemate developed once again between policymakers (centered in the executive branch) who stressed the financial viability of the industry and those who wished to rescue protectionist service and employment goals by employing new policy instruments and by transferring costs to government. Federal rail policy in the Northeast displayed important accelerationist characteristics: all railroads in the Northeast were considered as one system for purposes of planning, cutbacks were made in route mileage and employment, and federal rehabilitation aid was concentrated on the most economically viable lines.

Protectionist objectives dominated, however. Although USRA's planning process had a financially viable Conrail as its primary goal, it was a goal to be minimally satisfied rather than maximized. Cuts in service and costs were made only to the extent necessary to make the system self-sustaining according to financial projections. This ordering of goals did not originate with USRA; it was implicit in the Regional Rail Reorganization Act. It was, moreover, fully consistent with the long-standing protectionist policy of a minimally profitable rather than profit-maximizing rail industry. The goal of maintaining service to the vast majority of active shipping points was met by shifting costs of rehabilitation aid, labor protection, branch lines, and (at least temporarily) some operating expenses to the federal government. Maintenance of competition in the Northeast was less successful, but not because of lack of interest by USRA, DOT, and Congress.

The policy instruments chosen reflect this impasse. The desire of executive branch officials to avoid a permanent commitment in the form of nationalization or subsidies gave rise to instruments (such as redeemable preference shares and interest-deferrable loans) that perpetuated the illusion of a private sector solution and retained the option of a controlled transfer of some lines to solvent carriers. But Conrail's nominal owners (the estates of the bankrupt Northeast railroads) preferred to exercise their constitutional rights to compensation rather than maintain an interest in an apparently hopeless money loser.

Toward a New Rail Policy: The Rock Island and the Milwaukee Road

Another major rail crisis, this time in the grain growing area of the upper Midwest, confronted the federal government in the late 1970s. Two carriers—the Chicago, Rock Island and Pacific Railroad (known as the Rock Island) and the Chicago, Milwaukee, St. Paul and Pacific Railroad (known as the Milwaukee Road)—faced imminent shutdown and sought protection from creditors under federal bankruptcy laws. Congress did not follow the Amtrak and Conrail precedents by establishing public or quasi-public rail corporations in the Midwest. Instead, in a partial break with protectionist rail policy, it permitted substantial cuts in the number of route-miles served, limited the traditional benefits offered to labor, and allowed one corporation to go out of business.

The Midwest Rail Problem

The Rock Island and Milwaukee Road had major handicaps in adjusting to the changing U.S. transportation market. They depended heavily on agricultural (notably grain) traffic that is seasonal, highly unbalanced in one direction (from farm to export points), and requires a sizable branch-line network. They had too many competitors in their midwestern base and underutilized extensions outside that base.[48] Because of low revenues they were unable to maintain track and equipment properly, which led to further declines in service quality and traffic. To save themselves, the Rock Island and Milwaukee Road attempted in the 1960s to merge with other carriers, but neither merger was consummated. The Rock Island filed for protection from creditors under Section 77 of the Bankruptcy Act in 1975, followed by the Milwaukee Road in 1977.

48. Michael Conant, "The Future of the Rock Island Railroad," *ICC Practitioners' Journal*, vol. 44 (November–December 1976), pp. 51–59; and Conant, "The Future of the Milwaukee Road," *ICC Practitioners' Journal*, vol. 45 (March–April 1978), pp. 280–93.

As in the case of the Northeast bankrupts, the chances for income-based reorganization appeared slim.

In 1979 managers of the two carriers brought the Midwest rail crisis to a head. The Milwaukee trustee presented a reorganization plan that called for massive cutbacks in the railroad's system (dubbed "Milwaukee II"). A few months later, as part of its effort to stay afloat, the Rock Island attempted to institute unilateral work rule changes and a wage freeze. A strike by the United Transportation Union ensued, and management personnel took over running as many trains as possible. Both developments represented a direct challenge to existing policy: the government would have to accept major cuts in service and employment or undertake some direct form of federal support.

A Changing Political Environment

The political environment in the Midwest was much less favorable to a backdoor nationalization than it had been in the Northeast, however. Conrail was clearly the dominant carrier in the Northeast, but the Rock Island and the Milwaukee Road were surrounded by stronger, solvent competitors that were capable of hauling most of the region's traffic.[49] The two railways together employed fewer than 20,000 people in 1977, compared with Conrail's 95,000. These differences had important political implications. Loss of service and employment threatened costs that were primarily local rather than regional or national. Because solvent competitors existed in most Milwaukee Road and Rock Island markets, shipper commitment to service preservation was weak, and competing carriers opposed a government bailout. Rail labor was thus isolated in opposition to cutbacks.

In addition, government opposition to a bailout strengthened. The federal Department of Transportation viewed low traffic density caused by overcapacity as the source of the Midwest rail crisis, and it resisted efforts by the Midwest carriers to use rail rehabilitation funds authorized

49. The Rock Island and Milwaukee Road together carried only 7.3 percent of revenue ton mileage in the Western District in 1977, compared with the 43.7 percent carried by Conrail in the Eastern District. Interstate Commerce Commission, Bureau of Accounts, *Transport Statistics in the United States, 1977*, pt. 1: *Railroads* (ICC, 1977).

by the 4R act to bail them out.[50] Instead, it pressed for coordination of facilities by solvent and failing Midwest railroads, using rail rehabilitation funds as a financial incentive to restructure.[51] In short, the department sought to promote rather than to inhibit industrial adjustment.

The Interstate Commerce Commission generally supported the policy changes pushed by DOT. Transport deregulation was one of the major priorities of the Carter administration, and this goal was clearly reflected in its appointments to the commission. By early 1980, a majority of the commission was firmly committed to finding market-oriented solutions to the railroad industry's problems. Although the commission sometimes favored a slower transition than that favored by DOT to allow shippers more time to adjust, it did not serve as an institutional focus for opponents of service cutbacks, as it had with Amtrak and Conrail.

The balance of interests was different in Congress as well. The need to avoid "another Conrail" in the Midwest was stressed repeatedly.[52] Even more important were regional differences of interest. Amtrak and Conrail provided services deemed important in all regions of the country, but the Rock Island and Milwaukee did not. Nor did the two railroads, based largely in agricultural states, have the legislative clout of those in the Northeast. Moreover, even within the regions the two carriers served, there were divisions. The Milwaukee trustee's plan to save a "core" by massive route cuts pitted legislators from areas that would retain service (for example, Wisconsin and Illinois) against those that

50. For the department's views, see U.S. Department of Transportation, *A Prospectus for Change in the Freight Railroad Industry* (DOT, 1978), chap. 4. The dispute between the Rock Island and the department is discussed in *Milwaukee Road Bankruptcy,* Hearings before the Subcommittee on Transportation and Commerce of the House Committee on Interstate and Foreign Commerce, 95 Cong. 2 sess. (GPO, 1978), pp. 18–24, 71–101. The Rock Island had earlier sought a $100 million loan from USRA under Section 211 of the Regional Rail Reorganization Act. USRA refused the request on the grounds that the loan probably would not be repaid and would not prevent the Rock Island's insolvency.

51. Section 401 of the 4R act gave antitrust immunity to conferences called by the secretary to discuss rail coordination projects. The department in 1979 proposed that Title V assistance (excluding Section 511 loan guarantees) be given only where the secretary found that the project would promote a significant restructuring, and that solvent railroads be eligible for the funds. The department also backed legislation in the latter half of the 1970s to speed up rail reorganizations, acquisitions, and abandonments and to weaken the presumption under bankruptcy law that existing railroad operations should be continued.

52. *Reorganization of the Milwaukee Road,* Hearings before the Subcommittee on Transportation and Commerce of the House Committee on Interstate and Foreign Commerce, 96 Cong. 1 sess. (GPO, 1979), pp. 20–21.

116 POLITICS OF INDUSTRIAL CHANGE

would not (for example, Montana, Washington, and northern Iowa).[53] As a result, the "retentionist" pressures in Congress—so important in shaping Amtrak and Conrail—were substantially weakened.

The railroad industry was also divided. Some railroads would benefit from the preservation of "friendly connections" with the two bankrupt carriers; others feared competition with a federally owned or subsidized rail line. Some roads might even be able to purchase specific lines without having to take over the entire bankrupt system. Similarly, shippers on lines likely to lose service as a result of dismantling or reorganizing the two railroads had different interests from those on lines likely to be retained. The latter were understandably concerned that surviving railroads be as financially strong as possible and not be encumbered by unprofitable routes. The Department of Transportation encouraged this split by assuring shippers that the great majority of traffic would be retained by the purchase of viable track segments.

As a result of splits among shippers and the solvent railroads, rail labor was the only major group with a clear interest in rescuing protectionist policy. Isolated from shippers and railroads and lacking strong support in Congress, DOT, or the ICC, labor decided to concentrate on obtaining federal protection guarantees for workers who lost their jobs.

Labor also attempted to preserve rail service (and jobs) on many of the embargoed Milwaukee routes by the formation of a new employee-shipper-owned railroad. The proposed "New Milwaukee Lines" would require substantial federal assistance to finance the acquisition and rehabilitation of the Milwaukee's western lines. The plan had two flaws, however. First, it isolated rail labor from other interests, notably shippers and the Department of Transportation. DOT vehemently opposed the plan because it seemed to offer the same prospects for backdoor nationalization as Conrail. Second, the plan placed the onus on labor to come up with a scheme that the ICC and the bankruptcy court could accept as fair to the Milwaukee estate. Such an agreement proved unattainable.

53. See the contrasting bills introduced by Senators Larry Pressler of South Dakota (S. 839) and John Melcher of Montana (S. 1286) versus the approach of Senators Gaylord Nelson and William Proxmire of Wisconsin and Senator David Durenberger of Minnesota (S. 1492). *Milwaukee Railroad Financial Crisis,* pt. 2, Hearings before the Subcommittee on Surface Transportation of the Senate Committee on Commerce, Science and Transportation, 96. Cong. 1 sess. (GPO, 1979). See also Judy Sarasohn, "Congress Again Faces Rail Money Problems," *Congressional Quarterly Weekly Report,* October 13, 1979, pp. 2289–91.

Solutions Emerge

The initial federal responses to the threatened collapse of the Rock Island and the Milwaukee appeared to put them on the path followed in the Northeast. On September 20, 1979, President Jimmy Carter ordered Rock Island workers back to work for a sixty-day "cooling off" period under the National Labor Relations Act. On October 5 the ICC ordered a neutral carrier to take over management of Rock Island services under full federal subsidy. This directed service was expensive, costing the federal government between $11 million and $13 million a month, and it did little to solve the problem of the Rock Island's deteriorating physical plant.

At about the same time, an appeals court allowed the Milwaukee Road trustee's "Milwaukee II" reorganization proposal (which included the major service cutbacks) to take effect. Congress enacted the Milwaukee Railroad Restructuring Act on November 4 to restart service with federal assistance until the ICC and bankruptcy court could rule on the employee-shipper (New Milwaukee) plan. But the act was not purely protectionist. It set rigid deadlines for consideration of the plan, ensuring that federally financed service would not last past April 1.[54] The act also significantly eased the labor protection liability of the Milwaukee and provided federal funding for supplemental unemployment benefits and retraining of Milwaukee Road employees.[55]

54. Congress authorized a $10 million grant to restart all services briefly embargoed, and the Milwaukee Road trustee was forced to accept up to $75 million in federally guaranteed trustee's certificates to maintain those services. These certificates were to be subordinated to all creditors' claims, however. Thus the federal government would probably end up paying for the service. If the employee purchase plan was rejected, control over abandonments would be shifted to the bankruptcy court, which was likely to be more sympathetic to creditors.

55. Existing labor agreements would have made the Milwaukee liable for up to $521 million in payments, making a reorganization almost impossible. The Milwaukee Railroad Restructuring Act limited the liability of the estate to $75 million (financed by federal loan guarantees with high repayment priority) and provided $6.5 million in federal support for employee training and supplemental unemployment insurance. The act also gave furloughed Milwaukee employees a "right of first hire" with all other U.S. railroads for a one-year period, further reducing labor protection liability. Vacancies covered by affirmative action plans were exempted. Although employees still had recourse to the courts to obtain traditional labor protection benefits, the long delay before such benefits could be obtained through litigation provided a strong incentive for employees to accept the act's benefit program. See the Milwaukee Railroad Restructuring Act, 93 Stat. 736, sec. 8. See also secs. 9–15.

On balance, the Milwaukee Railroad Restructuring Act represented a victory for the Department of Transportation. Although the act led to greater federal expenditures than the department would have liked, it did follow the DOT strategy of shifting the responsibility for saving "excess" rail lines away from the federal government. The ICC unanimously rejected labor's New Milwaukee proposal on December 31, 1979. The commission, with the trustee and bankruptcy court, then began to transfer assets. Sales of lines were negotiated with several states and solvent railroads. At the end of February the Milwaukee embargoed 4,600 miles of track outside the "core."

While this restructuring was taking place, pressures increased to find a permanent answer to the Rock Island's woes. On January 25, 1980, Judge Frank McGarr finally ordered the trustee to prepare for liquidation of the Rock Island, and on January 31 the ICC voted 4-2 not to extend federally subsidized directed service past March 2.[56] By the time Congress became deeply involved in the Rock Island crisis early in 1980, these rulings had established a strong momentum for dissolution of the Rock Island. Legislators' attention had shifted to easing the transition process for Rock Island shippers, establishing a conveyance process for railroads interested in acquiring pieces of the Rock Island, and providing protection for Rock Island employees who lost their jobs. The last two issues were closely intertwined: no railroad was likely to close a purchase until it knew what responsibility it would have for former Rock Island employees working on those lines. While Congress spent two months wrangling over two provisions of the House bill that were unrelated to the needs of the Rock Island, directed service on the rail line expired.[57] The ICC, with strong backing from the Department of Transportation, refused further extensions of directed service and used creative but rather dubious statutory interpretations to allow other carriers to take over operation of portions of most Rock Island lines on a noncompensated basis.[58]

---

56. *Traffic World*, February 4, 1980, pp. 13–14, 107–09. For details of the trustee's proposal for reorganization, see *Traffic World*, January 7, 1980, pp. 68–69.

57. For details of the conflict, which involved efforts by Congressman James Florio to increase capital spending for rail passenger service, see *Traffic World*, April 7, 1980, p. 16.

58. Over the objections of some commissioners, the ICC first developed the notion of "emergency temporary operating authority." When the courts promptly ruled this beyond the commission's powers, it quickly substituted "uncompensated directed service." The wording was different, but the effect was the same. The notion of temporary authority was borrowed from provisions of the Interstate Commerce Act

By the time the Rock Island Transition and Employee Assistance Act (RITEA) was finally passed at the end of May 1980, the cutbacks in service and employment had already taken place. The act upheld these changes and instituted a labor protection arrangement similar to that on the Milwaukee.[59] It also provided $43 million (later raised to $65 million) to help noncarriers, such as states and employee-shipper groups, purchase lines of the Milwaukee and Rock Island, and $15 million to provide directed service on the two carriers' lines where there was a "transportation emergency" that could not be resolved through other means.

Major changes in the structure of the midwestern rail system have occurred in the wake of the Milwaukee Road and Rock Island failures. The slimmed-down "Milwaukee II" has been purchased by the Soo Line Railroad, the U.S. rail subsidiary of Canadian Pacific. Additional Milwaukee and Rock Island lines have been sold to solvent carriers, to shipper groups, and to states. Other lines are not being served at all.

It would be misleading to view the outcome of the Midwest rail crisis as a clearly market-oriented one, however. Of the more than $500 million in federal assistance (grants, preference shares, loans, and loan guarantees) authorized for the two railroads or prospective purchasers since 1975, $180 million was essentially palliative—operating subsidies to delay the closing of operations. An additional $65 million in redeemable preference shares was to help noncarrier entities buy Rock Island and Milwaukee lines. Almost $190 million in grants and loan guarantees was authorized for labor protection assistance. Thus most federal aid was consistent with longstanding protectionist goals: preserving service and protecting rail labor. Only a small portion of federal funding went into selective assistance for rail industry revitalization.

Indeed, the Rock Island and Milwaukee cases demonstrate the inability of any policy to satisfy the conflicting goals of carriers, shippers, and governments. It proved difficult to take any clear policy initiatives in the face of these differences. Movement toward market-oriented policies occurred largely because other options were blocked. The public enterprise option was rejected as a solution to the Midwest rail crisis primarily because of its identification with discredited protec-

---

dealing with motor and water carriers. See the summary of Commissioner George Stafford's dissent in *Traffic World,* December 17, 1979, pp. 38–39. The commission orders and court response are outlined in *Traffic World,* March 24, 1980, pp. 13–14, 18–19; March 31, 1980, pp. 15, 42–43.

59. 94 Stat. 399 (1980). The labor protection provisions of RITEA were overturned by the Supreme Court as a violation of the Constitution's requirement for uniform bankruptcy laws. See *Railway Labor Executives' Assn.* v. *Gibbons,* 455 U.S. 457 (1982).

tionist policy and the resulting opposition of the executive branch and rail industry.

Conclusions

By 1970 protectionist rail policies had helped to bring the U.S. rail industry to the verge of collapse. A massive infusion of federal funds would be required to preserve existing levels of rail service. But a federal operating subsidy or public enterprise was anathema to the Nixon White House and the OMB. An alternative set of rail policy proposals gradually emerged in the executive branch that focused on decreased regulation and selective assistance for rail rationalization. The administration resisted spending increases and stressed the financial viability of the rail network. Pitted against the administration were opponents of service cutbacks in Congress and (until the late 1970s) the ICC. The intense conflict over policy led to definitive action only when major service cutbacks were imminent. The compromises that were reached did not resolve the conflict, however; they simply defused it temporarily. This concluding section examines the consequences of that impasse for both industrial adjustment and instrument choice.

Nationalization and Industrial Adjustment

As chapter 1 pointed out, a successful accelerationist policy antici- pates and guides change rather than merely reacts to it; it prevents adjustment crises from occurring rather than responds to them after the fact. But the U.S. government, paralyzed by internal disagreements, showed little ability to anticipate and guide change in the Amtrak, Conrail, and Midwest rail crises. Once a major shutdown of services occurred or appeared inevitable, the government intervened, but then only to pick up the pieces with "solutions" that were a patchwork of incompatible protectionist, market-oriented, and accelerationist poli- cies.

The establishment of Amtrak showed awareness of the need for industrial change. For the first time, rail passenger service was consid- ered as a system rather than in terms of individual abandonment cases. The federal government created an institution to focus managerial attention on rail passenger service. About half of the remaining intercity trains—primarily long-distance trains, which were the most hopelessly uneconomic—were eliminated in one fell swoop. Perhaps most important, Amtrak removed much of the financial burden of passenger service from the railways. But the Amtrak planning process within the Department of Transportation was driven more by a desire to develop a politically acceptable compromise than by a realistic assessment of the financial realities facing the corporation. After Amtrak began operations, it lost even the semblance of being a vehicle for industrial adjustment, as Congress extended freezes on the basic route structure and added more routes. Nor did Amtrak's establishment lead to the development of "public needs" criteria for intercity passenger service: the creation of Amtrak politicized route decisions even more.

Similarly, the Conrail case revealed a mishmash of accelerationist and protectionist policies. Again, rail planners considered the Northeast rail network as a system. Thousands of miles of track were abandoned or sold to shippers, states, or passenger carriers (Amtrak and commuter rail authorities). A number of weak railroads were eliminated, which consolidated traffic on fewer main lines. Federal assistance financed the rehabilitation of Conrail, and a federally financed labor protection agreement helped to make the restructuring possible. But protectionist elements dominated. The United States Railway Association and the secretary of transportation were unable to compel solvent carriers to take over substantial portions of the bankrupts—despite the fact that the solvent railways already indirectly owned these lines through their control of bankrupt carriers.[60] The Conrail labor protection agreement went beyond transitional assistance. Its lifetime earnings guarantee inhibited labor exit from the industry and weakened labor's incentive to negotiate concessions that would have allowed some of the bankrupt lines to be conveyed to solvent carriers. Moreover, the USRA did not use the Conrail planning process to address labor productivity issues. Nor was the creation of Conrail accompanied by an effective deregulation of rates needed to make the Northeast rail system viable. In short, the Northeast rail crisis showed that the federal government has very limited resources to impose losses on private interests as part of an industrial adjustment package.

The Midwest crisis led to a greater restructuring of the rail industry

60. In the USRA's *Preliminary System Plan*, Norfolk and Western was to take direct control of the Erie-Lackawanna, which it already controlled through the Dereco holding company. The Chessie System was to take over certain lines of the Reading, which it controlled through stock ownership. See the *Preliminary System Plan*, vol. 1, pp. 40–41.

than either of the two earlier crises. This restructuring, however, was largely the result of federal inaction rather than federal initiative. Instead of forming protectionist coalitions, interest groups split, thus enabling the Department of Transportation and the Interstate Commerce Commission to resist protectionist pressures to a greater degree than they had before.

Why did federal initiatives in the three rail crises occur so far into the crises and have a predominantly protectionist cast? The reasons can be clearly traced to the absence of the political structures outlined in chapter 1 as requisite for accelerationist policy. Decisive government action in the United States requires a near consensus to overcome multiple veto points. The difficulty of reaching a consensus makes it very hard for the government to make any major change in the status quo, let alone impose concentrated losses. Multiple veto points created an obsession with consensus most evident in the USRA planning process.

Bureaucratic autonomy was lacking as well. Executive agencies were not trusted by Congress, let alone given decisionmaking autonomy. The rare exceptions (for example, the Department of Transportation's discretion in making the 1970 Amtrak route cuts) were generally not repeated. The planning of Conrail was not entrusted to DOT but to the United States Railway Association, especially created for that purpose. In fact, government agencies were sometimes relegated to bystander status as interest groups negotiated public policy directly among themselves. The most notable example is the negotiation of the labor protection agreement in the 3R act. One reason for this bystander role may have been the agencies' lack of unity. The Department of Transportation and the Interstate Commerce Commission took very different positions in the Amtrak and Conrail rail crises. Moreover, the federal government lacked strong mechanisms to compel compliance as became evident in the negotiations for conveyance of Conrail lines to solvent carriers. Constitutional restrictions on "taking" also gave Washington a weak hand in dealing with the railways.

Rail Nationalization as Instrument Choice

In responding to the rail industry crises of the 1970s, the federal government consistently chose the policy instruments requiring the least direct financial involvement. When regulation proved inadequate, the government's first reaction was generally to offer loan guarantees. These guarantees did not raise budget totals, and they gave the government top position among creditors. Most important, they did not represent a permanent commitment, and they preserved at least a semblance of a marketplace test of the companies' viability. These instrument choices often were clearly inappropriate to the task at hand. Loan guarantees, for instance, were used to finance operating expenditures when there was virtually no possibility of a short-term turnaround in the recipients' operations. Legislative criteria established to protect the integrity of those loan programs were altered to provide funds for the Delaware and Hudson and for the Milwaukee Road, while federal capital funding was diverted to provide service on the Rock Island.[61] In each case, Congress sought to avoid a separate appropriations process by rechanneling funds already available under existing legislation. But in so doing, Congress muddied the distinction between loans and grants and between capital and operating assistance while undermining the programs' original intent.

When public enterprise did emerge in the U.S. rail industry, it was through the evolution of institutional hybrids rather than as a result of a single identifiable choice or plan. The melding of public and private characteristics in Amtrak and Conrail was a means of "splitting the difference" in policy disputes and of delaying decisions on the extent and permanence of federal aid. Amtrak was established as a quasi-private corporation with a completely inadequate resource base, requiring it to return for additional funds shortly after it began operations. Conrail, too, was funded on the basis of overly optimistic financial projections. Public enterprise was not so much chosen as arrived at incrementally.

The patterns of instrument choice in the U.S. rail crises raise three questions. Why did the federal government accept public enterprise in the Amtrak and Conrail cases when it had rejected it for most industrial interventions in the United States? Why was public enterprise rejected in the Midwest after its emergence in the two prior rail crises? And why did public enterprise evolve from institutional hybrids rather than being chosen explicitly as in Canada?

61. Waivers in the criteria for ERSA funding were made for the Delaware and Hudson in the Regional Rail Reorganization Act of 1978, 87 Stat. 985, sec. 3(b), and for the Milwaukee Road in the Milwaukee Railroad Restructuring Act, sec. 7(d). Funding for directed service on the Rock Island was provided by changing criteria of the Rail Trust Fund established under Title V of the 4R act, sec. 104(b) (2).

While questions of instrument choice were closely intertwined with policy choices, the former were not simply a byproduct of the latter. The retention of protectionist principles in the mandates of Amtrak and Conrail eroded the private sector aspect of the institutional hybrids and made some reassessment of instrument or policy choice (or both) almost inevitable. But it was policy impasse rather than any specific policy that led to evolutionary nationalization. As Amtrak and Conrail drifted into greater dependence on government funding, Congress and the executive sought to tighten their control as a mechanism for asserting their respective policy concerns. Conflicting controls simply institutionalized government intervention without resolving the basic policy conflicts that had led to the establishment of the two corporations.

Ideology also fails to explain the patterns of instrument choice. Resistance to public enterprise was strong in all three rail crises, particularly among Republicans. In each case, however, ideological opposition was posed more in terms of empirical referents than in terms of general principle. The arguments marshaled against public enterprise included the huge deficits of Europe's nationalized railroads, the difficulties of imposing future service and labor cutbacks in a system beholden to Congress, and the likelihood that any aid program would become permanent. In retrospect, it is clear that these concerns were legitimate and justified.

Ideological explanations of instrument choice fail on several other grounds as well. Conservatives did not succeed in keeping the issue of public ownership off the political agenda or in preventing the (albeit backdoor) nationalization of Amtrak and Conrail. And ideology does not explain the differing outcome in the Midwest: the nationalization of Amtrak and Conrail is no more ideologically acceptable than the nationalization of Rock Island would have been.

In fact, the differing outcomes in the three cases are based on variations in societal and governmental interests and bargaining positions rather than on general attitudes toward public enterprise. As chapter 3 argued, owners and competitors of firms that are candidates for nationalization usually will resist use of public enterprise. Owners tend to prefer financial assistance mechanisms that allow them to retain control of their companies.[62] In the Amtrak and Conrail cases, however, the normally strong

---

62. This is the pattern that has been followed in the maritime and shipbuilding industries, where regulations limiting foreign competition and subsidies for construction

barriers to nationalization in the U.S. system were substantially weakened. Operators of intercity rail passenger service were anxious to get rid of the financial burden of those operations, and they did not feel threatened by an avowedly experimental corporation, operating in a clearly distinct segment of the rail business and contracting most of its operations to existing carriers. In the Northeast rail crisis, owners and creditors of the bankrupt carriers were more interested in being compensated for their rail properties (which appeared to be hopelessly uneconomic) than in retaining them. Competing carriers were in most cases also connecting lines that wanted to ensure that the Northeast rail system would not collapse. Moreover, in the cases of Amtrak and Conrail, the new institutional hybrids were perceived as offering the least direct government involvement practicable. The costs of nationalization for owners and competitors were, in short, both lower and less clear (because public enterprise evolved gradually) than in most instrument choice decisions.

The situation in the Midwest was very different: a government-funded "Farmrail" would have been a competitor rather than a connection for most railroads. In addition, the Rock Island and the Milwaukee Road carriers were much less important to the nation's rail system than Conrail. Thus rail nationalization in the Midwest presented a much more threatening precedent to owners and competitors than did Amtrak or Conrail. Furthermore, Midwest shippers were not united in favor of a government commitment to service retention; a broad coalition did not believe the possible benefits of government ownership outweighed its risks. Moreover, the policy implications of creating quasi-private enterprises in the rail industry had become much clearer by the late 1970s. If Comsat demonstrated that use of these institutional hybrids need not necessarily lead to greater government control, Amtrak and Conrail demonstrated that such an outcome was very likely in the rail industry.[63]

Government preferences regarding use of public enterprise differed in the Midwest crisis as well. Even when societal opposition is weak, nationalizations in the United States confront two constitutional obstacles: Fifth Amendment guarantees that private property cannot be taken for public use without just compensation and the system of checks and

---

and operations have been crucial in sustaining U.S. firms. See Gerald R. Jantscher, *Bread upon the Waters: Federal Aids to the Maritime Industries* (Brookings, 1975).

63. On quasi-private enterprise in the United States, see Lloyd D. Musolf, *Uncle Sam's Private Profit-Seeking Corporations* (Lexington Books, 1983).

balances that militates against control of a public enterprise by a single agency or branch of government. Amtrak and particularly Conrail had been seen as a way of getting around these costly strictures. These corporations proved, however, that "quasi-nationalization" was anything but inexpensive. DOT found that it could not control Amtrak and Conrail. It was therefore reluctant to repeat the experiment in the Midwest.

The government's inability to compel agreement in the United States was also an important influence on the pattern of instrument choice. Generally the existence of multiple veto points and the absence of stable legislative majorities work against nationalization; those who might suffer from it are able to block it. But in the Amtrak and Conrail cases the issue of government ownership was rarely addressed directly. Instead, each addition to funding and to government control was viewed as the minimum necessary to prevent a collapse of service, to preserve the stalemate between proponents of conflicting policies, and to avoid outright government takeover. Normal impediments to the creation of public enterprise were weakened because change was incremental.

Although conflict over instrument choice was weakened, conflict over policy was not. Public enterprise evolved in the Amtrak and Conrail cases because of continuing conflict over policy not in spite of it. In pluralist accommodation, policy disputes are often resolved by negotiation among the parties most directly affected by a dispute. Achieving agreement rather than policy coherence is the implicit goal of policymaking. The agreement is then accepted by government.

Pluralist accommodation often papers over policy conflict rather than resolving it. Gaining control of implementation thus becomes an important means of shaping policy. Generally, however, a stable equilibrium will be established, and all disputes will be "at the margin." In the Amtrak and Conrail cases, however, no such equilibrium was achieved, and inaction was politically impossible. This policy impasse gave both the executive and Congress a strong incentive to turn these government-sponsored enterprises into government-controlled enterprises—as long as it was they and not their opponents in the other branch exercising control. Public enterprise thus emerged as a byproduct not of specific policy choices, but of the failure to make such choices and of the efforts of rival political forces to control future choices.

The problems that arose after the establishment of Amtrak and Conrail convinced many legislators and ICC officials that a smaller and more market-oriented rail network was needed. The Department of Transportation, already committed to this objective, saw its failure to attain this goal through quasi-public enterprise as a sign that different policy instruments should be used. Thus the range of policy differences within the federal government was somewhat narrower in the Milwaukee Road–Rock Island collapse than in the earlier rail crises, and supporters of service retention lacked a strong institutional base within government. In the Midwest rail crisis, Congress primarily sanctioned courses of action already begun rather than resolved disputes. Executive-legislative impasse never emerged in the sharp form evident in the Conrail and Amtrak cases, nor did Congress enter into an escalating battle for policymaking authority. The absence of sustained policy impasse removed one of the major causes of the creation and evolution of institutional hybrids.

CHAPTER FIVE

Rail Nationalization in Canada: The Politics of Executive Dominance

THE CANADIAN pattern of railway ownership differs substantially from both the U.S. pattern of private sector dominance and the European pattern of public sector monopoly. At the beginning of World War I, the Canadian federal government owned only about 5 percent of the national railway mileage.[1] Currently, one federal Crown corporation and one private enterprise of roughly equal size dominate the rail freight industry in Canada with much smaller provincially owned and private sector firms sharing about 10 percent of the market. As in the United States, a federal public enterprise provides almost all of the intercity rail passenger service. This chapter examines the two major extensions of Ottawa's railway ownership in the twentieth century—the establishment of Canadian National Railways (CN) between 1917 and 1923 and VIA Rail Canada in 1977—and the consequence of those decisions for rail industry adjustment.

Strong parallels in the two Canadian nationalizations can be seen despite the more than fifty years between them. Although public enterprise was not a first choice in either case—less direct instruments were used initially—neither was it a last resort. In both cases there was strong support for public enterprise within the executive branch (cabinet or ministries), reflecting a belief that state enterprise was the most effective instrument to achieve the goals of the government of the day. And in Canada, unlike the United States, public enterprise was chosen explicitly and openly rather than through the evolution of quasi-public enterprises.

Executive support for public enterprise was matched by executive dominance in the decisionmaking process. In establishing Canadian

---

1. This excludes the National Transcontinental (the eastern division of the Grand Trunk Pacific), which was constructed by Ottawa, but scheduled for lease by the Grand Trunk Pacific.

128

National Railways and VIA, executive officials prevailed over strong external opposition to their choice of policies or policy instruments. In both cases, opponents had very limited resources to influence the choices made by the cabinet and virtually no effective resources once the cabinet had made its decision. Secure parliamentary majorities backing the government meant that Parliament had a negligible role in decisionmaking. Outside opposition influenced the scope and timing of nationalization, but it could not thwart the actions of a determined executive backed by a majority in the House of Commons.

Canadian National Railways: Industrial Crises and Political Compromise

The dawn of the twentieth century was a time of high hopes in Canada. Sir Wilfrid Laurier, the prime minister from 1896 to 1911, optimistically claimed that "the twentieth century is the century of Canada." Fulfilling that dream would require massive immigration to settle the Prairie provinces in western Canada. These settlers would provide markets for industry in central Canada. Settlement depended, Laurier believed, on further development of the western railway network, where the Canadian Pacific Railway (CPR) enjoyed a near monopoly. Because of its dominant position, the CPR had little incentive to construct branch lines that offered low return on investment but would encourage settlement. To stimulate competition, the government between 1903 and 1911 agreed to finance transcontinental extensions of two railways: the Grand Trunk, the major carrier in Ontario and Quebec; and the Canadian Northern, the largest competitor to the Canadian Pacific in the Prairies.

Cooperation between the two regionally based carriers was difficult because they were separated by more than a thousand miles of the Canadian Pacific rail monopoly north of Lake Superior. The obvious solution was either a merger or a cooperative arrangement for construction of a connecting line. The government sought to make cooperation a condition for federal financial assistance. When the two carriers could not agree, the government faced a difficult choice: abandon its goal of increasing rail competition in the West or sanction the creation of two additional transcontinental carriers in a very limited market. Given the optimistic mood of the times, it is not surprising that the latter path was taken. The transcontinental expansion of the Grand Trunk, authorized by Parliament in 1903, included an eastern division to be built by the federal government and leased to a subsidiary, the Grand Trunk Pacific. The Canadian Northern and the western division of the Grand Trunk Pacific were financed largely through the sale of fixed-interest securities (with substantial federal and provincial guarantees) rather than through equity or government grants.[2]

Giving financial assistance to both ventures was, in retrospect, a mistake. Heavy reliance on guarantees of fixed-interest securities proved equally unwise. This choice of policy instruments lowered the initial cost of the Laurier railway policy, but it also increased the risk of carrier collapse if credit tightened or revenues declined. By the time Laurier's Liberal party lost the 1911 general election, adverse developments—competition among Canadian bond offerings in London, tightening credit as fears of a European war grew, disadvantageous rate decisions, and rising construction costs at home—threatened the survival of the Canadian Northern and Grand Trunk Pacific.

The impending collapse of the two railways presented the new Conservative government of Prime Minister Robert Laird Borden (1911–20) with several options, all of them unpleasant. The first was to place the railways in receivership and allow them to reorganize with a reduced debt burden—the established practice in the United States. This would undermine London investors' confidence in all Canadian securities, and Canadian governments and industry were highly dependent upon London money markets. Receivership would also make raising additional funds to complete the new transcontinental lines even more difficult.[3] A second option, selling all or part of the failing lines to

2. See G. P. deT. Glazebrook, *A History of Transportation in Canada*, vol 2: *National Economy, 1867–1936* (Toronto: Ryerson Press, 1938; McClelland and Stewart, 1964), pp. 126–28; and A.W. Currie, *The Grand Trunk Railway of Canada* (University of Toronto Press, 1957), pp. 345–98. Financial arrangements for the eastern and western divisions of the Grand Trunk Pacific differed because the eastern division traversed an area with very little traffic-generating capacity, while the western division (Winnipeg to Prince Rupert, British Columbia) could draw traffic from existing settlements and hence was expected to be able to pay for itself as soon as it was completed.

3. At least two additional obstacles existed to the receivership option. First, many of the carriers' bonds were guaranteed by provincial governments, which would have to turn to Ottawa to avoid a default of their own. Second, the promoters of Canadian Northern were heavily in debt to a major Canadian bank, and receivership would have put the bank in danger of collapse as well. See T. D. Regehr, *The Canadian Northern Railway* (Toronto: MacMillan of Canada, 1976), pp. 366–69; John A. Eagle, "Sir Robert Borden, Union Government and Railway Nationalization," *Journal of Canadian Studies*,

Canadian Pacific, was equally unattractive. To do so would alienate western Canadians, who had sought effective competition to the CPR for more than thirty years. Although such a consolidation would reduce redundancy in rail facilities, any government that proposed it would be committing political suicide. A third option was to take over the Canadian Pacific along with the failing Canadian Northern and Grand Trunk. This plan, however, would alienate the CPR and its allies in the Montreal financial community, crucial allies of the Conservative party since the days of Sir John A. MacDonald (prime minister from 1867 to 1873 and from 1878 to 1891).

Given these political constraints, the government considered a temporary bailout and nationalization of the bankrupt railways to be the most promising courses of action. The two policies were pursued roughly in chronological order, with nationalization replacing temporary assistance in 1917. Between 1912 and 1916, the government extended several forms of assistance to the Canadian Northern and Grand Trunk Pacific, including direct loans, subsidies, and further loan guarantees. Permanent solutions were delayed by the inability of the cabinet to arrive at a consensus.

Borden himself viewed public ownership of the railways quite favorably.[4] In May 1915 he proposed to call a general election on the issue of nationalizing the Grand Trunk Pacific and Canadian Northern, but backed down when his cabinet colleagues opposed a wartime election. As the railways' financial situation worsened in the following year, Borden privately sought support from cabinet members for a nationalization of all Canadian railways (including the Canadian Pacific), but found that "there was little agreement among the Cabinet members he consulted . . . on adopting so drastic a measure."[5] Thus direct government operation was extended only when it did not conflict with carrier

---

vol. 10 (November 1975), p. 63; and G. R. Stevens, *Canadian National Railways,* vol. 2: *Towards the Inevitable, 1896–1922* (Toronto: Clarke, Irwin and Co., 1962), pp. 466–69, 481.

4. In 1904 Borden favored development of the Grand Trunk Pacific-National Transcontinental under government ownership. John A. Eagle, "Monopoly or Competition: The Nationalization of the Grand Trunk Railway," *Canadian Historical Review,* vol. 62 (March 1981), p. 3. In 1912 Borden offered to take over the entire Grand Trunk Pacific-Northern Transcontinental, but the Grand Trunk board of directors rejected this offer. Eagle, "Sir Robert Borden," pp. 60–61; and Stevens, *Canadian National Railways,* vol. 2, pp. 459–60.

5. Roger C. Brown, *Robert Laird Borden: A Biography,* vol. 2: *1914–1937* (Toronto: MacMillan of Canada, 1980), p. 49. See also pp. 41–42.

interests: in 1915 Ottawa gave control of the eastern division of the Grand Trunk Pacific to Canadian Government Railways (the successor to the Intercolonial) when Grand Trunk Pacific reneged on its commitment to lease the line.

Later, however, the government moved to nationalize the failing carriers over the objections of their owners. Borden decided to nationalize the Canadian Northern in 1917, and the purchase was completed late in 1918. The western division of the Grand Trunk Pacific was placed under the receivership of the minister of railways in March 1919 when its corporate parent threatened to shut it down. Nationalization continued after Borden's retirement that year. Arthur Meighen, the new prime minister (1920–21, 1926), was less enthusiastic than his predecessor concerning the virtues of public enterprise, but he supported nationalization of the Grand Trunk Railway in order to provide the expanded government rail network with an adequate feeder system in eastern Canada.[6] Parliament passed the Canadian National Railways Act authorizing consolidation of all government-owned carriers, in June 1919. With each extension of government ownership, there was criticism in Parliament, but the Borden government was able to use its majority in the House of Commons to secure victory. The cabinet and, to a much lesser extent, the Conservative (later Unionist) caucus in Commons were the only effective veto points on government decisions.

The increasingly aggressive Borden-Meighen nationalization policy resulted in part from the continuing decline of the Canadian Northern and Grand Trunk Pacific. But there were additional causes. Public opinion was opposed to further aid to privately owned railways. This was particularly true in the Prairie provinces, where farmers confronting local monopolies blamed railways second only to grain elevator companies for their economic woes.[7] By 1917, Borden felt that further aid to Canadian Northern without a government takeover was no longer

6. The Grand Trunk Railway, although not a direct recipient of government aid, was doomed by its guarantees to its subsidiary, the Grand Trunk Pacific. The takeover was consummated in 1920 after a bitter valuation process. For Meighen's views on public enterprise, see Roger Graham, *Arthur Meighen,* vol. 1: *The Door of Opportunity* (Toronto: Clarke, Irwin and Co., 1960), pp. 262–69.

7. The Canadian Council of Agriculture backed railway nationalization as early as 1910, and the Saskatchewan Grain Growers' Association endorsed nationalization in 1917. See W. L. Morton, *The Progressive Party in Canada* (Toronto: University of Toronto Press, 1950), p. 45; and Seymour M. Lipset, *Agrarian Socialism: The Cooperative Commonwealth Federation in Saskatchewan* (University of California Press, 1950; Doubleday, 1968), p. 78.

politically feasible.[8] In addition, the majority report of a royal commission on the railway problem recommended consolidation of the railways, not under direct government operation but under an independent government-owned company. The commissioners argued against either a public or private rail monopoly in Canada—not on the grounds of efficiency, but because the Canadian public would never accept it.[9]

A final factor shaping Ottawa's rail nationalization policies was the formation of the Union government of Conservatives and western Liberals under Borden's leadership after the 1917 election. The new government caucus and cabinet had greatly increased representation from western Canada, where support for public ownership of railways was particularly strong. Western representation in the cabinet also made a sale of some or all of the bankrupt carriers to the Canadian Pacific less likely, for any increase in CPR power was unacceptable to that region.[10]

The sequence of policy from short-term bail-out measures to nationalization has led most historians of the period to argue that nationalization was inevitable. As Donald Creighton put it, "Public ownership was not a first choice, but a last resort; and the hesitating steps with which the federal government took over the Canadian Northern, the Grand Trunk Pacific, and the Grand Trunk Railway were simply the inescapable consequences of the complete collapse of the ambitious Liberal railway-

8. Brown, *Robert Laird Borden*, vol. 2, p. 96.

9. The commissioners opposed direct government operation (that is, control by the minister of railways and canals) because they feared that in a democratic system political interference would be inevitable under such arrangements, to the detriment of both the political system and the railways. Railway Inquiry Commission, *Report*, pp. xliv–xlviii. The government, however, did reject the commissioners' suggestion that the company's board of trustees be self-perpetuating—hence independent of government control. Ottawa felt that it could not take all the risks of future deficits and capital costs without being able to change the board.

Ironically, Canadian Pacific backhandedly supported a nonpolitical nationalized railway system. Lord Shaughnessy, the president of the railway, suggested to Borden in 1916 and 1917 that Ottawa nationalize all railways in Canada, with CPR stockholders being guaranteed an annual dividend. Canadian Pacific would take over management of the unified system; Ottawa would make good any deficits. The plan was clearly motivated by Canadian Pacific's fear of competing with a government-owned rival, and it was rejected by the cabinet as politically impossible. Western Canada would never tolerate a reimposed CPR monopoly in any form. Nevertheless, Shaughnessy's plan did undercut arguments by Canadian Pacific and others that government ownership and efficient, businesslike operations are incompatible. On Shaughnessy's plan, see Graham, *Meighen*, vol. 1, pp. 151–52.

10. Eagle, "Sir Robert Borden," pp. 62–63; Stevens, *Canadian National Railways*, vol. 2, pp. 458–60; and Regehr, *The Canadian Northern*, pp. 428–35.

building programme of the previous decade."[11] All options short of nationalization had not been exhausted by the government, however. The most obvious area of potential relief was in regulation of rates. Rail costs rose dramatically during the war, but rate increases lagged behind. Requirements that government war-related traffic be carried free or at reduced rates exacerbated the carriers' difficulties.[12] Both Britain and the United States took account of unusual wartime conditions by guaranteeing railway rates of return, but this approach was not adopted in Canada. The government's failure to make major concessions in this area indicates that it perceived the political costs of rate increases to be higher than those of a railway takeover.

The fact that Ottawa did not limit its nationalizations after 1917 to the minimum necessary to keep trains running also casts doubt on the "last resort" argument. The nationalization of the Grand Trunk was prompted more by a desire to give Canadian National Railways better connections in eastern Canada than by a fear that the Grand Trunk could not exist as an independent railway.[13]

The choice of public ownership was, in short, neither a last resort nor a straightforward expression of government preference but a compromise. Canadian leaders were divided regarding the overall desirability and extent of railway nationalization. The governments of Robert Borden and Arthur Meighen were also constrained by the need to preserve unity in the cabinet and caucus and to maintain support from the voting public and the business community.

In creating the Canadian National Railway, federal decisionmakers carefully protected the fundamental interests of all groups. Shippers

11. Donald Creighton, *Canada's First Century* (St. Martin's Press, 1970), p. 139, quoted in Eagle, "Sir Robert Borden," p. 59.

12. Regehr, *The Canadian Northern*, pp. 397–405. For a discussion of the wartime rate case, see A.W. Currie, *Economics of Canadian Transportation* (Toronto: University of Toronto Press, 1954), chaps. 3–4. See especially pp. 56–57 for the Board of Railway Commissioners' refusal to take the financial needs of the Canadian Northern into account in the Western Rates Cases of 1914.

13. See Meighen's November 5, 1919, speech to the Montreal Canadian Club, reprinted in Graham, *Meighen*, vol. 1, pp. 309–32. On Ottawa's acquisition of the Grand Trunk, see also Eagle, "Monopoly or Competition." In choosing to nationalize, the Borden government rejected the Royal Commission minority report of A. H. Smith, which argued that Canadian Northern and Grand Trunk, confined to their original geographic strongholds, could become self-sustaining. Smith believed that only the "bridge" between the two north of Lake Superior was likely to require government aid indefinitely and the operation of that segment could be contracted out to a private company. Railway Inquiry Commission, *Report*, pp. xci–cii.

were guaranteed that most existing services and competition between railways would continue without a substantial increase in rates. The Canadian Pacific Railway was not nationalized, and it was given some protection against state-subsidized competition. Holders of Grand Trunk and Canadian Northern securities recovered some of their investments. And the federal government itself received a railway system that, although overbuilt and poorly integrated, had the potential to be fully competitive on a national basis with the Canadian Pacific Railway.

VIA Rail Canada: Policy Conflict and Executive Mobilization

Canadian National Railways had its origin in the failure of a rail policy during an adjustment crisis. The establishment of VIA Rail Canada, on the other hand, resulted from Ottawa's failure to implement a policy that could have prevented an adjustment crisis. If the federal government had carried out the market-oriented policies it had adopted in the National Transportation Act of 1967, federal subsidies for rail passenger service would not have exploded in the 1970s, and officials in Canada's Transport Ministry would not have sought new instruments to control the fiscal hemorrhage. Instead, the government failed to break with protectionist policies. As a result, subsidy payments posed an increasing burden on the federal treasury, the railroads grew more resentful over what they saw as a hopelessly uneconomic service imposed by government decree, and conflict worsened between Ottawa bureaucracies trying to impose different solutions to the problem.

Rising subsidies did not satisfy the railways, however. Their passenger service deficits continued to grow because the Canadian Transport Commission (CTC) compensated only 80 percent of losses. The losses were particularly heavy at Canadian National—about $40 million by 1977 or four times the level at Canadian Pacific. This difference stemmed in large part from differing corporate strategies in the 1960s. Whereas Canadian Pacific gave up and was allowed to abandon much of its service in the early part of the decade, Canadian National experimented with added service, new fare plans, and some new high-speed equipment into the late 1960s. By the mid-1970s, when the new top management at Canadian National had become firmly committed to minimizing its financial dependence on the federal government, discontinuances were much harder to obtain from the CTC.

Both Canadian National and Canadian Pacific put increasing pressure on the federal government to allow them to reduce services and to subsidize the full cost of passenger train losses. Both railways resisted the notion of a separate passenger corporation such as Amtrak on the grounds that passenger operations run by a different entity on highly used track would disrupt their primary business, freight operations.[14]

The railroads' complaints found a sympathetic hearing at the federal Department of Transport, now known as Transport Canada. Although Transport Canada and the CTC, as well as a number of Crown corporations, are considered part of the Transport Ministry for purposes of reporting to Parliament, the commission operates autonomously.[15] Transport Canada (along with the major budgetary agencies, the Ministry of Finance and the Treasury Board) found an increasing share of the Transport Ministry budget being spent on an activity over which they could exercise almost no control. Passenger subsidies were essentially an open-ended entitlement (barring cabinet intervention), with the CTC both controlling the flow of discontinuances and setting the criteria for compensating the railways.

The Canadian Transport Commission under Fire

By 1974, rail passenger subsidies approached $140 million, more than one and one-half times passenger revenues. As subsidies grew, Transport Canada and the budget ministries began to challenge the policies of the Canadian Transport Commission. The government's changing electoral fortunes made this easier: when the Liberal party won a majority of Commons seats in the 1974 general election, it became feasible to propose cuts in rail service without fear of imminent defeat. Changes would have to be made quickly, however, before the approach of the next general election. The appointment of Otto Lang as transport minister in 1975 was another impetus for change. Lang gave high priority to placing two

14. The railroads also disliked the fact that to receive a subsidy under the National Transportation Act they had to apply for a discontinuance, even if they did not want one or felt the CTC was unlikely to grant it. Applying for discontinuance was a public relations nightmare for the railways, particularly publicly owned Canadian National.

15. For a thorough study of the organization of the Transport Ministry, see John Langford, *Transport in Transition: The Reorganization of the Federal Transport Portfolio* (Montreal: McGill-Queens University Press, 1976).

of the Crown corporations in the Transport portfolio—Canadian National Railways and Air Canada—on a sound financial footing so that they would no longer require subsidies for deficits. To achieve this goal, unprofitable services would have to be cut.

The Department of Transport issued a comprehensive report on problems and policies in 1975 that called for a return to the MacPherson Commission's emphasis on commercial self-sufficiency for each mode of transportation, including a decline in the level of rail passenger subsidies. Noting that the CTC was about to begin its mandatory five-year review of all decisions that had required continuation of services, the report stated that "it would be unfortunate if this process were undertaken without some indication of government policy." The report recommended the establishment of "a working group of representatives of the Ministry, the Canadian Transport Commission and of Finance and Treasury Board to develop a plan of approach, and to develop a governmental directive to the CTC as a guideline for its required review." If this were not enough to challenge the independence of the CTC, the report also suggested that "the Minister should have and use authority to issue policy directives to regulatory or operating entities reporting to him, consistent with the principles in legislation."[16] In the same year, 1975, Transport Canada established a Rail Passenger Branch to develop a planning capacity in that field, thus challenging the CTC's monopoly on expertise.

The ensuing conflict between Transport Canada and the Canadian Transport Commission was not only a struggle over bureaucratic turf but also a fundamental disagreement over what served the public interest. The contrasting philosophies appear to be well understood by both sides. In a series of interviews conducted for this book, officials of Transport Canada's Railway Passenger Branch criticized the CTC for being oblivious to costs, for lacking any overall plan concerning what passenger trains should be doing, and for giving too much credence to nostalgic testimony at public hearings. Commission officials were equally critical of Transport Canada. One CTC staff member said, "They're all a bunch of dollar cutters over there. They call themselves planners, but all they're interested in doing is saving money. . . . They have a real missionary zeal: they think they're going to save the world."

16. Transport Canada, *An Interim Report on Inter-City Passenger Movement in Canada* (Ottawa: Information Canada, June 1975), pp. 124, 126, 150.

This bureaucratic conflict was a crucial element in the political process that led to the establishment of VIA Rail Canada. Transport Canada sought to impose new and quite different controls on rail passenger service than had existed under the CTC-administered subsidy program.

Transport Canada Takes Control

The railways, Transport Canada, and the Canadian Transport Commission all regarded the National Transportation Act subsidy program as a failure. Public enterprise, however, was not the inevitable outcome of that failure. VIA Rail Canada was not a first-choice solution for any of the actors involved. Transport Canada attempted to wrest control of discontinuances from the CTC and to force increased cooperation from and between the major railways. Canadian National and Canadian Pacific sought more discontinuances and full subsidy for all passenger train losses. The commission wanted to improve railway efficiency while protecting the public against massive cuts in service and itself against a major loss of authority. In the end, Transport Canada pushed for public enterprise because it saw no other way of reaching its goals.

Transport Minister Lang initially urged the commission to issue more discontinuance decisions and pressured the railways to improve service. In a major policy speech to the House of Commons on January 26, 1976, Lang called for a restriction of rail passenger service to markets where it could compete effectively. At the same time, he issued a directive to the commission for use in its review of discontinuance decisions, urging that the parallel Canadian National and Canadian Pacific transcontinental services be combined on a single line and supporting elimination of most local and regional services. To the railroads he offered to pay "100 percent of losses providing that efficiency in management and operations can be demonstrated." On the other hand, he threatened that unless service improved rapidly, he would consider "another organization to provide rail passenger service in Canada."[17]

Little immediate progress was made either toward improved service or full subsidy. The legal status of Lang's directive to the Canadian Transport Commission was questionable: although the National Transportation Act gives the cabinet authority to rescind or vary CTC orders, it does not mention giving directives for future orders. The Railway

17. House of Commons, *Debates,* 30 Parl. 1 sess., January 29, 1976, pp. 10437–39.

Transport Committee of the commission declared the directive to be "a very helpful statement of the intentions of the Government of Canada with respect to rail-passenger services, and . . . . one element of the 'public interest,' " but not binding on the commission.[18] The committee then largely ignored the directive in revising transcontinental passenger train service. Transport Canada pressed CN and CP to manage rail passenger service jointly, but the two carriers were unable to agree on a mutually satisfactory plan. When this option failed, a search for other management possibilities began. Canadian National then offered to set up a subsidiary to operate Canadian Pacific's passenger service as well as its own, but this plan was unacceptable to Transport Canada. The department wanted to ensure that Canadian Pacific would cooperate in the new venture. Most important, Transport Canada felt that a Canadian National subsidiary would not give the federal government adequate control over the services it was bankrolling.

With the elimination of these options, the establishment of a separate Crown corporation for rail passenger service seemed to Transport Canada to be the best means of increasing its control over rail passenger policy. This view was not universally shared: the Ministry of Finance and the Treasury Board opposed a separate corporation. They feared that expenditures for such items as sales operations, equipment purchases, and roadbed would, in the long run, increase government outlays for rail passenger service. Costs must be cut, they agreed, but they worried that a separate corporation would be even more difficult to control than the existing subsidy program. The rising costs of Amtrak south of the border were a ready object lesson.

Despite the reservations of the Ministry of Finance and the Treasury Board, Transport Minister Lang won cabinet approval for a separate Crown corporation.[19] VIA Rail Canada was incorporated on January 12, 1977. Officially, VIA was a subsidiary of Canadian National Railways. This was "the simplest way to set up the Corporation," according to VIA's first president, and VIA was intended to "operate at arm's length from the railways."[20] Its financial accounts were not consolidated with those of Canadian National.

The mere creation of a new corporation was not enough to enable

18. Canadian Transport Commission, Railway Transport Committee, *Eastern Trans-continental Passenger Train Hearings: Summary of Evidence,* January 1978, p. 48.
19. *Financial Post,* February 12, 1977.
20. Interview with Frank Roberts in the Toronto *Globe and Mail,* March 17, 1977.

Transport Canada to wrest control over rail passenger service from the CTC, however. To that end, the government of Prime Minister Pierre Trudeau made a curious insertion in a supplemental appropriations act passed by the House of Commons on March 22, 1977. Hidden amid one-line items funding various government agencies was a long item that clearly had very broad purposes despite the minute size (one dollar) of the appropriation. The item provided for direct contracts between the Minister of Transport and VIA Rail Canada for rail passenger services, full reimbursement to the railways for contracted services (rather than the 80 percent allowed for CTC-subsidized trains), and partial government financing of benefits for employees laid off because of reduced service.[21]

By burying an important piece of government legislation in a supplemental appropriations bill, the government was able to drastically limit debate on the measure in Parliament. With an election expected in less than a year, Transport Canada feared the political consequences of a major debate on rail passenger service and hence decided to "legislate by appropriation." The government's willingness to use this technique, despite protest from the opposition parties that it constituted an abuse of Parliament's privilege to debate, attests both to its sense of urgency over rising rail passenger subsidies and its awareness of the political sensitivity of passenger train policy.[22]

The appropriations bill sought to move the locus of passenger service decisionmaking from the CTC and to Transport Canada by allowing the Transport Minister to contract directly with VIA for management of rail passenger services. VIA, in turn, would contract with the railways for much of the actual train operations.[23] The bill did not withdraw the

21. *Canada Gazette*, pt. 3, vol. 2, no. 3 (1977), pp. 26–28.

22. See the statements of Stanley Knowles, House of Commons, *Debates*, vol. 120, no. 91, 30 Parl. 2 sess., March 21, 1977, p. 4160; and Don Mazankowski (the Progressive Conservative Transport critic), House of Commons Standing Committee on Transport and Communications, *Minutes of Proceedings and Evidence*, 30 Parl. 3 sess., no. 1, November 15, 1977, p. 16. See also the criticism by the Royal Commission on Financial Management and Accountability (Lambert Commission), *Final Report* (Ottawa: Supply and Services, 1979), p. 334.

23. The railways retained statutory responsibility to provide rail passenger service if VIA failed to do so. In a discussion paper prepared for the cabinet, Transport Canada argued that it was necessary to retain this provision of the Railway Act, even after transfer of equipment and employees substantially reduced the railways' ability to provide this service, to ensure continued cooperation by Canadian National and Canadian Pacific. Cabinet discussion paper, *VIA Rail Canada*, July 26, 1979, point 90.

CTC's veto over passenger train discontinuances. Thus commission decisions set a floor on passenger train operations and hence on the ministry's expenditures for rail passenger service. To end CTC jurisdiction over discontinuances would require an amendment to the Railway Act, which could not be done by the dubious mechanism of a one dollar appropriation. Nevertheless, the government's intent to replace CTC decisions with Transport Canada contracts was clear. Moreover, Transport Canada would replace the commission as "paymaster" for all services provided under contract with VIA, a modest shift in bargaining leverage.

Of equal substantive importance were the deliberate omissions in the legislation. Not addressed were VIA's financial structure, board of directors, the services to be operated, and whether VIA would own passenger equipment and employ train and engine crews directly or purchase their services under contract with Canadian National and Canadian Pacific. These omissions reflect a lack of consensus within the government concerning the future direction of VIA and a reluctance to put politically unpopular measures before Parliament. Transport Canada and the new management of VIA were both unwilling to "cast the organization in stone" until they had some sense of how it would run. The U.S. experience with Amtrak, changed by legislation almost every year since its creation in 1970 (with consequent political uproar), exemplified to the Canadians what should be avoided.

In December 1977 the Canadian government purchased VIA's stock from Canadian National Railways, making it a fully independent Crown corporation. But independence was not the government's intent in creating VIA. Its primary objective was to cut rail passenger services at minimum political cost by transferring them to an organization responsive to Transport Canada's priorities. Any attempts to cut service directly—either by cabinet order overruling decisions by the Canadian Transport Commission or by legislation removing commission jurisdiction over discontinuances—would have been very unpopular. But the establishment of a new Crown corporation joining Canadian National and Canadian Pacific services could be "sold" to the public as an effort to improve service. The government astutely downplayed its major objective: cutting costs and services. In essence, Transport Canada sought to ease public opposition to cutbacks (unsuccessfully, as will be seen in chapter 8) by portraying them in the politically nondivisive guise of a change in policy instruments.

Conclusions

The nationalization of Canadian National Railways and VIA Rail Canada shed light both on the Canadian government's response to industrial adjustment crises and on its policy instrument preferences and ability to obtain those preferences. Ottawa enjoyed substantial autonomy and flexibility in obtaining desired instrument choices, but was much less successful in promoting industrial adjustment.

Nationalization and Industrial Adjustment

In assessing the Canadian government's promotion of sectoral adjustment in the two nationalization decisions, it is important to keep in mind how Ottawa's pursuit of protectionist policies contributed to the adjustment crises. Certainly when Canadian Northern and Grand Trunk Pacific collapsed, it made sense for the government to unify those properties with railways it already owned. But Ottawa deserves much of the blame for that collapse. Successful accelerationist policy during the growth phase of an industry requires that government assistance be carefully targeted to avoid the development of overcapacity. Ottawa violated this principle by supporting both the Grand Trunk and Canadian Northern transcontinental extensions. After its creation, Canadian National exacerbated the overcapacity problem by entering a branch-line building competition with Canadian Pacific in the Prairies during the 1920s.

During the rail passenger impasse of the 1970s, the government officially adopted market-oriented policies through the National Transportation Act of 1967, but lacked the political will to implement them. The creation of a new public enterprise thus had ambiguous implications for industrial adjustment. Uniting CN and CP passenger services permitted consolidation of facilities and duplicative routes and gave the newly independent managers of VIA a stake in making the business as successful as possible, even if it meant incurring additional costs (for marketing, for example). On the other hand, the levels of rail service set by the restructuring effort clearly violated market principles. While Lang's 1976 directive to the CTC did lead the commission to carry out its first comprehensive review of rail passenger service, that review was not completed until mid-1979. Actual cuts in service and in subsidy levels were minimal in the first years after VIA was established. Creation of VIA changed the payment mechanism for rail passenger service, but it did not eliminate the requirement that passenger train discontinuances gain CTC approval. The commission remained very reluctant to grant discontinuances, and the cabinet to overrule them. Indeed, in 1978 the cabinet delayed CTC-ordered cuts in western transcontinental service for a year because a federal election was imminent.

The Canadian National Railways and VIA Rail Canada cases buttress the claim made in chapter 1 that while united government may be necessary to pursue an accelerationist industrial policy successfully, it is not sufficient. The Laurier government did not have to give aid to both railway projects, but it did not want to see them fail. The federal cabinet could have signaled the CTC that more passenger train discontinuances were in order, but it failed to do so. In both cases, the fact that accelerationist actions would have had strong region-specific effects was a powerful motivating factor. Fearing the political repercussions of service cuts, Ottawa used its power to diffuse and disguise costs rather than to impose them.

Nationalization as Instrument Choice

The CN and VIA nationalization decisions exhibit differences as well as similarities. One notable difference is in the role played by top elected officials. The federal cabinet and, in particular, the prime minister, were much more involved in the creation of Canadian National Railways than in the establishment of VIA Rail Canada sixty years later. This difference is not surprising. Despite its growing drain on the federal treasury, VIA was a much less important issue. In addition, the development of a specialized bureaucracy enabled the Ministry of Transport to resolve disputes at a lower level, subject to ratification by the minister of transport and the cabinet.

The similarities in the creation of CN and VIA are equally striking. In both cases, the federal government chose less direct instruments first— instruments that lowered short-term financial costs as well as political costs. When these instruments failed, Ottawa could have taken remedial action short of nationalization (rate relief and temporary subsidies in the case of CN; cabinet waivers of CTC decisions in the case of VIA) that would have achieved most of its goals. But the high political costs of these alternatives led to their rejection in favor of a Crown corporation approach.

While there was substantial precedent for government ownership in Canada, its role in the establishment of Canadian National and VIA was permissive, not compelling. This heritage of government ownership increased the legitimacy of public enterprise as a policy instrument, but it did not force policymakers to adopt that approach. There was a serious, sustained search for alternative policy instruments in both cases. Nor did Canadian decisionmakers couch their support for public enterprise in ideological terms. They favored public enterprise because they felt they could control it. Control, however, does not mean that policymakers sought to manage day-to-day operations. Rather, they felt that their broad policy goals would be implemented faithfully and efficiently, not sabotaged by an enterprise pursuing divergent goals of its own or of a variety of clientele. (Indeed, in the case of VIA, the creation of a Crown corporation was seen as an effective mechanism to counter a "deviation" from government goals under the Canadian Transport Commission's regulation and subsidy powers.) Executive branch decisionmakers in Canada believed that public enterprise offered the most acceptable balance between managerial autonomy and government control over financial commitments in specific problem situations. The balance struck between the two goals differed in the cases discussed here: managerial autonomy was more important in the creation of Canadian National Railways, control over financial commitments in the establishment of VIA. What is crucial is that executive decisionmakers thought public enterprise could achieve either goal or both simultaneously.

Once mobilized in support of a public enterprise approach, executive branch officials in Canada dominated the instrument choice process. Like most countries with a parliamentary system, Canada has few veto points where opponents can force a stalemate once the cabinet has made a decision. In the case of VIA, executive dominance was reinforced by the multiple channels open to Ottawa for establishing Crown corporations. By setting up VIA as a Canadian National subsidiary, and then gaining approval of service contract arrangements through a one dollar appropriation, the Trudeau government managed to avoid parliamentary scrutiny almost completely.

The distribution of affected interests enhanced the ability of Canadian executive branch officials to nationalize CN and VIA. In the case of

Canadian National, organized interests saw both concentrated costs and concentrated benefits accruing to themselves from nationalization—a potential stalemate situation. Prime Minister Borden, who saw takeover of the Canadian Northern, Grand Trunk Pacific, and Grand Trunk as the first step toward a possible public rail monopoly, gained support from shipper interests, particularly western farmers, many of whom had a very different goal—namely, ensuring continued competition for the Canadian Pacific Railway. The Borden government's need to consolidate its newly gained political support in the Prairies made impractical any choice that appeared to cater to the private sector railways.

The government was able to override opposition from several parties by a variety of means. Canadian Northern had pledged most of its stock to the government for loans it could not repay. It continued to exist at Ottawa's sufferance; thus its owners could do little to resist a takeover. The Grand Trunk Railway was British-owned, and it had alienated Canadian political leaders by its failure to fulfill its obligations with respect to the Grand Trunk Pacific. As a result, the company had few domestic political resources. Ottawa needed to be concerned only that compensation to owners of Grand Trunk securities be large enough to avoid damaging Canada's credit rating in London.

The most important opponent of railway nationalization was the Canadian Pacific Railway, which had strong allies in the Montreal business community. While these interests clearly lost, they did not fare too badly: Canadian Pacific itself was not nationalized, and it retained its status as a rate-making yardstick, which guaranteed that it would be profitable despite state-owned competition. Such a side payment would have been much harder to make in the United States with its plethora of strong and weak carriers.

Ottawa's task was much easier in the creation of VIA. Only the major railways and rail labor unions had a concentrated stake in the nationalization decision, and negotiations were limited to these parties. The labor unions were bought off with a government-assisted attrition agreement. Canadian National (already federally owned) and Canadian Pacific preferred to retain more control over operations on their tracks, but since both railroads were suffering high losses under the existing subsidy arrangement, they accepted the offer of 100 percent subsidy in exchange for increased federal control.

In short, what emerges is a picture of a government that views public enterprise as compatible with its own goals, leads the building of coalitions to support that policy instrument choice, and is able to prevail over substantial opposition in imposing that choice.

U.S.-Canada Contrasts in Instrument Choice

Differences between rail nationalization in the United States and Canada can be largely attributed to the two nations' political and industrial structures. Intense regional pressures in Canada helped place public enterprise on the government's agenda by creating more situations requiring long-term railway aid. Ottawa has faced strong demands to equalize disadvantaged regions' access to markets by aiding the construction of railways with little or no profit potential. Only public enterprise and subsidies to the private sector have appropriate economic attributes for this task. In the United States, on the other hand, the most durable regional cleavage—that between the North and the South—led to a congressional alliance of Southern Democrats and Republicans with the goal of limiting the scope of government (especially federal) power rather than providing regional benefits. Thus public enterprise rarely reached the public agenda in the United States.

Differing political institutions contributed to these policy differences. Ottawa, with its disciplined parliamentary parties, has been able to provide benefits directed at individual regions. In the United States, looser party structures generally require log rolling or a broad geographic spreading of benefits within programs. Thus assembling winning coalitions for programs of direct aid to railways is a more difficult task and has rarely succeeded.

Fragmentation within the U.S. federal government made nationalization less likely for two additional reasons. First, leaders in the executive branch did not believe that they would be able to exercise the same degree of control over government-owned firms as their Canadian counterparts; firms would therefore be prone to ruinous group demands imposed through Congress. Thus U.S. decisionmakers believed that two of the primary theoretical advantages of public enterprise—control and flexibility—would be lacking in practice. In Canada, on the other hand, the attributes of control and flexibility were important incentives for using public enterprise.

Second, the weakness of multiple veto points within Canada's federal government and the existence of multiple channels for creation of state enterprise in that country also made it easier to impose instrument choices on recalcitrant actors (for example, the board of directors of the Grand Trunk Railway) once the cabinet reached a decision. Indeed, the case of VIA Rail Canada illustrates that Ottawa has multiple channels for establishing Crown corporations with virtually no parliamentary input. Explicit nationalization in the United States is hindered by the need for a broad consensus among groups and agencies to overcome multiple veto points in the system and by the requirement that each new public enterprise be created by separate statute. Moreover, efforts to nationalize existing firms are constrained by Fifth Amendment guarantees of prompt and adequate payment and a legal process that is long and costly, as the lengthy litigation over Conrail illustrates.

But what of the role of ideology in instrument choice? U.S. and Canadian officials view public enterprise differently. Does this not support the ideological explanation of U.S.-Canada differences? It does so only if decisions were based on general attitudes about the role of government in the economy rather than on a realistic assessment of the merits of various instruments and the obstacles to their successful implementation in individual cases. Yet the latter considerations were critically important. Canadian and U.S. officials reached different conclusions about the merits of public enterprise because their political systems differ: Canadian officials felt that they could control their creations, U.S. officials did not. As chapters 7 and 8 will show, leaders in both countries were largely correct in their perceptions.

There is a substantial kernel of truth within the ideological explanation, however. The heavy reliance on regulation in the United States is consistent with the idea that rival private interests can be mediated by government, obviating the need for positive state action. Canada's use of public enterprise reflects a perceived need for an activist state. More important, however, are the social realities that underlie those Canadian beliefs: intense regional cleavages; a small, open economy; and internally cohesive, competitive levels of government.

CHAPTER SIX

Determinants of Public Enterprise Behavior

ON THE SURFACE, public enterprise appears to be an ideal vehicle for promoting change within an industry. Strong mechanisms of control are needed to accelerate industrial adjustment. But government ownership is not sufficient, and perhaps not even conducive, to bring about industrial change. Indeed, one of the most common views of public enterprise is as the "politicians' free lunch"—an inherently inefficient, patronage-ridden vehicle used to raid the public treasury for narrow political ends.[1] Other analysts argue that state-owned enterprise is similar to private enterprise, more concerned with the "bottom line" than with the public welfare.[2] Still other observers see public enterprise as concerned primarily with implementing some government-mandated notion of the public interest. These differing assessments reflect very real behavioral differences in government-owned firms. This chapter attempts to explain those differences in terms of the same causal factors stressed in chapters 1 and 3.

The incentive structure provided to enterprise managers, often inadvertently, is the key to predicting and controlling enterprise performance—not the presence or absence of specific control mechanisms. The goals of public enterprise managers are almost certain to be distinct from those of their political masters. Adjustment goals, for example, will be of interest or relevance to enterprise managers only insofar as they are translated into constraints on enterprise behavior. Our concern therefore must be with how the government's adjustment goals—market-oriented, protectionist, or accelerationist—are integrated into the strategy and

1. Kenneth Walters and R. Joseph Monsen, "The Nationalized Firm: The Politicians' Free Lunch," *Columbia Journal of World Business*, vol. 12 (Spring 1977), pp. 90–102.
2. Harvey Feigenbaum, "Public Enterprise in Comparative Perspective," *Comparative Politics*, vol. 15 (October 1982), pp. 101–22.

behavior of government-owned firms. The analysis here is therefore firm-centered rather than government-centered.

The managers of public enterprises have three broad strategic options: security, autonomy, and public service. The choice they make is largely determined by the enterprise's financial dependence on government and by the government's command structure for the enterprise. Distinctive national political institutions and patterns of interests contribute to substantial within-nation similarities and cross-national variations in public enterprise strategy and behavior. These political constraints strongly influence the ability of individual governments to use public enterprise as an instrument for accelerating industrial adjustment.

The major limitation on public enterprise as an instrument of industrial adjustment is not any inherent inefficiency or lack of accountability on the part of government-owned firms. Nor is it simply governments' tendency to press multiple, inconsistent goals upon reluctant public enterprise managers. Rather it is the danger that state-imposed constraints provide incentives for enterprise managers to adopt corporate strategies that are neither efficient for the firm nor sufficiently attuned to industrial adjustment goals.

Strategic Options for Public Enterprise

Few economists assert that the sole objective of firms is to maximize profits. The assumption that firms attempt to maximize profits seems particularly inappropriate for public enterprises, which must respond to a variety of conflicting demands.[3] Government agencies may seek to

3. Economists have argued that firms may have a variety of often conflicting goals, including maximization of sales, management perquisites, and potential for future profits. See C. M. White, "Multiple Goals in the Theory of the Firm," in Kenneth E. Boulding and W. A. Spivey, eds., *Linear Programming in the Theory of the Firm* (MacMillan, 1960), pp. 181–201; and Oliver Williamson, *The Economics of Discretionary Behavior: Managerial Objectives in a Theory of the Firm* (Markham, 1967), chap. 4. For a comparison of the goals of private sector enterprises with those of public bureaucracies, see John T. Tierney, *Postal Reorganization: Managing the Public's Business* (Boston: Auburn House, 1981).

Although this study posits a broader set of goals than those associated with a private firm, it does view a public firm as a unitary rational actor. A public enterprise will conduct comprehensive searches for policies that will maximize achievement of its goals. Such simplifications can be misleading, however. Organizational inertia may prevent a firm from maximizing preference satisfaction. Moreover, this approach

involve them in projects that are politically rewarding but economically unrewarding or risky. Central budgetary agencies want to minimize demands on the treasury. Labor unions pressure state enterprises to increase wages, consumers (whether individuals or firms) champion low prices for their output, and suppliers seek guaranteed markets. These conflicting pressures tend to be self-reinforcing. Once enterprises become financially dependent on government, they are less able to resist additional demands.

Public enterprise behavior is determined by a complex process. *Management goals* (a series of ends that senior managers would ideally like to achieve) are converted into a workable *corporate strategy,* which in turn is implemented through specific *policies* in areas such as pricing, capital allocation, and labor relations. Outcomes reflect the interaction of enterprise policy and the firm's environment. Both governmental and nongovernmental influences constrain enterprise choice at each stage, but this chapter will focus on the governmental determinants of enterprise strategy.[4] These influences will be discussed in detail after the three goals, and the strategies and policies likely to result from each goal in its "pure" form, are outlined (see table 6-1).

Security

Corporate survival is obviously a sine qua non for achievement of other goals. Enterprise managers are therefore likely to value the security goal above all others.

At first glance, security might not seem a major concern of public enterprise managers. Many public enterprises (Conrail, for example) are rescue operations of bankrupt firms, which shows that not even minimal profitability is necessary for public firms to survive. Yet state enterprises occasionally have been dismantled, particularly those established during

---

underplays the extent to which enterprise strategies may grow out of (and engender) intrafirm conflict over goals. The model assumes a degree of control by top managers that may not be achievable in practice. Indeed, senior management may itself be divided. For a discussion of public enterprise as a unitary rational actor and a presentation of alternative approaches, see Renato Mazzolini, *Government Controlled Enterprises: International Strategic and Policy Decisions* (Wiley and Sons, 1979).

4. Governments may also intervene directly in specific policy and project decisions—that is, in policy implementation as well as in agenda-setting and problem definition. Indeed, public enterprise managers adapt their strategies to anticipate and avoid disruptive interventions. Such managerial adaptation is entirely consistent with the approach taken here.

Table 6-1. *Public Enterprise Strategies and Goals*

Item	Security	Autonomy	Public service
Overall corporate goal	Maximize probability of enterprise survival; minimize threats to enterprise budget and managerial tenure.	Maximize decision-making autonomy of enterprise managers.	Maximize total social welfare as defined by government or by enterprise managers.
Strategy to maximize goal	Increase political support from entities controlling resources needed by enterprise.	Decrease enterprise's resource dependence on government; maximize corporate profitability.	Develop and implement trade-offs among specific public service goals.
Enterprise policy toward:			
Unprofitable operations	Drop or add operations based on expected political rewards; use profitable operations to cross-subsidize politically rewarding ones; respond to political business cycle.	Drop unprofitable operations or transfer them to another entity.	Add or drop services based on public service goals rather than profitability.
Allocating capital	Maximize political rather than economic return on capital; expand investments as elections near.	Maximize return on investment.	Maximize attainment of specified mix of public service goals subject to capital constraint.
Employment	Seek labor support by holding steady or increasing employment, especially as elections near.	Improve labor productivity; reduce employment.	Trade off employment goals against profitability and other mandated goals.

the Great Depression and during wartime. The survival of Amtrak and Conrail has also been threatened repeatedly.

The more common threat to a public enterprise's security is to its management or budget. Differences in policy or politics can lead to the dismissal of enterprise managers. For example, Sir Henry Thornton was forced to resign as president of Canadian National Railways in 1932 because of a dispute with the Bennett government over CN's policies. Avoiding budget cuts is a constant problem for many public enterprises, especially those dependent upon annual appropriations (for example, Amtrak). The absence of a secure source of income makes long-range planning difficult. Winning and maintaining political support for the tasks they perform and for their own role as the best agent for completing those tasks is likely to prove more important for a public enterprise than making a profit.[5]

Most organizations will not be content with bare survival, however. Thus security-oriented public enterprises will try to build stable coalitions of support that will defend them against outside attack and protect them from excessive demands. Because the fate of specific state enterprises is rarely a voting issue in legislative elections,[6] the constituencies relevant to government-owned firms are those government agencies, political parties, and interest groups that control resources needed by them. In building coalitions, security-oriented public enterprises will attempt to obtain agreement on a "base" of operations and, if necessary, government financial assistance.[7] Operations are likely to gain inclusion in an enterprise's base less as a result of the benefits it provides to society than because of its effectiveness in building a support coalition. Firms that have formed stable coalitions tend to make only incremental policy adjustments in an effort to maintain their support, while threatened enterprises are likely to attempt to broaden their support by expanding their operations (and hence their clientele). Managers of security-oriented enterprises may relinquish decisionmaking authority in order to avoid being caught in the political crossfire of conflicting demands. With less discretion, managers may be able to avoid political blame for failing to make a profit.

Strategic choice affects specific policies in each of the areas outlined

5. Indeed, governments in most advanced capitalist societies are reluctant to assign a task to public enterprise when private capital can be attracted in expectation of a profit. There are exceptions. The purpose of the state tobacco monopoly in France is to raise revenue for the government. Profit maximization is particularly likely when most sales (minerals and petroleum, for example) are to foreign purchasers. In such cases, there usually is less domestic pressure to keep prices down, or a two-price system may be employed.

6. Two possible exceptions to this rule are the creation of Hydro-Quebec, an issue in the 1962 provincial election in Quebec, and the proposed dismantling of Petro-Canada, a minor issue in the Canadian federal elections of 1979 and 1980.

7. On the concept of a budgetary base, see Aaron Wildavsky, *The Politics of the Budgetary Process*, 3d ed. (Little, Brown, 1979), p. 17.

in table 6-1: dropping unprofitable operations, allocating capital, and employment. Security-oriented public enterprises would be likely to add or drop services and products to gain political support, regardless of the effect on profitability. They would cross-subsidize money-losing but politically rewarding operations with the proceeds from profitable operations. Rewards will be skewed toward actors controlling resources necessary for the survival of the enterprise and its management. And in times of conflict over policy, security-oriented public enterprises would try to stimulate growth to increase their clientele. Decisions on the allocation of capital in these firms would be based on political rather than economic rates of return. To ensure labor's support, they would increase employment or at least hold it at a stable level.

The efforts of a public enterprise to build a consistent set of policies will also be undermined by variations over time in the strength and type of outside demands. Most notably, the incumbent administration can be expected to pressure state firms to resist politically embarrassing moves such as service cutbacks, price increases, and layoffs when an election is near; immediately after an election, the administration is more likely to emphasize fiscal restraint. Studies of government finance have widely documented the effects of this "political business cycle."[8]

Autonomy

Alternatively, public enterprise managers may respond to external demands by attempting to maximize their decisionmaking authority vis-à-vis the government. Only when an enterprise is able to make its own decisions are the firm's interests (as perceived by its managers) likely to receive adequate attention.[9] In order to increase their firm's autonomy, managers may claim a special expertise that government agencies cannot match or warn that they will be unable to compete if government imposes burdens on them.[10]

8. See, for example, Edward P. Tufte, *Political Control of the Economy* (Princeton University Press, 1978).

9. On this point, see Tierney, *Postal Reorganization*, chap. 1.

10. Firms financed by revenue bonds may build coalitions of support among bankers and bondholders who will object to burdens being placed on the firm. Annmarie Hauck Walsh, *The Public's Business: The Politics and Practices of Government Corporations* (MIT Press, 1978). Similarly, officials of Air Canada and Canadian National Railways have supported the sale of a minority shareholding to the public, which would "force" the enterprise to consider the interest of those investors.

The most direct means of promoting public enterprise autonomy is to reduce the enterprise's financial dependence on government. Financial dependence inevitably creates vulnerability to outside demands. Capital that government provides free or at below market rates is usually obtained at the expense of promises to invest in projects with a low or negative rate of return, thus reinforcing the cycle of dependence. Minimal profitability (including enough income to meet future capital needs) is an essential prerequisite for public enterprise autonomy,[11] and improving profitability must be the centerpiece of an autonomy strategy.

The policy implications of this strategy are very different from those of a security-oriented one. Autonomy-oriented enterprises will attempt to drop unprofitable operations or transfer them to some other entity. Similarly, capital will be allocated to improve corporate profits through investments that provide the highest rate of return, regardless of their social effect. Diversification into new markets may be an important way of increasing profitability. As Annmarie Walsh notes with reference to U.S. enterprises,

> Public corporations . . . seek to insure their own success. When certain projects succeed, they try to expand similar types of projects and to abandon or avoid having to continue more problem-ridden programs. Many public corporations try to "cream," to take over only the richest parts of the public sector. Their motive is not so much greed for excess revenues as a desire for a secure cash flow and an eagerness to avoid difficult jobs and dependence on public appropriations.[12]

In addition, autonomy-oriented firms can be expected to press aggressively for improvements in labor productivity and to cut employment whenever practical.

Public Service

Both autonomy and survival goals imply that the public enterprise and its managers are motivated solely by organizational or personal self-interest. While it would be naive to ignore such motivations, it seems equally shortsighted to assume that no conception of public service enters into the policies of government-owned firms.

11. Yair Aharoni, "Managerial Discretion," in Yair Aharoni and Raymond Vernon, eds., *The State-Owned Enterprise in the Western Economies* (St. Martin's Press, 1981), pp. 184–93.
12. Walsh, *The Public's Business,* p. 11.

Ideally, a state enterprise oriented toward public service would be governed by a mandate that includes a precise set of measurable goals, rules for making trade-offs among those goals, and opportunity costs of each goal. The objectives included in the enterprise's mandate may include adjustment objectives (for example, high-risk investments during the industry's growth phase, consolidation of operations in the declining phase) or "public needs" objectives (for example, regional development and maintaining employment). The enterprise would use these decision criteria to maximize societal welfare (as defined by its mandate), to the extent its resources allowed. If, for example, the conflicting goals spelled out in the act establishing Conrail (such as preservation of service, rationalization of facilities, reduced government expenditures, and maintenance of employment) included a set of trade-offs among goals, then general criteria could be applied to matters such as track abandonments and layoffs of workers. Although the results might not be economically efficient, enterprise managers would have clear decision rules to apply consistently in a variety of contexts.

Although explicit calculations might not be made in all cases, a public service–oriented enterprise should be distinguished by its attempt to apply general criteria of societal net benefits to specific decisions rather than respond to political pressures relating to individual situations. But the conditions necessary to carry out a detailed analysis on a spectrum of issues are rarely, if ever, met in practice. A variety of problems interfere. Government often defines its goals very vaguely. There may be no measures that can accurately tie effects to actions, let alone a common currency that permits trade-offs among goals. And the impact of enterprise activities often cannot be precisely known in advance. Public service criteria tend to be helpful as minimum standards rather than as strict rules for making marginal decisions between programs and projects. It is not difficult to reach a consensus that Air Canada should provide a national route structure, for example; but the public interest is not a clear guide on the question of serving, say, Medicine Hat, Alberta, or Trois Rivières, Quebec.[13]

The most serious obstacle to a public-service-oriented strategy is the inability or unwillingness of government to give public enterprises clear guidelines with respect to the trade-offs that inevitably must be made. In

13. For a brief discussion of how the decisions to serve these cities were actually made, see John Baldwin, *The Regulatory Agency and the Public Corporation* (Ballinger, 1975), pp. 103–44, 155–57.

most cases, enterprises are handed incompatible goals and left on their own to sort them out. Obviously, this approach has certain advantages for the government: an exhaustive set of goals avoids offending anyone. But it can be disastrous for the enterprise because it gives proponents of each goal legitimacy to advance their own interests, with no accepted criteria or procedures for resolving those clashes.[14] In such a situation, political (that is, security) considerations win out over service goals that lack political allies.

The pursuit of public service by state enterprise is thus likely to be similar to the notion of bureaucratic "essence" developed by Morton Halperin. Organizations develop strong notions of mission that they will defend against external pressures, even if it means an overall decline in the size of their operations and budget. This essence or mission represents the goals of top managers and is relatively impermeable to external political pressures.[15] The specific goals embodied in the public enterprise's essence will rarely be questioned or altered by the firm, which will resist a trade-off of these goals with others. The use of public enterprise as a policy instrument thus poses a twofold problem: not only must government-owned firms be made to stress public service over autonomy and security, but they must also supplant the firm's own notion of mission with a consistent mandate established by government. There is a third problem if a public service–oriented enterprise is to be an effective vehicle for industrial adjustment: government must place adjustment objectives above other goals in its mandate for the enterprise. This is a tall order for government as well as public enterprise.

A tremendous variety of goals can be embodied in the mandate or essence of a public enterprise that is oriented toward public service. This makes it more difficult to draw policy implications for these firms than for those emphasizing security and autonomy. The following hypotheses seem reasonable, however. Public service–oriented firms will drop operations that do not contribute, or that contribute least, to the set of goals established by or for the firm. Capital allocation will be skewed toward attaining the firm's goals, even when they provide low political or economic returns. Emphasis on job creation and preservation

14. See Howard Raiffa, "Decision-Making in the State-Owned Enterprise," in Aharoni and Vernon, eds., *State-Owned Enterprise in the Western Economies*, pp. 54–62.

15. Morton Halperin, *Bureaucratic Politics and Foreign Policy* (Brookings, 1974), pp. 26–28.

will depend on whether those goals are included in the corporation's mandate. An enterprise with a specifically accelerationist mandate is likely to drop unprofitable operations, shift capital out of low productivity sectors and into high-risk ventures with growth potential, and institute labor-saving innovations.

Choosing Enterprise Strategy

Although security, autonomy, and public service were presented earlier as options for public enterprise managers, those managers are limited in their choice of strategies. Some values, notably autonomy, may be precluded by a firm's environment. In such cases, managers either can work toward achieving attainable goals, or they can attempt to change constraints. When constraints permit, managers generally prefer an autonomy strategy. This section will outline how governmental constraints influence managerial choice and the conditions under which enterprises are likely to switch strategies.[16]

Management Preferences

Security is the most highly valued goal of managers because it is a prerequisite for achieving all other goals; if an organization does not have good prospects for survival, it is unlikely to be able to obtain needed resources. And while some public enterprise managers may wish to put themselves out of a job, most presumably will not. Once some degree of organizational security is achieved, enterprise autonomy is likely to be the second most valued goal. Organizational and personal incentives are very influential. Organizations can never respond completely to all the demands placed upon them. Therefore, they try to reduce the need to

16. The typology presented in table 6-1 and discussed here assumes that the behaviors resulting from the three strategies can be distinguished from one another. This may not always be easy. Actions that can help preserve a firm's coalition of support may also be useful in meeting its service goals. In fact, firms are likely to see the two as inseparable. Similarly, an accelerationist public service strategy may closely resemble an autonomy-profits strategy. There are, however, guidelines that can be used to distinguish strategies. First, the process of policy formation as well as outcomes can be examined to determine influences on enterprise decisions. Second, cases can be focused upon that require clear choices between strategies. The case studies of U.S. and Canadian railways in the following chapters employ these guidelines in an intensive study of a few firms.

comply.[17] Public service is usually the least valued goal of state enterprise managers because it is less closely tied to organizational and personal well-being than security and autonomy. In practice, managers pursue a mixture of goals. They will not completely satisfy their desire for security before thinking about public service, for example.

Managers' attempts to convert their goals into a workable corporate strategy are complicated by the fact that successful pursuit of each of the three strategic options outlined earlier achieves not only the goals it stresses, but some elements of the others as well. A public service strategy, for example, can help a public enterprise gain some autonomy and security if the firm has a reputation for expertise in its policy area. The autonomy-profits strategy may engender security by removing financial dependence on government, while a security strategy may allow managers discretion in a narrow range of choices. In this situation, managers of public enterprises are likely to prefer an autonomy strategy because it maximizes the two goals that they value most: security and autonomy (see the following table).

| Strategy | Results in: | | |
pursued	Security	Autonomy	Public service
Autonomy	High	High	Uncertain
Security	High	Low	Uncertain
Public service	High	Low	High

If the enterprise can reduce its dependence on outside agencies for resources, it can reduce its vulnerability to those agencies' demands. Moreover, managers who have worked in the private sector are likely to view profitability and autonomy as inherently good. And emphasis on profitability provides clearer decision rules (and hence a better protection against political criticism) than is likely to be available when the other goals are pursued. The difficulty of responding simultaneously to social and economic mandates has been cogently stated by a former president of CN Rail:

> How do you make decisions . . . when it is suggested that capital be spent, with only partial cost recovery, on projects that significantly improve service to a sector of the Canadian public? How far do you go in this direction? When

17. Jeffrey Pfeffer and Gerald Salancik, *The External Control of Organizations* (Harper and Row, 1978), p. 43.

are you adding unduly to the taxpayer's burden? If you decide to reject the proposal, are you failing to fulfill the mandate given to you by your shareholders?[18]

An autonomy-oriented strategy rests on the form of accountability with which the enterprise manager is likely to be most comfortable: the accountability of the "bottom line."[19]

The security strategy, by contrast, has serious drawbacks. The price extracted for political support may be quite high, which makes construction of a support coalition difficult. And reliance on government financial assistance almost certainly forecloses attaining the highly valued goal of autonomy. Thus managers are likely to choose a security-oriented strategy only when they believe that an autonomy strategy is unlikely to succeed.

The public service strategy also has important shortcomings. It is difficult to identify what is in the public interest; there are many publics, each offering a different notion of the public interest. An enterprise that attempts to define and implement its own (or any one public's) conception of the public interest is likely to find itself under political attack, threatening its security. Moreover, a precise specification of goals and careful evaluation of an enterprise's performance may show many of its programs to be inefficient or ineffective, again posing a threat to its security. And, like the security strategy, the public service strategy usually precludes organizational autonomy by making the enterprise dependent on public funds.

A public service strategy is likely to be chosen only under three conditions. First, it may be chosen if an enterprise is highly dependent upon a single government agency that is able to impose its own goals and make the enterprise into little more than an operating entity. In this situation, the "tutelary" agency provides the public enterprise with relatively clear decision rules (often by removing much decisionmaking authority) as well as resources and political protection (that is, security). This may be accomplished through a contractual relationship, as has been tried in Canada and France.[20] Second, unusually strong leaders

18. R. R. Latimer, "Bottom-Line Railroading," address to the thirteenth annual meeting of the Canadian Transportation Research Forum, June 12, 1978, p. 2.

19. This assumes, of course, that a successful bottom-line performance is possible. When price controls are in force, for example, and prospects for profits are slim, managers will naturally seek other standards of judgment.

20. See John Sheahan, "Experience with Public Enterprise in France and Italy," in William Shepherd, ed., *Public Enterprise: Economic Analysis of Theory and Practice*

(for example, David Lilienthal of the Tennessee Valley Authority and Henry Thornton of Canadian National Railways) may be willing to take the risks of defining and implementing the enterprise's own notion of the public interest. As a result, a strong "organizational culture" develops that the enterprise is willing to defend against outside attack.[21] Third, public service strategy may be chosen if the firm's political masters can reach a strong consensus on both the ends and means to be employed in the public interest.

The corporate strategy and policies that a public enterprise chooses will depend heavily on the strength of the constraints it faces. In a highly constrained environment, a public enterprise will need to stress organizational security. In an unconstrained environment, it would be likely to allocate resources differently, devoting primary attention to the autonomy of the enterprise (or, less frequently, to public service). But seldom are public enterprises able to implement their first-choice strategy. Security becomes the strategy of many government-owned firms by default rather than by preference. Autonomy and public service strategies both require fairly special conditions that most government-owned firms do not enjoy. Conflicting demands and resource dependence thus make security the dominant goal and strategy for many government-owned firms, especially those whose activities confer concentrated benefits or costs on well-organized groups.

Government Constraints on Enterprise Choice

The strategic choices made by state enterprise managers are strongly influenced by the constraints imposed by their owner governments. Two sets of constraints are of particular importance: the financial dependence of the enterprise upon the state and the government's "command structure" for transmitting orders to the enterprise. Each will be examined in turn.

FINANCIAL DEPENDENCE. Public enterprises that are unable to generate

(Lexington, Mass.: Lexington Books, 1976), pp. 156 ff. A contract system is now in use between Transport Canada and both CN Marine and VIA Rail Canada.

21. On the concept of organizational culture, see Harold Seidman, *Politics, Position, and Power: The Dynamics of Federal Organization*, 2d ed. (Oxford University Press, 1975). For examples of organizational culture, see Philip Selznick, *TVA and the Grass Roots* (University of California Press, 1949; Harper and Row, 1966); and Herbert Kaufman, *The Forest Ranger: A Study in Administrative Behavior* (Johns Hopkins Press, 1960).

sufficient revenue for operating and capital needs will be dependent upon government for their survival—and hence more vulnerable to government surveillance and interference. To some extent, the profit potential of an enterprise is set by the market in which it operates, but markets and the roles of public enterprises in them are substantially determined by the government. Government-set mandates, whether contained in statutes or conveyed informally, establish the baseline for the services that public enterprises are required to perform. Moreover, these enterprises are generally not allowed to diversify outside their lines of business. In the United States, for example, a number of private sector railroads have diversified into sectors that offer higher rates of return on their investments, and some have gotten out of the rail business entirely. The Consolidated Rail Corporation, on the other hand, is prohibited by the Regional Rail Reorganization Act of 1973 from engaging in nontransportation activities as long as more than 50 percent of its debt is owed to or guaranteed by the federal government. The lack of profitable activities to offset its losses increased Conrail's financial dependence on the federal government.

Governments can also enhance the profit potential of a public enterprise in several ways. Perhaps the most common method is granting it a monopoly or guaranteed share of profitable markets. A notable example is the limitation on entry by CP Air, Canada's largest private sector airline, into the transcontinental passenger market. This entry barrier gave Air Canada income that could be used to cross-subsidize its unprofitable routes.[22]

Governments may also provide guaranteed access to capital or statutory operating subsidies for nonremunerative services. The Canadian National Railways Capital Revision Act of 1952, for example, required the Canadian government to purchase stock equal to 3 percent of Canadian National's revenues for each year until 1960.[23] Another example is the statutory operating subsidies the U.S. Postal Service receives for specific public services, such as rural delivery, which allow it to earn a profit in most years.

Variations in the financial constraints on state-owned enterprises strongly influence enterprise behavior. A *high level of government support* (as a percentage of enterprise revenue) will lead toward a security

22. This restriction on CP Air has gradually been relaxed. See John Baldwin, *The Regulatory Agency and the Public Corporation*, chaps. 9 and 11.

23. *Revised Statutes of Canada*, 1952, chap. 311.

strategy; if the level of government support is low, an autonomy strategy is more likely. Government funding promotes uncertainty concerning the scope of legitimate public demands on the enterprise and the degree to which it should be responsive to those demands. The greater the firm's financial dependence on the government, the greater the uncertainty.

The impact of government funding can be modified in several ways. First, the lower the *visibility of government support,* the greater the likelihood that enterprise managers will be able to choose an autonomy strategy. Governments can support public firms directly—notably through subsidies—or they can give them an opportunity to earn monopoly profits (for example, limitations on competition to Air Canada). Because this kind of support is not as visible as direct aid, it usually does not stimulate "excessive demand" to the same extent.[24]

Second, the *less discretion* a government has in supporting a public enterprise, the more likely the enterprise will pursue an autonomy strategy. If a public enterprise must construct a new support coalition every year to win funding, it will probably need to emphasize political returns in its allocation of resources. If it is guaranteed that support by constitution, statute, or long-term contract, it can be much less concerned with building support.

Third, if government assistance is *targeted to a specific service or market,* managers are likely to choose a public service strategy in that sector and an autonomy strategy elsewhere. Subsidies for specific unprofitable operations give the enterprise clear direction and tend to increase its responsiveness to the agency granting support. "Service-specific" subsidies also lessen the need to cross-subsidize unprofitable operations with profitable ones, however. They thus allow public enterprise managers to segment their operations and their corporate strategies, emphasizing public service for some and autonomy for others. In theory, unrestricted subsidies should give managers even more discretion by allowing them to allocate resources as they see fit. In practice, however, nontargeted subsidies stimulate the conflicting demands from a firm's political environment: when the purpose of the grant is not clear, everyone believes that he is entitled to benefit from it. The major impact of unrestricted subsidies is to weaken incentives for the enterprise to

24. Regulation-imposed cross-subsidies can maintain their low profile only so long as the losers from cross-subsidies see no alternative to the status quo. When they do see an alternative, as Canadian airline passengers have as a result of airline deregulation in the United States, the visibility of the subsidy is increased.

operate efficiently without providing clear decision rules on how the money should be spent.[25] Weak incentives to improve financial performance may make the enterprise more security-oriented.

Finally, *the greater the parity of governmental assistance to public and private firms* in an industry, the more likely the firm is to be able to pursue an autonomy strategy. If a public enterprise is not receiving special favors but is being compensated on the same basis as private sector firms, it may be able to resist excessive political demands by claiming that it needs to be able to compete on even terms with those firms. Canadian National Railways, for example, receives hundreds of millions of dollars each year in VIA contracts and grain transportation subsidies, but it can claim that Canadian Pacific is receiving the same treatment. Air Canada, on the other hand, while its transcontinental near monopoly was not a direct subsidy, clearly was receiving favorable treatment.

GOVERNMENT COMMAND STRUCTURE. The structure through which a government transmits commands to an enterprise also helps determine the strategy managers choose. These mechanisms can take a variety of guises, both formal (ministerial directives, contracts and subsidies, appointment of directors and managers) and informal (pressure from ministers and legislators).[26] The precise mechanisms of control are less important than the strength and dispersion of controls. All else being equal, if a government's command structure for an enterprise is *weak,* an autonomy strategy is more likely. As noted earlier, enterprise managers will pursue an autonomy strategy if they can. More important than the potential strength or weakness of the controls is whether or not they are actually exercised. If a government agency possesses mechanisms for controlling the choices of an enterprise but fails to exercise them for a prolonged period (or announces that it will eschew them in the future), the firm will modify its behavior in the direction of an autonomy strategy. On the other hand, if the government exercises *strong and centralized* control over an enterprise, a public service strategy probably will be chosen. In this situation, chances of an enterprise receiving a clear mandate are maximized—for example, if a single ministry has a monop-

25. See Howard Darling, *The Structure of Railroad Subsidies in Canada* (Toronto: York University Transportation Centre, 1974), pp. 35–39.

26. On the variety of potential mechanisms for government influence over public enterprise, see Harold Seidman, "Public Enterprise Autonomy: Need for a New Theory," *International Review of Administrative Sciences,* vol. 49, no. 1 (1983), pp. 65–72.

oly on giving orders to a firm. Of course, even a single source may give inconsistent or unclear commands.

If the government's command structure for an enterprise is *strong and dispersed,* however, the enterprise is likely to be security-oriented. Multiple channels of influence increase the probability that a firm will receive—and will be forced to respond to—inconsistent commands. Divided control is perhaps the most common command structure for government-owned firms. Even when primary control (for example, appointments to the board of directors, approval of budgets) is limited to a single agency, conflicting demands are likely to be conveyed through other channels. Central budgetary agencies with power over an enterprise's budget and regulatory agencies may seek to impose policy priorities different from those of the agency with direct authority. The costs that these agencies impose on the public enterprise may indeed be a "free lunch" if those costs come out of another agency's budget.

Legislators also tend to view public enterprise benefits in distributive terms—that is, in terms of what they will do for their constituencies. This viewpoint further increases the pressure on government-owned firms. Ironically, then, the complexity of the modern state and a system of checks and balances within government may provide incentives for government-owned firms to follow an inefficient strategy.[27]

Changing Strategies

The framework presented in the preceding section analyzed public enterprise behavior in a static environment. But several conditions might lead to a change in public enterprise strategy over time. First, a change in government constraints—in funding mechanisms or in the method of selecting a firm's board, for example—may alter the incentives of enterprise managers. Second, a change in market or general economic conditions (such as an increase in demand for a firm's products) may also alter managerial incentives by changing the degree to which the enterprise is financially dependent on government, although government has not directly changed constraints. Finally, changes in management may contribute to a change in constraints. Public enterprise managers

27. On the influence of a divided command structure on enterprise strategy, see Raiffa, "Decision-Making in the State-Owned Enterprise."

are by no means totally passive in their choice of goals and policies.[28] They often come into conflict with their owner governments and are concerned with expanding their options as well as adjusting to constraints.[29] Constraints, however, do set limits on corporate strategies. Managers are therefore most likely to have discretion if organizational inertia in the past led an enterprise to forgo opportunities to move to a preferred strategy when the firm's environment would have allowed it.

Political Systems and Constraint Patterns

Variations in government-imposed constraints lead to differing choices of enterprise strategy. This does not mean, however, that all enterprises owned by a government have similar constraints and hence pursue similar strategies. All federally owned enterprises in Canada do not pursue public service strategies; all federal U.S. enterprises do not pursue security strategies. Within-nation variations exist, first, because financial dependence on government varies substantially across industries. Most national oil companies are profitable; most nationalized railways are not.

Second, enterprises differ in the degree to which their decisions are distributive—that is, confer benefits that "can be disaggregated and dispensed unit by small unit, each unit more or less in isolation from other units and from any general rule."[30] Airline and passenger train routes, for example, are highly distributive and are likely to spark intense interest by local legislators, firms, and governments. The insurance rates charged by the Pension Benefit Guaranty Corporation, on the other hand, are much less likely to spark controversies. In the absence of such conflicts, public enterprises probably will not face strong pressures (associated with the security strategy) to build a support coalition by distributing specific benefits.

28. The literature on managerial discretion is growing. See Williamson, *The Economics of Discretionary Behavior;* and Jean-Luc Migue and Gerard Belanger, "Towards a General Theory of Managerial Discretion," *Public Choice,* vol. 17 (Spring 1974), pp. 27–43.

29. See Jean-Pierre Anastassopolous, "The French Experience: Conflicts with Government," in Aharoni and Vernon, eds., *State-Owned Enterprise in the Western Economies,* pp. 99–116.

30. Theodore J. Lowi, "American Business, Public Policy, Case-Studies and Political Theory," *World Politics,* vol. 16 (July 1964), p. 690.

Finally, government command structures are largely the product of factors unique to each enterprise. Governments have attempted to codify the mechanisms through which they transmit commands to public enterprises (for example, the Government Corporations Control Act in the United States and the Financial Administration Act in Canada). But most enterprises are established by separate statute (or, in Canada, by cabinet order), which often specifies the relationship between firm and government in excruciating detail.[31] These enterprise-specific command structures reflect the prenationalization history of the firm (if any), current fads in public administration theory, and political goals of the government in power—all of which may vary over time and across industries.

Nevertheless, a nation's patterns of interests and institutions do have a distinctive influence on public enterprise strategies. Governments characterized by heavy reliance on checks and balances are particularly likely to give public enterprises conflicting commands, thus forcing them to adopt a security-oriented strategy. Federal corporations in the United States are much more likely to be caught in executive-legislative disputes than are Canadian corporations. In a parliamentary system of government, executive dominance is the norm. The difference is one of degree: federal Crown corporations may be caught in disputes among ministries, but the lines of authority are likely to be fairly clear. The Canadian practice of making specific ministers accountable to Parliament for the behavior of individual corporations, and of including corporation budget requests within that ministry's budget, reinforces these lines of authority.[32]

31. Moreover, Canada's Financial Administration Act distinguishes between three types of Crown corporations—departmental, agency, and proprietary—each with a different set of controls. Some Crown corporations (for example, deHavilland Aircraft of Canada) are not included in any of the act's categories. See *Revised Statutes of Canada*, 1970, chap. F-10. Amendments adopted in 1984 to the Financial Administration Act modified these categories slightly. See also John Langford, "Crown Corporations as Instruments of Policy," in G. Bruce Doern and Peter Aucoin, eds., *Public Policy in Canada* (Toronto: MacMillan of Canada, 1979), pp. 239–74. On the diversity of command structures for U.S. public enterprises, see Harold Seidman, "Public Enterprises in the United States," *Annals of Public and Co-operative Economy*, vol. 54, no. 1 (1983), pp. 3–18.

32. The responsible ministers do not always have strong levers of control over the corporations within their portfolios, but this system makes it somewhat more difficult for other ministers to press their own claims. Where strong ministerial controls are present, a tutelary relationship, and a public service–oriented strategy on the part of the

In the United States, on the other hand, endemic fragmentation of power creates conflicting lines of authority; executive agencies, congressional committees, and appropriations subcommittees all contend for power. Individual members of Congress, often unfettered by party discipline, have the power as well as the electoral incentive to pursue local interests. This, in turn, enhances the ability of societal groups to press their own, unaggregated demands on the enterprise through government channels sympathetic to their cause. Such an institutional environment is conducive neither to enterprise autonomy nor to a stable tutelary relationship between a single agency and an enterprise.[33]

Canada's strong regional interests make central control difficult, however. Although the provincial governments do not serve as official sources of commands for federal Crown corporations, federal agencies, and the enterprises themselves, must pay constant attention to criticism from the provinces and attempt to defuse it whenever they can. Policies with important region-specific consequences are particularly likely to be subject to such interference, creating conflict and contradiction in the mandate given to the enterprise.

Enterprise Strategy and Industrial Adjustment

Thus far, public enterprise strategy has been examined from the viewpoint of the enterprise manager. Now it will be considered from the perspective of industrial adjustment policy. Clearly, enterprise strategy has implications for adjustment: an enterprise seeking to build a broad political coalition through a security-oriented allocation of resources is unlikely to be an effective tool for sectoral adjustment because it will be reluctant to impose concentrated costs on any one group. Under what conditions, then, can public enterprise serve as a vehicle for accelerating industrial adjustment, and are these conditions present in the United States and Canada?

enterprise, may develop. Where controls are absent, or are not exercised, Crown corporations may be able to pursue an autonomy strategy.

33. This does not necessarily mean that the U.S. government will have more security-oriented public enterprises than Canada, however. As chapter 3 argued, the U.S. government has avoided establishing public enterprises in many of the sectors in which distributive pressures are most intense. In Canada, on the other hand, the federal government has viewed public enterprise as a cost-effective mechanism for responding to intense distributive pressures from the regions.

Table 6-2. *Industrial Adjustment Consequences of Enterprise Strategy and Government Policy Choice*

Enterprise Strategy	Government sectoral policy		
	Protectionist	Market-oriented	Accelerationist
Autonomy	Market-oriented	Market-oriented	Market-oriented (accelerationist if industry is restructured)
Public service	Protectionist	Market-oriented	Accelerationist
Security	Protectionist	Protectionist	Protectionist

As noted earlier, government-owned firms have goals distinct from those of their owner governments. If government goals and enterprise strategies conflict, managers tend to pursue their own strategies—unless, that is, the government provides incentives for, or compels, them to bring their objectives in line with those of government. A government that wishes to use public enterprise to accelerate industrial change must ensure that constraints on the enterprise are consistent with that goal rather than working at cross-purposes.

It would be overly simplistic to identify the three enterprise strategies outlined in this chapter directly with the three types of industrial policy—market-oriented, protectionist, and accelerationist—outlined in chapter 1. But there clearly are relationships among them. Table 6-2 outlines the probable industrial adjustment consequences for each combination of enterprise strategy and sectoral adjustment policy. It is assumed that enterprises will pursue their own constraint-determined strategies when they conflict with the government's overall sectoral policies. Accelerationist outcomes may occur in two sets of circumstances (shown in the righthand column of the table).

An autonomy-oriented strategy is likely to produce outcomes consistent with a market-oriented sectoral policy. Such an enterprise will follow market signals and minimize demands for financial assistance from government. It is unlikely to undertake actions that pose high risks or net costs on the firm, even though these actions may promote overall sectoral adjustment. Nevertheless, an autonomy strategy may result in substantial industrial change, especially if the enterprise previously was constrained to serve protectionist ends. A case in point is British Prime Minister Margaret Thatcher's efforts to give British Steel and the National Coal Board more autonomy in cutting their labor forces and closing unprofitable operations.

An autonomy-oriented enterprise can serve as a vehicle for accelerationist policy, however, if nationalization is used to alter the structure of an industry—for example, by combining the operations of several firms to permit economies of scale and to allow the use of the most efficient facilities of several predecessor firms. Thus an autonomy strategy by the firm can produce a more financially viable industry than would have existed under the previous industry structure. Accelerationist outputs emerge as a byproduct of this strategy. Conrail, for example, was supposed to allow consolidation of rail traffic on fewer lines, eliminating redundant facilities.

A security-oriented public enterprise is likely to engage in protectionist behavior, regardless of the government's overall sectoral policy. As the enterprise seeks to build a political support coalition, it will try to avoid imposing concentrated losses (for example, plant closings and layoffs) during industrial adjustment crises.

Only when a public enterprise is pursuing a public service strategy are its goals fairly certain to coincide with those of government. Unless the enterprise has strong leaders capable of developing and implementing their own conception of public service, its goals are likely to reflect the industrial adjustment preferences (or nonpreferences) of the government agency with supervisory responsibility for the firm.[34] If an agency can impose an accelerationist, public service strategy on a public enterprise, accelerationist policy should result.

As table 6-2 makes clear, public enterprise will serve as an effective vehicle for accelerating industrial change only if government transmits clear accelerationist incentives and commands to the enterprise or restructures an industry by nationalizing several firms. These actions invariably require imposing concentrated losses on some sectors of society. A government is most likely to succeed in imposing costs if it is united and its bureaucrats enjoy both expertise and autonomy and have strong mechanisms to compel compliance. The U.S. government, characterized as it is by multiple veto points and bureaucracies that lack autonomy, is unlikely to attempt, let alone succeed in compelling, accelerationist behavior on the part of its publicly owned firms. Much the same is true of the Canadian government, although for somewhat different reasons, notably regional pressures.

---

34. Of course, sponsoring agencies may give public needs objectives precedence over adjustment goals because adjustment goals have constituencies only at times of crisis. Moreover, when adjustment goals are addressed, agencies are unlikely to choose accelerationist policies because such policies require imposition of concentrated costs.

The disturbing conclusion of this analysis is that to the very considerable extent that governments press protectionist goals upon public firms, enterprise responsiveness and economic efficiency are likely to conflict with one another. As the case study chapters that follow make clear, government constraints on public enterprise in the North American rail industry have been used to promote protectionist objectives rather than accelerationist ones. In the rail freight industry, Canadian National Railways and Conrail have pressed their owner governments to follow more market-oriented policies in recent years, as they have moved toward autonomy-profit strategies themselves. The money-losing passenger carriers, Amtrak and VIA, on the other hand, have had to fight hard simply to attain a secure political environment.

CHAPTER SEVEN

Public Enterprise in the Rail Freight Industry

THE VERY different political environments and institutions in the United States and Canada strongly influence their choice of policy instruments. This chapter and the one that follows examine whether national differences exist in the behavior of the two countries' public enterprises. Because the rail freight and passenger industries differ in character—notably in their potential for profitable operations—they will be considered separately. This chapter compares two firms engaged primarily in transporting rail freight—Canadian National Railways and, in the United States, the Consolidated Rail Corporation (Conrail). Chapter 8 will examine the two intercity passenger carriers—Amtrak and Via Rail Canada. Both chapters will focus on the influence of government constraints on overall corporate strategy and their impact on corporate decisions in three areas: unprofitable operations, capital expenditures, and employment. The final section of each chapter will compare the corporate strategies of the two enterprises and evaluate their capacity to act as vehicles for industrial adjustment.

In the case of the two freight railways, recent changes in government constraints have led them to pursue an autonomy strategy. Canadian National and Conrail, in turn, have pressed their owner governments for a more market-oriented rail policy.

Canadian National Railways

Canadian National Railways (CN) is by far the oldest and most highly diversified of the public enterprises examined in this study. In addition to its Canadian rail operations, CN owns several U.S. railroads and has interests in telecommunications, hotels, trucking, and oil exploration.

Although Canadian National is less diversified than its private sector rival, Canadian Pacific, Ltd. (CP), the two companies are similar enough that CP is almost inevitably used as a "yardstick" for evaluating CN.[1] Indeed, Canadian Pacific serves as a yardstick for Canadian National's management as well as for government and the public. In the 1920s, CN managers sought to emulate CP's high standards for physical plant and operations. In the 1980s, CN's management has tried to match attributes of Canadian Pacific that only recently have seemed within reach: profitability, diversification, and considerable autonomy from government-imposed obligations.

Canadian National has enjoyed substantial success in meeting these goals. It has earned profits in most years, albeit with considerable aid from government subsidies and contract payments. Changes in federal transportation policy as well as in its own management were instrumental in improving CN's financial performance. It is the interaction of the two factors that is crucial. Following the model developed in chapter 6, this chapter argues that relaxation of financial and command structure constraints by Ottawa enabled CN managers to develop and implement a more autonomy-oriented strategy and policies.

Corporate Development, 1923–67

Canadian National Railways began its corporate existence under severe financial constraints. Afraid of harming Canada's credit standing in the City of London, the federal government required CN to take over the publicly held debts of its predecessors. The Board of Railroad Commissioners' policy of using Canadian Pacific as the rate-making yardstick also contributed to the almost unbroken string of deficits of the company, which had a heavier burden of redundant and low-density lines than CP. Moreover, Canadian National was expected to serve both as a "cradle" for infant enterprises (notably Trans-Canada Airlines, now Air Canada) and as a dumping ground for unprofitable services that the federal government did not wish to operate directly (for example,

1. At the end of 1982, Canadian National's rail properties (CN Rail, Grand Trunk, and TerraTransport) totaled 83.3 percent of net corporate property investment, with other transportation divisions (CN Marine, CN Trucking, and CN Express) comprising another 4.4 percent; the rail properties of Canadian Pacific, Ltd. (CP Rail and Soo Line) totaled 21.2 percent and other transportation divisions (CP Air, CP Ships, and CP Trucks) totaled 12.5 percent of net corporate property investment. Canadian National Railways, *Annual Report, 1982;* and Canadian Pacific Railways, *Annual Report, 1982.*

the Canadian Merchant Marine after World War I, the Hudson Bay Railway, and the Newfoundland Railway). Consolidation of the properties of the insolvent and government-owned carriers was completed in 1923. Under the aggressive management of Sir Henry Thornton, Canadian National began an extensive, and expensive, program of upgrading and expansion based "less on what it could afford than upon the standards and services in effect on the Canadian Pacific."[2] Thornton's Canadian National had a strong sense of mission to promote national development, supported by the government of Prime Minister W. L. MacKenzie King. With the onset of the Great Depression and the victory of R. B. Bennett's Conservatives in the 1930 general election, Thornton was forced to resign as president at the request of the minister of railways, the board of directors was replaced by three trustees, and operations were drastically slashed. When the Liberals returned to power in 1935, many of these changes were reversed. A recapitalization in 1937 wiped out most of Canadian National's debt to the government, but the company's financial problems remained. Only during the traffic boom years of World War II did it meet interest payments on all of its publicly held debt.

After the war, Canadian National's heavy burden of interest on debt made an overall (that is, after interest charges) surplus rare, although it was often able to earn an operating profit. From 1946 to 1975, CN earned an overall profit in only four years and then only because another recapitalization in 1952 significantly reduced interest charges.[3] After the 1952 recapitalization, the railway again borrowed heavily on bond markets and again was unable to retire its publicly held debt as it matured. Although the federal government refinanced this debt, Canadian National's interest payments continued to take between 5 percent and 8 percent of revenues. This interest burden and the company's low pay-back

2. Leslie Fournier, *Railway Nationalization in Canada* (Toronto: The MacMillan Company of Canada, 1935), p. 124. See generally chaps. 8–11. Particularly costly was a competitive struggle between the two carriers to add branch-line mileage, primarily in Alberta and Saskatchewan, during the 1920s.

3. Even when CN earned a profit, it had to turn over after-tax-and-dividend earnings to the federal government. Canadian National Railways Capital Revision Act of 1952, *Statutes of Canada*, 1952–53, chap. 36, sec. 9. The cabinet at its discretion could direct the application of earnings to retire CN's debt. Until 1978, the government had a statutory obligation to meet the company's operating shortfalls. Canadian National Railways Act, *Revised Statutes of Canada*, 1970, chap. C-10, sec. 37(4). Subsection 37(5) prohibits CN from using for operating purposes funds appropriated by Parliament for capital expenditures.

potential precluded a return to private capital markets, forcing CN to rely on its meager internal resources and annual stock purchases by the federal government to finance its capital spending.[4]

The federal government was obligated from 1952 to 1960 to purchase preferred shares in CN equal to 3 percent of the company's revenues, and it continued the arrangement after 1960 on a discretionary basis. When the government failed to provide funds in 1972 and 1973 (a period of minority government), CN was severely strapped for capital funds.[5] There was limited room for growth and less for diversification. At the same time, CN's debt-laden capital structure, the confusing flow of funds from the government to CN and back again, and cross-subsidies made it difficult to assess the company's performance on anything other than an incremental basis.

Changing Constraints

FINANCIAL CONSTRAINTS. Three legislative changes—the National Transportation Act of 1967, the Canadian National Railways Capital Revision Act of 1978, and the Western Grain Transportation Act of 1983—have drastically altered the government's financial constraints on Canadian National, giving its managers much more freedom to pursue an autonomy-oriented strategy.

The National Transportation Act gave the railways greater pricing freedom and required that all rates (except statutory grain rates) be at compensatory levels. The act also gave CN (and CP) stable, statutory compensation for two of the largest drains on their revenue—unprofitable passenger services and branch lines (80 percent of losses for the former, 100 percent for the latter), where the Canadian Transport Commission (CTC) determined that such operations should be maintained in the public interest. The service-specific subsidies did not cover all of CN's deficits on these operations, but by 1976 they totaled more than $255

4. These internal resources were primarily depreciation and sale of retired assets. Depreciation served as a source of funds for CN in the following manner: the federal government met CN's deficits (including depreciation charges, a noncash item), and the corporation did not pay taxes due to its deficit status. Thus depreciation reserves were available for investment after subsidies were received to balance deficits. The 1978 recapitalization act changed this situation.

5. Moreover, the beneficial effects of the preferred stock purchase were largely offset by CN's interest payments to the Government of Canada: from 1967 to 1976, CN received $434.5 million for preferred shares, but repaid $384.2 million in interest charges. House of Commons, Standing Committee on Transport and Communications, *Minutes of Proceedings and Evidence*, 30 Parl. 3 sess., issue 18, April 4, 1978, p. 56.

million (14 percent of CN's Canadian rail revenues), enabling CN to earn a modest profit of $12.9 million. The Western Grain Transportation Act of 1983 eliminated CN's (and CP's) remaining grain transportation losses.

Figure 7-1 shows the changing pattern of government support for Canadian National between 1969 and 1984. Although the level of payments grew dramatically during this period (both absolutely and as a percentage of total expenses), general and discretionary subsidies were replaced by statutory, service-specific subsidies and by contract payments from the federal government and VIA Rail Canada. Nongovernmental operating revenues and other corporate income fluctuated between 85 and 92 percent of total expenses, except during years of severe economic downturn (1974–75 and 1982, for example). General subsidies, primarily in lieu of freight rate increases, and payments to meet yearly deficits declined gradually and disappeared after 1976. But service-specific subsidies, quite small as late as 1972, grew from 3.4 percent of expenses in 1971 to 18.7 percent in 1975 before being partially replaced by contract payments. Beginning in 1984, federal payments to CN for carrying grain are considered operating revenues rather than subsidies. The implication of this analysis is clear: the percentage of operating expenses met by CN revenues was fairly stable during the past decade, dipping only during the economic downturns of the mid-1970s and early 1980s. Canadian National's "profits" came directly from the federal treasury, as Ottawa began to pay directly for activities that CN had been cross-subsidizing. The same, it might be added, was true of Canadian Pacific.

Although CN's newfound profitability has been touted by management for its effects on corporate morale, its major impact has been political. Subsidy payments are statutory, not subject to the whims of Parliament or the government of the day. The corporation does not have to defend the annual appropriation in Parliament: that is the job of the Canadian Transport Commission or, in the case of contract payments, the Department of Transport. And CN does not receive special treatment: Canadian Pacific is compensated on the same basis (although CP's subsidies have been smaller, largely because it retained fewer rail passenger services before they were transferred to VIA).

The Canadian National Railways Capital Revision Act of 1978 further weakened the financial constraints on Canadian National.[6] The act

6. *Statutes of Canada*, 1977–78, chap. 34.

Figure 7-1. *Sources of Revenue for the Operating Expenses of*
Canadian National Railways, 1969–84[a]
Percent of operating expenses

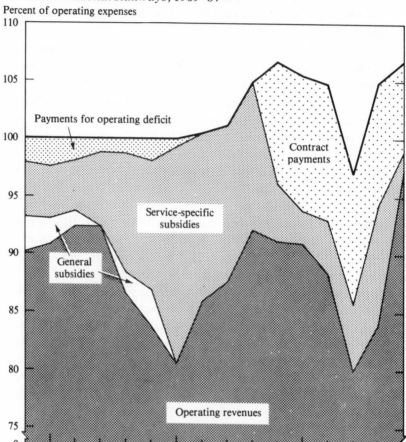

Source: Canadian National Railways, *Annual Report,* various years.

a. Total operating expenses include direct operating expenditures, depreciation, and interest on debt (less interest received on loans to Air Canada) for all consolidated companies, including U.S. holdings. For 1982, expenses exclude write-off of investment in Central Vermont Railway and Cast. *Operating revenues* include revenue from all consolidated companies, including U.S. holdings, as well as contract payments from VIA Rail Canada (1977 and 1978 only) and from the Government of Ontario for GO Transit, and subsidies from the Province of New Brunswick for Black's Harbor–Grand Manan ferry service. *General subsidies* include normal payments initiated by the National Transportation Act of 1967 and, for 1973 and 1974, subsidies given in lieu of general freight rate increases. *Service-specific subsidies* include payments under the Railway Act for passenger service, branch lines, and "At-and East" grain rates. (Data are not corrected for Canadian Transport Commission overpayments in 1974 and 1975. Corrected figures would show slightly lower payments under service-specific subsidies and correspondingly higher government payments for operating deficits.) This category also includes payments under the Maritime Freight Rate Act and the Atlantic Region Freight Assistance Act, subsidies for Canadian National's ferry operations in the Maritimes (before their replacement by contract payments in 1979), and, for 1978 only, payments from the Province of Quebec for the operation on Montreal commuter service. *Contract payments* include contract revenues received by CN Marine from the Government of Canada, and by CN Rail from VIA Rail Canada. *Payments for operating deficit* include statutory payments from the Government of Canada to meet corporate losses.

converted $808 million in government-held CN debt to equity, substantially lowering CN's interest charges. It also ended the government's practice of purchasing CN preferred shares every year. The act allows CN to retain up to 80 percent of its after-tax earnings and to borrow to meet income deficits. In essence, it ended the corporation's dependence upon the government for capital grants, while cutting the confusing back-and-forth flow of funds (interest payments from CN to Ottawa, preferred share receipts from Ottawa to CN) that complicated assessment of CN's performance.

Figure 7-2 shows the shifts in the sources of CN capital funding between 1973 and 1984 as a percentage of total funds provided. Canadian National's ability to retain earnings and to raise money on North American and European debt markets has largely ended its dependence on Ottawa for capital funding. Government capital funding is now restricted to service-specific assistance for projects that are not commercially viable (for example, rehabilitation of Prairie branch lines and purchase of new vessels for Atlantic ferry operations). Indeed, general government capital assistance to the corporation is becoming negative as CN slowly liquidates its government-held debt. The combination of high interest rates and low return on rail investment is likely to pose severe financing problems for CN in the future, however.[7]

COMMAND STRUCTURE CONSTRAINTS. The governmental command structure imposed on Canadian National is fairly decentralized although potentially quite strong. These constraints also have been weakened in recent years—not through a formal shift in authority, but because the Ministry of Transport has allowed CN greater autonomy.

The cabinet system of government effectively limits parliamentary control of Crown corporations to reviewing budgets, examining annual reports, asking questions of the appropriate minister during question periods, and debating (but rarely altering) appropriations requests for the enterprise.[8] Most of the formal powers over Canadian National are

7. For example, in 1981 CN placed an offering of $150 million (U.S.) 14 percent sinking fund debentures. This replaced part of a maturing $300 million (Canadian) 4 percent bond issue guaranteed by the Government of Canada. CN's interest burden will rise accordingly. Canadian National Railways, *Annual Report, 1980*, pp. 38, 44.

8. The 1978 CN recapitalization act requires that the CN annual report be referred to the Standing Committee on Transport and Communications of the House of Commons to ensure that members of Parliament provide oversight—and can air their constituency concerns—at least once a year. But since control of legislation is in the hands of the government of the day, the committee's major power is the power to embarrass.

Figure 7-2. *Sources of Funding for the Capital Expenditures of Canadian National Railways, 1969–84*[a]

Percent of total funding provided

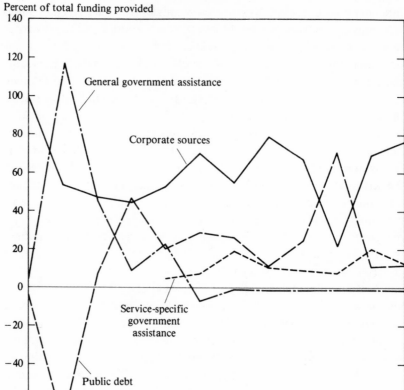

Source: Canadian National Railways, *Annual Report*, various years.

a. Funds provided from all four governmental and nongovernmental sources total 100 percent. Negative percentages represent repayment of principal on debt. For example, in 1974 Canadian National Railways retired $200 million in maturing bonds, which were refinanced by the Government of Canada. Data include current portion of long-term debt but exclude short-term bank loans, cancellation of CN investment in Air Canada, and 1977 conversion of $808 million in CN debt to the Government of Canada into equity. *Corporate sources* include retained earnings, depreciation, disposal of assets and investments, sale of rolling stock purchased in previous years and leased back, repayment of advances, and miscellaneous sources. The year 1980 includes maturing of a $108 million term deposit to retire a bond issue maturing in 1981. *Public debt* includes net changes in principal on bonds and debentures, equipment trust certificates, and loan and promissory notes. It excludes changes in capital lease obligations except those recorded by the company as long-term debt. *General government assistance* includes 4 percent preferred stock purchases (ended in 1977 by the CN Recapitulation Act) and net changes in principal on loans and advances from the Government of Canada. *Service-specific government assistance* includes stock purchases by the Government of Canada for purchase of vessels by CN Marine and capital for the rehabilitation of Prairie branch lines. It excludes capital grants for the Newfoundland containerization program.

vested in the cabinet, which approves CN's capital budget on the recommendation of the ministers of transport and finance and the president of the Treasury Board.[9] A recent amendment to the Financial Administration Act gave the cabinet authority to issue directives to most Crown corporations, including CN.[10] Finally, the cabinet appoints Canadian National's board of directors and its president.[11] Board appointments have been used less as a means of influencing corporate policy than as a reward to stalwarts of the governing political party and as an instrument for ensuring symbolic representation for all regions of Canada. Active public servants are not appointed to the CN board, as they are to the board of VIA Rail Canada.

CN managers complain that board members are motivated primarily by a desire not to embarrass the minister who appointed them. As one explained in an interview for this study:

No one asks whether these people can help CN when they are being appointed. They are selected because of loyalty to the right political party. A lot of these people are really small businessmen—the village druggist. The sums of money we are talking about really terrify them. So they tend to withdraw.

With no expertise and little external direction from government, the board serves as a weak, reactive check on management. When asked if the board ever turns down management initiatives, one top CN official replied, "They can't, because they don't do their homework," although management does consult with the board and generally does not ask for things that it thinks might get turned down.

The appointments process is quite different for the company's senior managers. Each of the last three chief executives of Canadian National Railways has been appointed from within the company, although the current head, J. Maurice LeClair, had come from the federal Treasury Board Secretariat less than three years before his appointment to the top job at CN.[12]

9. Financial Administration Act, *Revised Statutes of Canada,* 1970, chap. F-10, sec. 70(2). In addition, the cabinet approves any construction of branch lines by CN. Lines more than twenty miles require parliamentary approval as well.

10. *Statutes of Canada,* 1983–84, chap. 31, sec. 99. The cabinet also must approve any CN acquisitions or sales of other companies. The cabinet can entrust to Canadian National for operation "any railways, properties or works, or interests therein, that may be vested in or owned, controlled or occupied by Her Majesty" without advance notice to or approval of the company. Canadian National Railways Act, secs. 19, 22–31.

11. Canadian National Railways Act, sec. (7)1. Until 1984, the president was officially selected by the CN's board, subject to cabinet approval, but it was still a government decision.

12. The posts of board chairman and president of Canadian National Railways were

Most of the government's detailed supervision of CN—for example, review of capital budgets and diversification and expansions—is carried out by the Transport Ministry, and it is through the minister that the company reports to Parliament. Consultation occurs on major corporate decisions, and when possible the company advises the minister in advance of developments, such as layoffs, that might lead to hostile questions in the House of Commons question period.

Over the past decade, transport ministers have generally chosen not to exercise the formal and informal levers of control over Canadian National that have been available to them, emphasizing cooperation rather than command. The MacPherson Commission and ensuing National Transportation Act set this tone with their rejection of the notion that railways should be used as instruments of national development.[13] This policy has affected CN in several ways. First, there has been an effort to identify money-losing transportation services more carefully. Second, the ministry sought to place the Crown corporations in its portfolio—notably CN, Air Canada, and the Canada Ports Corporation— on a more commercial basis, rather than use control of budgets as a device for maintaining accountability.[14]

---

held by the same person until 1974. When Robert Bandeen became president and chief executive officer in that year, a separate chairmanship was established as a largely honorary post. The chairmanship was generally given to individuals with a high public profile (for example, a former Liberal cabinet minister and a former commander of Canada's armed forces). In 1985 the new Progressive Conservative government fired the chair of the CN board, Elizabeth Hewes, a Liberal. Rather than appoint a new outsider to the post, CN President Maurice LeClair became chairman, while retaining his post as chief executive officer. Ron Lawless, a career employee of Canadian National and the president of CN Rail, became president and chief operating officer of the entire company.

13. The commission's philosophy was never fully reflected in government behavior, but the National Transportation Act weakened the legitimacy of government action unless corporations suffering from such actions were compensated. Although a review of transport policy by the ministry in 1975 urged that increasing emphasis be given to the goals of accessibility and equity (particularly in Canada's less developed regions) in relation to the goal of efficiency stressed by the MacPherson Commission, it also argued that government should assume costs whenever carriers were required to operate unremunerative services. See Transport Canada, *Transportation Policy: A Framework for Transport in Canada* (Ottawa: Information Canada, 1975), pp. 28–29. See also E.J. Chambers, M.J. Dunn, David Gillen, and D.G. Tyndall, "Bill C-20: An Evaluation from the Perspective of Current Transportation Policy and Regulatory Performance," *Canadian Public Policy*, vol. 6 (Winter 1980), pp. 47–62.

14. This approach is evident in Transport Minister Otto Lang's testimony before a House of Commons committee in 1978: "It is a little strange to me to hear other

This is not to say that the potential levers of power for transport ministers have disappeared simply because recent ministers did not use them. Indeed, the last transport minister under the Trudeau and Turner governments, Lloyd Axworthy, caused consternation both in Canadian National and in Transport Canada because he was seen as violating the noninterventionist understandings that had grown up between the corporation and his ministry. The reasons for the change are evident: as one of only two Liberal MPs elected in 1980 from the four western provinces, Axworthy had to be concerned with improving the governing party's image in the West and with improving his own shaky prospects for reelection.[15] But his actions and rhetoric led to a high level of tension within the company. As one CN official put it:

> Axworthy is absolutely ruthless in his political desires. He lets his bureaucrats know this. What helps politically comes first. His thrust is to be the Minister of Transport for Manitoba [his home province]. He looks after that first; if other things can be done after that he will do them.

Sentiments like these underscore CN management's realization that although legislative changes have given the firm much more financial autonomy than in the past, that freedom is precarious.

Moreover, the Canadian government does not speak with a single voice on transportation matters. The Canadian Transport Commission is also a major source of government commands to Canadian National, and its priorities are different from those of Transport Canada.[16] The commission's reluctance to allow service cutbacks—along with the cabinet's unwillingness to use its authority to override the commission's decisions—have imposed heavy financial burdens on the corporation. With authority over the railways divided between the transport minister and a regulatory commission oriented toward the preservation of services

---

members from the Conservative Party say that it now wants accountability when in fact we are getting the right kind of accountability which is a dividend performance. . . . The policy today is clear, which is, that we expect that a government, if it wants some non-economic performances from the railway, will in fact pay for those rather than suddenly try to run them in and hide them away in the mixture of railway operations." Commons, Committee on Transport and Communications, *Minutes,* 30 Parl. 3 sess., issue 23, April 19, 1978, p. 20.

15. See Andrew Nikiforuk, "Axworthy Delivers," *Maclean's,* January 16, 1984, p. 16; and James Rusk, "The Axworthy Empire," *Globe and Mail* (Toronto), December 4, 1984, p. 1.

16. Although officially part of the Transport Ministry for purposes of reporting to Parliament, the CTC operates autonomously. See Hudson Janisch, *The Regulatory Process of the Canadian Transport Commission* (Ottawa: Supply and Services, 1978).

(the CTC), federal rail policy has usually been made on an ad hoc basis in response to pressures on specific issues—notably abandonment of branch lines and of passenger service.

Provincial governments also attempt to influence CN decisions. They generally do not exercise regulatory or financial control over CN,[17] but rather pressure the company both directly and through federal agencies and members of Parliament. The provinces tend to view Canadian National more as a public service than as a commercial enterprise.[18] "Ottawa-bashing" rivals hockey as Canada's favorite sport, and the provincial premiers are its Team Canada. Service cutbacks by CN give provincial governments an opportunity to upbraid the federal government for its cavalier treatment of their provinces.

Both the federal and provincial governments limit Canadian National's freedom to curtail unprofitable operations. But CN's profitable core of operations and the subsidy programs and other policies enacted in recent years have put it in a relatively strong position to adjust those burdens.

Corporate Strategy

Chapter 6 argued that a relaxation of financial and command structure constraints will lead a public enterprise to move toward an autonomy strategy. The case of Canadian National Railways supports this view.

During its early years, Canadian National was viewed by government and viewed itself as an instrument of national development. Profitability was subordinated to national purpose. This role was eroded, however, as Canada's transportation system matured, and railways became less important to the country's economic development. Canadian National's

17. There are some exceptions. The provinces of Ontario and Quebec subsidize rail transit service in the Toronto and Montreal metro areas, respectively. Some CNM, Inc., ferry operations are under a management contract with the province of New Brunswick. CN Roadcruiser bus service was regulated by the Newfoundland Public Utilities Board until 1976.

18. See, for example, the Commission on the Costs of Transporting Grain by Rail (Snavely Commission), *Report* (Ottawa: Supply and Services, 1977), vol. 1, pp. 96–97; and Canadian Transport Commission, Railway Transport Committee, *Eastern Transcontinental Passenger Train Hearings: Summary of Evidence* (Ottawa: CTC, 1978), p. 7. The Province of Newfoundland has stressed the obligation to take over ferry and railway operations contained in the Terms of Union. See the *Report of the Commission of Inquiry into Newfoundland Transportation* (Sullivan Commission) (Ottawa: Supply and Services, 1978), chap. 2.

continuing dependence on government led to a period of drift in which CN reacted to government initiatives rather than lobbying actively for policies in its own interests. The criticisms expressed by one Canadian National official sound very much like private sector criticisms of public enterprise:

> We went through a double stage in the 1960s of fairly high losses and a very low-key style. We didn't say "boo" to anyone and we didn't make our position well known. And the Company didn't mind that we didn't make money. The senior people didn't mind. They saw the railway as a public service. Deficits were a way of life for CN.

CN was by no means lethargic: it was an industry leader in areas such as containerization and the use of computers. And some policy changes were taking place. But articulation of a clearly autonomy-oriented strategy did not occur until the retirement of CN President Norman MacMillan in 1974. Under the new president, Robert Bandeen, CN pursued a dual strategy. It gave primary stress to the goals of autonomy and profitability. Management well understood, however, that it would have to continue many money-losing operations in the public interest. CN has not been willing to define any notion of public service. Instead, it has attempted to separate these unprofitable operations from its other services and to obtain clear government direction and complete compensation for them. A cogent statement of this philosophy appeared in the 1976 *Annual Report:*

> Canadian National can best serve the interests of the people of Canada if a clear distinction is maintained between those of its services which are expected to be profitable and those which must be operated on a non-profit basis as a matter of public policy. . . . It should not be up to the management of CN to decide on subsidy programs to assist certain regions, commodities, or loss-making services; such decisions should be in the hands of Parliament. CN should be able to concentrate on operating its services efficiently, receiving full compensation for any function performed as a public service and with incentives built into the subsidy system.[19]

At the same time, management endorsed privatization (selling stock to the public) as a way of enforcing "the corporation's objective of operating along commercial lines."[20]

19. Canadian National Railways, *Annual Report, 1976,* p. 13; see also *Annual Report, 1980,* p. 5.
20. Canadian National Railways, *Annual Report, 1976,* p. 13; and Robert Bandeen, "The Ways and the Means," address to the Empire Club of Canada, Toronto, Canada, February 10, 1977. ·

Under Bandeen, Canadian National implemented its autonomy strategy by reorganizing into a number of "profit centers" (for example, rail, trucking, express, and communications), which improved managerial accountability and, equally important, highlighted areas of government-imposed financial losses. CN has lobbied hard to convince the government that without relief from these burdens the company would have to cut back on capital expenditures or, as happened at the end of the 1950s, incur debts that Ottawa would eventually have to refinance.[21] This is the message of what CN officials refer to as their "missionary work" with government: costs imposed on CN are real, and government should face them now rather than later. Lying behind this message is the hope that if program costs are clearly identified and paid directly by the government, the government may decide that those with little social justification are not worth the cost and eliminate them. The days of low-key style are no more.

Canadian National's revised strategy has important political and economic implications. First, by dividing its business into public service and profit-oriented sectors, CN is claiming that government should not interfere in a large part of its business. Second, the corporation is seeking to avoid decisionmaking in areas that are politically sensitive and thus lower its political profile. Third, by eliminating cross-subsidization, CN hopes to become even less dependent upon the government in the future.

The departure of President Bandeen in early 1982 does not appear to have led to major changes in Canadian National's commercial orientation, although his successor, Maurice LeClair, does have a different style. LeClair does not share his predecessor's open disdain for politicians and bureaucrats and is more likely to get personally involved in negotiations with the federal government. LeClair is also less enthusiastic about privatization, believing that it would mean selling off the most profitable nonrailway operations that currently help to meet the railway's huge requirements for capital funds.[22] But these same beliefs have led him to continue support for Bandeen's diversification policies and to resist federal proposals for increased government control over self-supporting Crown corporations.[23]

21. Canadian National Railways, "The President's Review," *Annual Report, 1980*, pp. 6–8.

22. Canadian National Railways, *Annual Report, 1982*, p. 7.

23. See J. Maurice LeClair, "Crown Corporations: A Time for Debate," address to the Toronto Canadian Club, Toronto, October 17, 1983.

Policies and Outcomes

The relationships between government constraints and public enterprise strategies outlined in chapter 6 suggest two broad hypotheses relevant to Canadian National Railways. First, there should be notable differences in the behavior of CN and comparable private sector firms prior to passage of the National Transportation Act of 1967. Second, the relaxation of constraints on Canadian National beginning in the late 1960s should narrow these differences, particularly after the management change at CN in 1974. This section tests those hypotheses against CN's experiences in three decisionmaking areas: unprofitable operations, capital expenditures, and employment.

UNPROFITABLE OPERATIONS. Public enterprises pursuing an autonomy strategy will try to drop unprofitable operations and resist the addition of new ones.[24] Canadian National has been hindered in its efforts to implement this strategy. Many of its most unprofitable operations are concentrated in regions that see themselves as aggrieved. Moreover, services provided by CN are viewed as part of the bargain under which these regions agreed to enter the Canadian confederation.[25]

Canadian National's corporate strategy represents an attempt to adapt to this environment by eliminating unremunerative services through exit, pricing, or cost-cutting measures, or, where these options are not viable, by gaining stable compensation from government. CN's efforts to cut unprofitable operations have generally run as follows: (1) make internal changes to highlight losses for government; (2) encourage impartial inquiries (by Royal Commissions, for example) that will give added weight to CN's claims; (3) undertake good faith initiatives to show that losses are not due to managerial shortcomings and that the service is truly hopeless; (4) attempt to enlist government agencies as allies in cutting the services; (5) if that fails, bring continuous pressure for relief;

24. To reduce corporate losses, an autonomy-oriented public enterprise may not need to eliminate a service: raising prices or cutting costs may achieve the same end. But each of these options is politically sensitive for state-owned firms and equally so for government, since the latter must acquiesce in if not actively approve such change.

25. The promise of a railway from central Canada was an important lure for entry by Nova Scotia and New Brunswick into the Dominion of Canada in 1867. British Columbia agreed to join in 1871 on the condition that a transcontinental railway be built. Prince Edward Island signed on in 1873 when the Dominion government agreed to take over the debt of the province's railway and operate it. The federal government agreed to operate the Newfoundland Railway under the Terms of Union with that province in 1949.

Table 7-1. *Income (Loss) Statement by Division, Canadian National Railways, Selected Years, 1973–84*[a]
Millions of Canadian dollars

	1973	1975	1977	1979	1981	1982	1983	1984
CN Rail	21.3	23.2	206.7	234.6	206.7	(43.3)	260.7	304.4
CN Passenger[b]	n.s.	(70.9)	(49.9)	(9.2)	n.s.	n.s.	n.s.	n.s.
TerraTransport[c]	n.s.	n.s.	n.s.	(24.8)	(28.8)	(32.4)	(34.6)	32.9
CN Express[b]	n.s.	(39.3)	(33.8)	(47.2)	(39.9)	(40.6)	(25.4)	n.s.
Grand Trunk Corp.	6.5	3.5	28.6	29.6	40.5	(54.5)	(12.2)	14.3
CN Communications	17.0	22.8	25.2	25.5	31.9	32.1	34.5	39.3
CN Trucking	3.4	6.6	2.3	3.2	(0.3)	(5.8)	(7.9)	(29.8)
CN Hotels[d]	4.4	3.6	2.3	(1.6)	0.9	(0.7)	(2.8)	(2.3)
CN Marine	...	...	...	8.8	9.3	16.5	19.8	21.9
CN Exploration	n.s.	n.s.	n.s.	n.s.	4.1	11.1	10.3	16.1
CN Real Estate[e]	n.s.	n.s.	n.s.	17.5	10.5	11.3	10.5	14.9
Miscellaneous[f]	(4.1)	147.5[g]	7.2	(25.0)	(39.7)	(116.7)	(40.6)	(38.2)
Interest	(69.8)	(113.4)	(154.8)	n.s.	n.s.	n.s.	n.s.	n.s.
Total	(21.3)	(16.4)	29.3	211.5	195.2	223.0	212.2	307.8

Source: Canadian National Railways, *Annual Report*, various years.
n.s. Not a separate division or not reported separately.
a. All figures are pre-income tax.
b. Included in CN Rail prior to 1975. Express included in trucking beginning in 1984.
c. Included in CN Rail prior to 1978.
d. CN Tower included beginning in 1978; prior to 1978, Tower included in Miscellaneous.
e. Included in Miscellaneous prior to 1979.
f. Loss beginning in 1978 consists primarily of interest on debt not assigned to divisions and treated as a separate item prior to that year.
g. Includes $151.7 million in subsidies for services rendered under the National Transportation Act in prior years.

and (6) if the pressure fails, compromise on a second best solution that relieves CN of most of the financial burden—usually by shifting it to government. Although Canadian National has not moved as rapidly as a private firm might, it has managed in the past few years to reverse its traditional role as a dumping ground for unprofitable operations.

CN's rail freight operations—carried out through CN Rail in Canada and Grand Trunk Corporation in the United States—have generally shown profit over the past decade, as table 7-1 indicates. Other profit centers show substantial losses, however, notably CN Express (parcel and less-than-truckload freight delivery), rail passenger service, and TerraTransport (rail freight, bus, and express services on the island of Newfoundland). Other operations have been marginal performers, notably Hotels and CN Marine.[26] CN's strategy of creating separate profit centers to highlight areas of sizable deficits is also evident in the table. The proliferation of reporting categories is a product of the Bandeen era. Canadian National sought relief from a number of government-imposed burdens simultaneously, but the sectors of largest loss, and those for which the political environment seemed ripest for change, received the most attention.

Canadian National's biggest financial drain in the mid-1970s was not in operations at all, but in interest payments. As noted earlier, CN's campaign in Ottawa for a more favorable capital structure resulted in the recapitalization of 1978.[27] CN also lobbied hard for relief from passenger deficits, either through full subsidy or increased discontinuances.[28] This pressure on the government and the Transport Ministry's concern over rising subsidies for passenger trains led to the creation of

26. CN Marine became a separate Crown corporation on January 1, 1985.

27. The resulting conversion of government-held debt to equity caused CN's net interest expenses to drop $59.6 million between 1977 and 1978. In exchange, the corporation agreed to the termination of the government's annual purchase of preferred shares for capital spending, which would have brought CN about $87 million in 1978. Canadian National thus sacrificed cash flow for improvements in the bottom line and decreased dependence on government.

28. This campaign was the culmination of a shift that began under Bandeen's predecessor. In the mid-1960s, while Canadian Pacific was getting rid of trains as rapidly as possible, Canadian National mounted an innovative marketing program to attract additional traffic. CN was initially reluctant to petition for passenger subsidies under the National Transportation Act because the act required that it first apply to discontinue the service in question. Mounting deficits caused the railroad to seek aid for all intercity passenger services in 1970 and 1971. By this time the CTC granted few discontinuances. CN was granted subsidies, but they covered only 80 percent of losses, and Canadian National's losses on passenger operations rose throughout the early 1970s.

VIA Rail Canada in 1977. While CN still runs passenger trains, it does so on contract with VIA, which in turn contracts with Transport Canada. Canadian National's losses have essentially been eliminated, as has the political liability of applying for discontinuances.[29] Yet actual cuts in service levels by VIA have been much less than those sought by Transport Canada.

Canadian National also has become more aggressive in trimming its physical plant. While CN's route structure actually grew between 1955 and 1975, Canadian National managed to cut its system at a faster rate than CP between 1975 and 1980.[30] Many of these cuts were made in the face of intense regional opposition. The intertwined regional issues of the Crow's Nest Pass grain rates and uneconomic Prairie branch lines are the classic example. Moreover, Canadian National could not easily make grain carrying a separate division to highlight losses as it had done with other functionally distinct (CN Express, CN passenger) or geographically distinct (TerraTransport) entities. After the moratorium on branch-line abandonments in the Prairies was lifted in 1975, however, CN abandoned more Prairie rail mileage than CP.[31] Canadian National also joined Canadian Pacific in strong support of a reform of grain rates, advocating that any subsidies be paid to shippers rather than to carriers.[32] The Western Grain Transportation Act of 1983 subsidizes

29. Most of the increases in contract payments and decline in service-specific subsidies shown in figure 7-1 for 1979 and 1980 are due to changes in the method of financing rail passenger service.

30. Canadian National's route mileage increased 1.2 percent between 1955 and 1975 as CN built or leased new "roads to resources," primarily in northern Canada. In the same twenty-year span, CP's route mileage declined by almost 4 percent, while rail mileage in the United States declined by about 10 percent. CN and CP route mileage shrank 6.7 percent and 5.0 percent, respectively, between 1975 and 1980; U.S. carriers' route mileage shrank by another 14 percent. As an amalgamation of several systems, CN had more than its share of redundant lines, notably the dual transcontinental line north of Lake Superior, a region that originates very little traffic. Canadian National also has substantially more mileage than Canadian Pacific in the low traffic density Maritime provinces. Statistics Canada, *Railway Transport*, pt. 3: "Equipment, Track and Fuel Statistics," catalogue 52–209 (Ottawa: Statistics Canada, various years); and the American Association of Railroads, *Railroad Facts, 1984 Edition*. These figures do not reflect the purchase by CN of Northern Alberta Railways in 1980, which previously had been jointly owned by CN and CP.

31. CN cut road operated in Manitoba, Saskatchewan, and Alberta from 10,178 miles to 9,168 miles (9.9 percent) between 1974 and 1978, while CP Rail's road decreased from 8,481 miles to 7,921 miles (6.6 percent). Statistics Canada, *Railway Transport*, pt. 3: "Equipment, Track and Fuel Statistics," various years.

32. R. A. Bandeen, presentation to the Grain Handling and Transportation Commis-

carriers rather than shippers and reregulates rather than deregulates grain rates. Nevertheless, the nationalized carrier again gained equal treatment with CP rather than serving as a dumping ground for unprofitable operations.

Regional pressure has also been the major deterrent in Canadian National's efforts to drop unprofitable rail services on the island province of Newfoundland, a region where it does not compete with CP. These operations have been hopelessly unprofitable for a number of reasons,[33] but the federal government until recently succumbed to political pressures against cutting them. Ottawa has also been reluctant to subsidize these services because earlier subsidies under the National Transportation Act proved to be palliatives that were difficult to remove, perpetuated inefficiency, and sapped the federal budget.

Canadian National has long lobbied Ottawa for further relief from its Newfoundland losses.[34] In 1979 it formed the TerraTransport profit center to highlight those losses. At one point in its lobbying effort, CN considered putting the Newfoundland Railway up for abandonment. Ottawa's reaction was swift and negative. As one CN senior manager explained: "We wrote to Lang and said we were considering this. They wrote back and said 'You will not do this.' It was the nearest thing to a directive we have ever gotten."

More recently, CN proposed containerization of most cargo moving in and out of Newfoundland as a means of cutting costs, while easing a potential phase-out of rail operations. The provincial government countered with a proposal to rebuild the Newfoundland Railway to standard

---

sion, Saskatoon, Saskatchewan, October 15, 1975, pp. 10–11. Subsidizing shippers would further reduce the government's payments to CN and give grain producers an incentive to choose the lowest cost transportation alternative, which in turn would encourage rationalization of the system as farmers abandoned high-cost grain elevators and branch lines.

33. The Newfoundland Railway was entrusted to CN in 1949 as part of the Terms of Union under which Newfoundland joined Canada. Its shortcomings include a roundabout route, low traffic density, poor engineering standards, and narrow gauge tracks that do not easily accommodate standard gauge railcars from the mainland. Competition from truckers and subsidized steamship companies has further eroded the rail market.

34. The appointment of the Sullivan Commission on Newfoundland Transportation was largely a response to CN pressure, and the commission's recommendation that the railway be phased out, with the federal government assuming losses in the meantime, was consistent with CN's position. The provincial government was vehemently opposed, however, and Ottawa rejected the shutdown proposal.

gauge—estimated to cost at least $750 million.[35] This proposal had virtually no chance of adoption, but it was effective as a political weapon on the island and as a bargaining chip in negotiations with the federal government. Ottawa eventually agreed to fund CN's containerization plan.

Newfoundland rail freight operations thus illustrate CN's strategy as well as the limitations on such a strategy. Canadian National has attempted to gain federal support to help it meet provincial demands for service retention and low fares. In Newfoundland CP did not ally with CN to pressure Ottawa, because the problem was not shared by the private sector carrier. CN has not been willing to challenge the federal government directly, as a rail abandonment application would surely do. Finally, Ottawa's approval of such cutbacks depends as much on political concerns as upon economic concerns.[36]

Canadian National enjoyed greater success in cutting CN Express. Once an adjunct of rail passenger operations, CN Express is now almost completely a trucking operation. It became a heavy money loser as its market share was eroded by more specialized carriers. In 1980 a new CN Express management team brought in by Bandeen decided to concentrate the division's service on large, multipiece shipments and line hauls between major markets. CN countered the expected political uproar over cuts in Express service and employment by threatening a total shutdown.[37] A few terminal closures were delayed under pressure from Ottawa, but major cutbacks did occur, and in 1984 CN Express was merged completely into CN's independently operated trucking company.

In short, Canadian National Railways has successfully eliminated or gained subsidies for many unprofitable operations, particularly since 1975. It has been especially successful in cases when it was able to build alliances with Canadian Pacific, notably over intercity passenger service and grain traffic. Clearly, the federal government has been much more

35. Sullivan Commission, *Newfoundland Transportation*, p. 191.

36. Constitutional concerns are also important to Ottawa. Abandoning the New-foundland Railway would undoubtedly provoke a court battle with the province over the federal government's obligations under the Terms of Union to maintain the railway in perpetuity. The two governments have already been in court over the issues of constitutional reform and ownership of offshore resources. Ottawa is not anxious to add another dispute to the list, particularly on an issue so close to the heart of Newfoundlanders.

37. See the *Financial Post*, December 13, 1980, p. 25; December 20, 1980, p. 16.

willing to negotiate comprehensive solutions that meet the needs of both carriers than to address problems unique to CN (for example, Newfound-land).

CAPITAL EXPENDITURES. Variations in corporate strategy should also lead public enterprises to different investment policies. These differences should be particularly noticeable in multidivisional firms like CN. A security-oriented public enterprise will presumably attempt to preserve the existing balance of investments among its divisions or, when there is conflict, invest in the divisions that will broaden the firm's political support. Funds generated by profitable divisions will be "exported" to finance the capital needs of operations with a low or negative return on investment (ROI). Divisions with a high rate of return should not receive a greater share of corporate capital funding than unprofitable divisions. On the other hand, for enterprises oriented toward public service, specific social benefits replace political returns as the primary criterion for decisionmaking. Capital imports and growth in net investment will occur in divisions providing high "social returns" regardless of those divisions' return on investment.

The goals of a public enterprise pursuing an autonomy strategy should be very different from those of a security- or service-oriented firm. Divisions of high expected ROI should import capital and experience growth in net investment. Divisions offering low ROI should be capital exporters and shrink in size, as the firm sells off, scraps, or disinvests in those operations. Specifically, such a firm should (a) increase investment in sectors that are likely to offer the highest rate of return at a given level of risk, including (b) diversification where it contributes to that goal; (c) disinvest in unprofitable operations; (d) avoid new ventures that may offer political or social returns but have little chance of being profitable; and (e) adjust its total capital expenditures to fit the firm's resources. The following discussion of CN investment policy will be organized around these five points.

Canadian National faces serious economic and political obstacles in any attempt to implement an autonomy-oriented investment strategy. The most important constraint is the railway itself. Rail operations are highly capital intensive. Most rail investment cannot be deferred if the system is to be kept in good operating condition. Disinvesting in plant and equipment, common among U.S. railroads, is politically risky for Canadian National. And the railway's low level of return on overall investment has meant that little money is available for diversification.

The CN divisions with high losses (for example, TerraTransport) will continue to drain CN's investment funds unless they can be eliminated entirely or government subsidizes them fully. Finally, CN will always be prey to political pressures to reinvest in the transportation sector. Canadian Pacific, on the other hand, has allocated most of its capital spending to nontransportation ventures. To avoid direct financial dependence on Ottawa over the long term, CN must earn commercial rates of return on its transportation investments.

Maximizing investment in profitable sectors. It was argued earlier that autonomy-oriented public enterprises will shift resources into divisions that earn a higher return on investment. (Of course, a declining marginal return on divisional investment may weaken this tendency.) Unfortunately, capital expenditure and investment return data for CN's various profit centers are sketchy, particularly prior to 1975. Moreover, the broad nature of several of the divisions (notably CN Rail) aggregates many of the investment decisions to the point where such data become meaningless. Data from 1979 to 1984, however, make it possible to draw tentative conclusions concerning Canadian National's investment strategy. Table 7-2 shows the relationship between return on divisional assets (as an indicator of expected return on investment) in a given year and both divisional imports or exports of capital and the rate of growth of divisional assets.

A weak negative relationship exists between importation of capital and return on assets, contrary to what the autonomy strategy would predict. CN must continue to invest in its unprofitable divisions and to do so requires funds from outside those divisions. But more important, there is a strong positive relationship between return on assets and the rate of investment growth. Consistent with the autonomy strategy, the company is pouring more money into profit centers with a high rate of return (by CN standards) than it is into marginal or unprofitable sectors.[38] Although the federal government views the railway as the primary mission of the company, CN does not appear to be investing more in the

---

38. The correlation between divisional return on assets and a division's share of total corporate investment, defined as investment in a division divided by corporate investment, was also calculated for this analysis. A high correlation would have supported the argument that CN is pursuing an autonomy strategy, pouring the bulk of its money into the most profitable divisions. But because CN's divisions are of very unequal size (CN Rail assets in 1983 were approximately 140 times those of CN Express), the impact of profit center size on distribution of investment funds among divisions obscures the impact of division profitability.

Table 7-2. *Division Profitability and Investment Patterns, Canadian National Railways*[a]

Independent variable	Dependent variable	R^2	Significance
Divisional return on assets (*DRETURN*)[b]	Divisional import of capital funds (*IMPORT*)[c]	−0.18	0.102
Divisional return on assets (*DRETURN*)[b]	Rate of divisional investment growth (*INVGROW*)[d]	0.57	0.00
CN Rail (controlling for divisional return on assets)	Rate of divisional investment growth (*INVGROW*)[d]	−0.10	0.24

Source: Canadian National Railways, *Annual Report,* 1981–84.

a. The table uses a pooled set of financial data, with a total of 54 observations drawn from the years 1979 to 1984. The divisions included are CN Rail, Grand Trunk, CN Communications, CN Trucking, CN Express (until 1983), CN Hotels, CN Marine (until 1983), TerraTransport, and, beginning in 1981, CN Exploration and CN Real Estate.

b. The variable *DRETURN* is a measure of the divisional return on assets for a given year in comparison to the overall corporate rate of return on assets in that year. It is calculated with the equation

$$DRETURN_{ij} = (EARNINGS_i / ASSETS_i)_j - CORPRETURN_j,$$

where for every year j, $EARNINGS_i$ is the pretax income or loss of division$_i$, $ASSETS_i$ is the value of the assets of division$_i$, and $CORPRETURN$ is the quotient of corporate earnings and corporate assets, that is, the rate of corporate return on assets. The rate of corporate return is subtracted from the divisional return rate rather than used as a divisor because in 1982 the overall corporate return was negative. Dividing divisional rate of return by corporate rate of return to standardize *DRETURN* would have resulted in a positive *DRETURN* value for divisions with losses, and a negative value for profitable divisions.

c. *IMPORT*, the value of a division's "imported" funds, that is, funds other than those generated within a division as a percentage of total divisional investment, is expressed as

$$IMPORT_{ij} = [INVEST_i - (EARNINGS_i + DEPREC_i) - STOCK_i]_j / INVEST_{ij},$$

where for each year j, $INVEST_i$ is the total divisional investment, $EARNINGS_i$ the net income or loss for the profit center (division), $DEPREC_i$ the depreciation in value of division assets, and $STOCK_i$ the funds provided by issuing stock to the Government of Canada for capital projects of that division. STOCK applies solely to CN Marine, the only division for which such an arrangement exists with the federal government. $EARNINGS_i$ and $DEPREC_i$ are both sources of funding internal to the division. $DEPREC_i$ is counted as an expense but is not a cash item. $STOCK_i$ can be attributed to that division although it is not strictly speaking generated by it. When division losses are greater than the funds generated by depreciation allowances, those losses should be counted as an operating expense to be borne by the rest of the corporation rather than as a negative capital source. Otherwise, values of $INVEST_{ij}$ could be greater than 1.0 (that is, more than 100 percent of divisional investment could be attributed to sources external to the division). Hence all negative values of $(EARNINGS_i + DEPREC_i)$ have been recoded to 0.

d. *INVGROW*, the rate of investment growth within a division, is standardized by the size of division assets, and is calculated with the formula

$$INVGROW_{ij} = (INVEST_i - DEPREC_i)_j / ASSETS_{ij},$$

where $DEPREC_i$ represents the corporation's estimate of the decline in value of its assets in year i as those assets are worn out or become obsolete.

railway than profit maximization would dictate. Once divisional return is controlled for, CN Rail investment is not growing more rapidly than that of other divisions.

Commercial motivations clearly dominated Canadian National's decision to expand its U.S. rail holdings. CN inherited railways in New England and the Midwest from its bankrupt predecessors. In 1980 Grand Trunk Western, the largest of CN's U.S. lines, purchased the Detroit, Toledo and Ironton Railroad, extending CN's rail properties as far south as Cincinnati. Grand Trunk also bid for the remnants of the bankrupt Milwaukee Road, but bowed out when two other carriers (including CP's U.S. rail subsidiary) placed significantly higher bids. Nevertheless, the willingness of the federal cabinet to approve Canadian National's U.S. rail expansions indicates the extent to which political barriers to CN investment decisions have weakened.

Canadian National's independently operated trucking subsidiaries, on the other hand, have encountered political barriers to expansion. Once again, it is the provincial governments rather than Ottawa that have placed the obstacles. Canadian truckers are regulated provincially, and many trucking firms and provincial governments have resisted extension of railway-owned trucking operations. In particular, Canadian National was unable for many years to obtain license authority between Montreal and Moncton, New Brunswick. This prevented full coordination of a transcontinental trucking network. (CP's trucking subsidiaries, by contrast, enjoy full transcontinental authority.) In 1981 CN's trucking subsidiary agreed to purchase a Quebec-based trucking concern, Les Entreprises Bussières Ltée., filling the Montreal-Moncton gap. However, the Quebec government told CN that to win provincial approval it would have to find a Quebec-based partner in the private sector. When CN was unable to do so, the Quebec government decided to purchase half of Bussières itself, making it an equal partner with CN while entrusting day-to-day management to a CN trucking subsidiary. The provincial transport minister explained this action as consistent with the Parti Québécois policy of keeping centers of economic decisionmaking in Quebec and acquiring "observation posts" in the provincial transportation industry.[39] The Bussières purchase further illustrates the impact of provincial governments on Canadian National's decisionmaking and the willingness of CN to accommodate a variety of government interests.

Diversification. CN's status as a public enterprise and its deficits up to 1975 severely limited diversification into new types of businesses. The range of CN operations and the percentage of revenues derived

39. Jay Bryan, "Quebec, CN Partners in Trucking Firm," *Gazette* (Montreal), January 3, 1981, p. 17. For CN's view, see Commons, Committee on Transport and Communications, *Minutes,* 32 Parl. 1 sess., issue 22, January 22, 1981, pp. 30–31, 49–53. Although CN executives interviewed for this study stated that provincial representatives on the Bussières board had not prevented decisions from being made on a commercial basis, the lack of complete ownership prevented CN from including the Bussières holdings in unification of CN trucking operations. In 1985 CN agreed to sell its stake in Bussières in exchange for the right to a trucking corridor across Quebec.

from them were about the same in 1975 as they were in 1955.[40] Canadian Pacific, on the other hand, made major changes in its corporate investments during this period.

CN's recent attempts to move into new fields have not fared well. In 1975 CN purchased a minority interest in the parent company of the Cast container shipping line that operates across the North Atlantic out of the port of Montreal. CN's investment in Cast sparked repeated protests from Maritime politicians, who feared that the CN-Cast partnership would divert traffic from the port of Halifax, which is also served by Canadian National.[41] President Bandeen sought to increase CN's minority stake in Cast (one of the few areas where he encountered strong resistance from the CN board), while Cast encountered repeated financial difficulties as a result of fierce rate competition. CN participated in a financial rescue of Cast in 1982,[42] but it wrote off its investment in Cast's parent company. In 1983 CN planned to join with the Royal Bank of Canada, Cast's major secured creditor, to keep the company operating and reduce competition by purchasing a major nonconference competitor, Sofati Container Line, and merging it with Cast. The cabinet failed to issue an order allowing the Sofati purchase, however, and CN's negotiations with Cast and the Royal Bank collapsed shortly thereafter. Royal Bank ended up with full control of both Cast and Sofati, although CN continues to carry both lines' containers.[43]

Canadian National also ran into difficulties in its efforts to diversify

40. Moreover, the few attempts that CN made to diversify in earlier years, such as the CN Tower telecommunications project and the ill-fated Metro Centre real estate development in Toronto, provoked strong protests in Parliament: the national railway should use its scarce resources to purchase rolling stock and not to build "monuments."

41. Cast's very low rates also led to protests in the U.S. Congress that it was diverting traffic from U.S. ports. See *Canadian Cargo Diversion*, Hearings before the Subcommittee on Merchant Marine of the Senate Committee on Commerce, Science and Transportation, 97 Cong. 2 sess. (GPO, 1982).

42. CN bought Cast's Montreal terminal facilities for $10 million (leasing them back to Cast) and an option to purchase a 75 percent interest in its container (but not ship) fleet. The terminal operation was sold back to Cast's successor company in September 1983. See Jane Boyes, "Understanding and Rate Concessions: The Keys to Cast's Survival," *Containerisation International*, vol. 16 (June 1982), pp. 52–53.

43. On the negotiations between CN, Royal Bank, Cast, and Sofati, see the *Globe and Mail* (Toronto), June 6, 1983; June 12, 1983; and June 14, 1983. See also Commons, Committee on Transport and Communications, *Minutes*, 32 Parl. 1 sess., issue 96, May 12, 1983, pp. 12–15, 44–48; issue 100, June 21, 1983; issue 101, June 28, 1983, pp. 10–20. On the sale of Sofati to the reorganized Cast, see *Globe and Mail* (Toronto), August 5, 1983; August 6, 1983.

into nontransportation sectors, notably petroleum. CN has substantial oil and gas properties in western Canada. In the past CN had acted as a passive landlord in exploiting these properties, but in 1980 it developed plans for increasing this role by purchasing huge Gulf Canada from its American parent. CN managers bypassed their board of directors by obtaining approval directly from their minister and the prime minister, who saw CN's proposal as consistent with Ottawa's National Energy Program to "Canadianize" ownership of the country's petroleum resources.[44] But after federally owned Petro-Canada purchased Petrofina in 1981, concern grew in Ottawa that Canadianization of the oil industry was beginning to look like nationalization. As a senior CN official involved in the negotiations put it, "The government felt vulnerable—they cut us off overnight." Denied the opportunity to purchase Gulf Canada, CN has decided to take a more active role in its oil-producing properties through formation of a new division, CN Exploration.

Disinvestment. Private sector firms are likely to disinvest in unprofitable operations by deferring maintenance and by refusing to replace worn-out assets.[45] When revenues fall short of short-term variable costs, more severe forms of disinvestment—sale or scrapping of assets—may be required. With public enterprise, political or public service objectives often override economic incentives for disinvestment. Canadian National has enjoyed mixed success, disinvesting slowly in several sectors and in others obtaining government capital assistance (partially in response to its disinvestment). It has not, however, completely eliminated its responsibility to invest in unprofitable operations.

Canadian National has been most successful with its rail passenger service, first forgoing new investment and then selling its equipment to VIA.[46] Similarly, Canadian National and Canadian Pacific were unwilling

44. See the statement by Transport Minister Jean-Luc Pepin in Commons, Committee on Transport and Communications, *Minutes,* 32 Parl. 1 sess., issue 24, March 26, 1981, pp. 39–40. For CN's view, see Bandeen's statement in issue 22, January 22, 1981, pp. 33–34. See also *Globe and Mail* (Toronto), December 19, 1980; and Ian Anderson, "Selling Patriotism at the Gas Pumps," *Maclean's,* February 16, 1981, pp. 38–39.

45. See Michael Conant, *Railroad Mergers and Abandonments* (University of California Press, 1964), p. 118.

46. Although the Canadian Transport Commission could require carriers to maintain passenger services (subject to review every five years), it could not give carriers incentives to purchase new rolling stock. Canadian National last ordered new equipment in 1966, although it did rehabilitate some equipment in later years. By the time VIA Rail Canada was formed in 1977, most CN passenger equipment was more than twenty years old. This equipment was sold to VIA at net book value.

to rehabilitate Prairie branch lines or purchase new rolling stock for grain hauling until the Crow's Nest Pass rates were changed. Both carriers followed minimum maintenance policies, even on lines guaranteed against abandonment until the year 2000.[47] Because grain transportation problems in the Prairies were shared by CN and CP, Ottawa once again tried to develop comprehensive solutions rather than pick up CN's grain-related losses as part of a general subsidy to the public enterprise. Moreover, Canadian National was able to convince the federal government that capital costs could not be hidden or cross-subsidized. During the 1970s, Ottawa responded to these railway concerns by subsidizing branch-line rehabilitation and purchasing grain hopper cars. Then in 1983, it modified the Crow's Nest Pass rates to make grain traffic profitable again. Since 1981 CN has also received federal assistance to finance containerization of rail traffic into and out of Newfoundland.

Avoiding investment in unprofitable ventures. The reluctance of Canadian National's management to get involved in unprofitable investments was evident in a 1980 conflict over construction of a major new rail line to the Sukunka coal fields in northeastern British Columbia.

When the Canadian coal producers and the Japanese steel companies planning to buy it announced that they could not close a deal without concessions on transportation costs, Premier William Bennett of British Columbia pressed Ottawa for an increase in aid over the original federal-provincial agreement.[48] Although reluctant to set a precedent for subsidizing exports, federal officials offered a $70 million construction grant. Premier Bennett first threatened to go it alone, then offered to let CN take over construction of the new line. CN agreed, but only on terms that ensured it a commercial return. Premier Bennett vetoed the proposal with a verbal blast at CN for "shirking its responsibility to promote new areas of the country."[49] The British Columbia government eventually

47. Grain Handling and Transportation Commission (Hall Commission), *Grain and Rail in Western Canada,* vol. 1, pp. 58–59, 101. CN began a small upgrading program in 1972, amounting to about $35 million over five years.

48. The original division of responsibilities negotiated by Ottawa and the British Columbia provincial government assigned the federal government most of the responsibility for port improvements in Prince Rupert (to be recovered through user charges), while CN was to upgrade its line into Prince Rupert and acquire the necessary rolling stock, again with an expectation of a commercial return. The provincially owned British Columbia Railway (BCR) would upgrade its portion of the route and build the line into the coal fields. For a more detailed discussion of this conflict, see R. Kent Weaver, "The Politics of State Enterprise" (Ph.D. dissertation, Harvard University, 1982), pp. 458–66.

49. Bruce McLean, "Bennett Will Go It Alone on Coal Route," *Province* (Van-

financed the coal line itself through the British Columbia Railway (BCR), while the federal government compromised on port charges.

The coal line dispute illustrates once again the attempt by provincial governments to use Canadian National for their own symbolic (of a distant and hostile Ottawa) and substantive ends. Even more striking is the contrast between the two publicly owned railways and their treatment by their owner governments. The BCR played "agent" to the provincial government's "principal": decisions on whether the railway would build the coal line were made by the provincial government rather than by railway management, apparently on short notice and with minimal consultation. When the BCR management expressed reluctance to participate in the coal line development, it was simply ignored.[50]

Canadian National encountered heavy pressure from the federal ministers involved in the project to lower their rates.[51] Nevertheless, it enjoyed substantial latitude in its cost calculations, rate-setting, and final decision on whether to construct the coal line. The case thus shows that governments can resist pressure to use public enterprises for political ends and that these firms can win considerable decisionmaking autonomy when their goals are not inconsistent with those of the government.[52]

Adapting capital spending to resources. The final and most important test of an autonomy strategy is management's ability to adapt its investments to available capital resources (retained earnings and debt backed by future earning power). Either management or government must ensure that commercial disciplines are applied to overall capital expenditure levels as well as to specific investment decisions. This is something that Canadian National was not able to do in the past. Indeed,

---

couver), June 15, 1980; see also "CNR Lacked Foresight, Says Bennett," *Colonist* (Victoria), June 26, 1980.

50. Glenn Bohn, "BCR Shies at Building Coal Line," *Sun* (Vancouver), July 11, 1980.

51. Given the Liberal party's sorry state in the West, the cabinet desperately wanted to make sure that Ottawa would not be blamed for a collapse of the coal development. A senior CN official involved in the negotiations thus described the effect of this federal pressure: "We probably lowered our rate sooner than we would have, and charged a bit less than we would have."

52. Additional evidence that CN is no longer viewed as a dumping ground by the federal government comes from the case of the Maislin trucking line. When this major Canadian carrier was threatened with bankruptcy in the summer of 1982, Ottawa extended a loan guarantee to allow it to stay in operation. A senior federal minister made discreet inquiries to see if CN's management would be interested in adding Maislin to its trucking operations. They were not, and the matter was dropped. (Interviews with CN executives.)

critics in Parliament of CN's 1978 recapitalization charged, with some justification, that the company responded to its recapitalization in 1952 by going on a spending spree that necessitated a repeat of the earlier bailout.

In their efforts to gain relief from uneconomic operations such as grain transportation under the Crow's Nest Pass rates, Canadian National's managers have repeatedly stressed the need to make investments in the railway, notably to increase main-line capacity in western Canada. They have argued that without such relief they will have to obtain an infusion of new equity from the government or the public, incur additional debt that the company probably could not repay, or forgo investments. CN's managers are using the threat of the last two options (debt requiring eventual bailout or noninvestment) to persuade Ottawa to adopt one of the first two options (relief or new equity). But experience suggests that if the company's managers are forced to choose between overburdening the company with debt or noninvestment, they are more likely to choose the debt option. Indeed, CN's debt ratio (debt as a percent of total capital) rose from 36 percent in 1980 to almost 45 percent in 1984. CN's current management claims that it has reduced and stretched out future capital outlays to hold the debt ratio at 48 percent.[53] It remains doubtful, however, whether that level of debt can be serviced and whether capital outlays can in fact be reduced in the face of persistent government pressure to invest. If they cannot, CN's autonomy strategy will inevitably be eroded.

EMPLOYMENT. Employment is another area in which autonomy-, service-, and security-oriented public enterprises adopt different policies. Autonomy-oriented firms will attempt to maximize labor productivity and reduce employment when possible. More specifically, these firms respond to technological change and economic downturns by trying to decrease employment, at a rate similar to that of private firms. Public service–oriented firms retain excess employees when this is part of the firm's mandate. Thus employment trends for those firms are likely to be unresponsive to the electoral cycle and less responsive to the business cycle than those for comparable private sector firms. Security-oriented

53. Canadian National Railways, *Annual Report, 1984*, pp. 7, 11. In the disastrous downturn of 1982, CN officials claim to have slashed projected total capital spending by $250 million, but investments were only $14.4 million lower than those in 1981. CN's debt ratio (long-term debt as a percentage of total capital) rose from 36.8 to 44.5 in one year.

200   POLITICS OF INDUSTRIAL CHANGE

firms will generally attempt to hold employment levels steady or increase them to win labor union support. Thus in an industry that is enjoying rapid productivity increases, employment is likely to shrink less over time in public sector firms than in private ones. Such a public enterprise may also be responsive to government requests to avoid layoffs at sensitive points in the electoral cycle (notably election years and, in parliamentary systems, periods of minority government). Employment changes may also be responsive to changes in party control of government.

Canadian National provides an excellent testing ground for these rival hypotheses. Technological changes and changes in consumer preferences have slashed labor requirements throughout the North American rail industry. Moreover, cuts affect some regions more than others; in Northern Ontario, for example, entire communities were created by the railway, and they are utterly dependent upon it for their economic survival. Some regions lack highway access. As the change from steam to diesel locomotives made longer runs between servicing possible, some of these communities lost their raison d'être, and the skills of boilermakers and of many other railway workers became obsolete.[54] Railway workers are well organized, and their leaders know that failure to respond to members' concerns can lead to a loss of control over the union.

These impediments to improving labor productivity are partially balanced by the fact that Canadian National and Canadian Pacific negotiate labor agreements together, and CP can claim that contract provisions must be compatible with black ink. Canadian Pacific has generally taken the lead in pressing for productivity improvements.[55] CN has made significant employment cuts in recent years. But Ottawa still intervenes in the firm's affairs, usually through informal information

54. See the *Report of the Industrial Inquiry Commission on Canadian National Railways "Run Throughs"* (Freedman Commission) (Ottawa: Queen's Printer, 1965); and A.W. Currie, *Canadian Transportation Economics* (Toronto: University of Toronto Press, 1967), chap. 15. The regional problem has an additional aspect: railway workers are paid a nationwide wage rate—a princely sum in areas like Newfoundland. Workers in such areas have virtually no chance of transferring their skills to other industries at a similar wage.

55. For example, Canadian Pacific eliminated firemen on certain freight service locomotives early in 1957 and suffered a strike in the process. CN continued operating during the strike; the strike was settled by a royal commission, and the commission's settlement was eventually applied to CN. Canadian National, however, took the lead in instituting run-throughs of former division points in the early 1960s, resulting in a brief wildcat strike in 1964. See the Freedman Commission report, pp. 22–24.

gathering. Layoffs by the major transport companies inevitably prompt queries from the opposition parties during the House of Commons question period, and accurate information is needed to avoid embarrassing the minister.[56]

Occasionally, Ottawa intervenes directly. In 1979 CN attempted to lay off more than 300 employees of its Newfoundland Railway operations. The federal government ordered CN to delay the layoffs and agreed to pay a portion of employees' salaries while negotiations proceeded on a comprehensive attrition agreement in Newfoundland. A special agreement was reached that applied both to the employees declared redundant under the present system and to the reduction of an additional 300 employees expected with containerization.[57] A similar intervention by Transport Minister Jean-Luc Pepin in 1981 delayed the closing of two CN Express terminals in the Maritime provinces.

Data comparing CN and CP labor productivity over time are consistent with a shift in CN strategy toward an autonomy orientation. The summary results are presented in figure 7-3.[58] There are some problems with the high aggregation of outputs used in developing the productivity measures.[59] It is clear, however, that CN's overall level of employee

56. As an aide to a former transport minister put it: "If CN was going to lay off workers in New Brunswick or Newfoundland, I would call them up and find out what was going on, and see if changes could be made. . . . We were at pains never to treat CN and CP differently . . . [but] if I were going to call CN or Air Canada about a layoff, I would feel a lot more comfortable than in calling CP or CP Air."

57. The federal government agreed to pay up to $10 million under this agreement. Commons, Committee on Transport and Communications, *Minutes,* 32 Parl. 1 sess., issue 30, April 9, 1981, p. 68.

58. Passenger and express personnel were excluded because of problems of data comparability. CN included express service workers in its railway employment statistics in the early 1960s, while CP counted them separately. Data on the categories of railway workers most likely to be affected by those reporting differences have therefore been excluded in developing the summary index shown in figure 7-3. Excluded are freight shed personnel, motor vehicle mechanics, drivers and helpers, and garage servicemen. Including passenger service data does not significantly change the relationship between CN and CP productivity from 1957 to 1977. After 1977, however, productivity measures for passenger service became unrealistic as both companies rapidly transferred passenger service to VIA.

59. See Douglas W. Caves and Laurits R. Christensen, *Productivity in Canadian Railroads, 1956–1975,* Report 10-78-16 (Ottawa: Canadian Transport Commission, Research Branch, 1978), pp. 28–34, 51. Specifically, commodity type and length of haul are likely to influence the inputs required for railway service. If one railway has significantly longer hauls, or a larger share of bulk commodities in its traffic mix, its labor requirements per ton-mile should be lower. When ton-miles are weighted to take

productivity in nonpassenger service operations is consistently lower than that of CP from 1957 to 1983. A cyclical pattern to the relationship can be seen. CN is furthest from matching CP's productivity in years of economic downturn (for example, 1975 and 1982). There is a downward trend through the 1960s and early 1970s in CN's performance relative to CP's that is reversed after 1975, coinciding with the change in CN's management.

Figure 7-4 shows that these patterns vary significantly among employment categories. CN Rail has done quite well with train and engine crew personnel such as conductors, brakemen, engineers, and firemen, where operating practices are regulated very strictly by contracts that CN and CP share with the unions. In the categories most affected by attrition agreements between rail labor and the carriers (firemen and brakemen), CN has outperformed CP, sometimes by substantial margins. Where work rules are governed less closely by joint contracts (for example, road maintenance, professional, and clerical personnel), CN lags seriously behind.

The data developed here provide little support for the security model, which suggests that public enterprise employee productivity will grow less quickly than comparable private enterprises. This assertion is contradicted by the faster rate of labor productivity growth for CN than for CP after 1975. Nor does employee productivity vary with the electoral cycle, the party in power, or the security of the government's mandate. To measure the influence of political variables, the productivity ratio was regressed separately on three dummy variables, as presented in table 7-3. Although this analysis is limited by the small number of observation years (1957–83), the results are helpful. Minority governments, election years, and governing parties do not significantly influence changes in the CN/CP labor productivity ratio at the 95 percent level of confidence.

On the other hand, the economic cycle (as measured by changes in CN and CP freight ton-miles) does have a significant impact on changes in the labor productivity ratio: when CN's traffic levels rise at rates equal to or greater than CP's, CN's productivity rises relative to CP's; when

---

account of differing costs, the ratio of CN to CP ton-miles in 1967 increases from 1.263 to 1.345. This suggests that differences between CN and CP labor productivity may be somewhat less than shown in figure 7-3. Similarly, the aggregation of ton-miles and passenger miles as an output measure for some categories of workers ignores the different labor requirements for the two types of traffic.

Figure 7-3. *Labor Productivity of Canadian National Railways Relative to That of Canadian Pacific, 1957–80*[a]

Percent

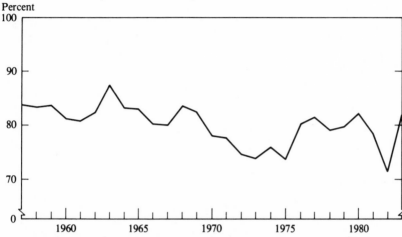

Source: Statistics Canada, *Railway Transport*, pt. 3: "Equipment Track and Fuel Statistics," catalog 52-209 (for data on miles of track operated); pt. 4: "Operating and Traffic Statistics," catalog 52-210 (for data on revenue freight ton-miles and passenger miles); pt. 6: "Employment Statistics," catalog 52-212 (for employment data) (Ottawa: Statistics Canada, various years). All data for 1982 and 1983 are from "General Statistics" catalog 52-215.

a. The labor productivity ratio equals

$$\sum P_{ij}\left(\frac{N_{ij}}{T_j}\right),$$

where P_{ij} is the ratio of CN to CP employee productivity for a specific category of workers i, in a year j; N_{ij} is the number of CN workers in category i in year j; and T_j is the total number of CN workers in year j.
The CN/CP productivity ratio within categories of workers is expressed in the following equation:

$$P_{ij} = \frac{O_{ni}}{L_{ni}} \div \frac{O_{pi}}{L_{pi}},$$

where O_{ni} is the output of CN workers in category i, L_{ni} is the number of CN workers in that category, O_{pi} is the output of CP workers in the same category i, and L_{pi} is the number of CP workers in that category.
The output measures used for the various categories of workers are as follows: revenue ton-miles for road freight crews (conductors, brakemen, engineers, firemen, and helpers); the sum of revenue ton-miles and revenue passenger miles for general workers (including executives, professionals, police, and store personnel, as well as all others listed under "general" in Statistics Canada classifications), station agents, yard personnel (including yardmasters and assistants, switch tenders, hostlers, yard foremen and helpers, yard engineers and motormen, yard firemen and helpers), equipment maintenance personnel (excluding coach cleaners), and miscellaneous transportation personnel (including train dispatchers, clerks, floating equipment employees, and other employees listed in categories 46-64 of catalog 52-212 and listed elsewhere in this figure); and total miles of track operated (including trackage rights) for road maintenance personnel. Excluded are passenger service personnel (road passenger conductors, brakemen and baggagemen, engineers and motormen, firemen and helpers, sleeping and parlor car personnel, dining car personnel, and coach cleaners), baggage, parcel room and station attendants, restaurant personnel, news agents, freight shed personnel, motor vehicle mechanics and helpers, garage servicemen, and revenue motor vehicle drivers and helpers.

the two carriers' traffic falls at equal rates, CN's labor productivity falls faster. Canadian National appears to have pursued a public service strategy for the early part of the 1957–80 period: although the company's actions do not seem to have been influenced by short-term political events, it cut employment less than CP in employment categories not

Figure 7-4. *Productivity of Canadian National Railways Relative to That of Canadian Pacific in Four Areas, 1957–83*

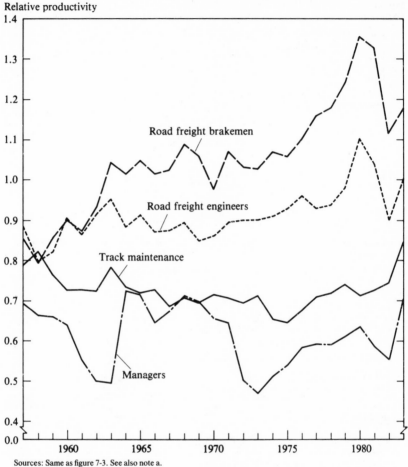

Relative productivity

Sources: Same as figure 7-3. See also note a.

closely governed by work rules, and, during recessions, it allowed productivity to fall rather than laying off workers to the same extent as CP did. But as noted earlier, differences between the two carriers grow smaller after 1974, consistent with a shift to a more autonomy-oriented strategy.

CN's employee productivity relative to CP's has improved since the depressed levels of 1974–75. Although CN is still far from achieving equal levels of productivity, it is generally keeping pace with its private

Table 7-3. *The Effects of Political and Economic Variables on Changes in the Relative Labor Productivity of Canadian National and Canadian Pacific*[a]

Independent variable and summary statistic	Equation			
	(1)	(2)	(3)	(4)
Independent variable				
Constant	−0.01	−0.01	−0.003	−0.002
	(−0.86)	(−0.39)	(−0.28)	(−0.3)
Election year	0.03	. . .	. . .	. . .
	(1.33)			
Minority government	. . .	0.01	. . .	. . .
		(0.45)		
Governing party	. . .	. . .	0.01	. . .
			(0.37)	
Changes in CN traffic levels	. . .	. . .	. . .	0.66
				(7.26)
Changes in CP traffic levels	. . .	. . .	. . .	−0.66
				(−7.50)
Summary statistic				
R^2 (corrected)	0.03	−0.03	−0.04	0.69
Durbin-Watson	2.0	2.1	2.1	1.9

Sources: Same as figure 7-3.

a. n = 25 in all models. *Election year* equals one in an election year, zero otherwise; *minority government* equals one in years of a government with a minority in Parliament, zero otherwise; and *governing party* equals one during years of Conservative government, five-tenths in years when governments change, and zero during Liberal government years. The numbers in parentheses are *t*-statistics.

sector counterpart in a period of increasing freight traffic and falling rail employment—a significant achievement for a public enterprise.[60]

Conclusions

Canadian National has been slower than Canadian Pacific to cut unprofitable operations, to diversify into new businesses, and to lower

60. Both CN and CP increased their "total factor productivity" much faster than comparable U.S. carriers between 1963 and 1974. Douglas W. Caves, Laurits R. Christensen, and Joseph A. Swanson, "Economic Performance in Regulated and Unregulated Environments: A Comparison of U.S. and Canadian Railroads" (Evanston: Northwestern University, Transportation Center, 1980), p. 22. CN actually increased its "total factor productivity" faster than CP between 1957 and 1975. Judging by changes in the cost shares of factor inputs, it appears that these relative productivity gains occurred in inputs other than labor. Douglas W. Caves and Laurits R. Christensen, "The Relative Efficiency of Public and Private Firms in a Competitive Environment: The Case of Canadian Railroads," *Journal of Political Economy*, vol. 88, no. 5 (1980), pp. 958–76.

employment. These differences, however, have declined and in some cases have reversed since the late 1960s—particularly since 1974 when a corporate strategy oriented toward autonomy and profitability began to emerge. For the most part, the Canadian government has encouraged development of this strategy.

CN's policies have had several important economic and political effects. First, CN has been able to carry out significant industrial adjustment in many of its operations. It has also managed to avoid receiving any major new "gifts" of unprofitable operations in the past decade. Where such operations have been maintained, CN has been able to minimize the need to cross-subsidize many of them by separating them out and transferring them to other entities (VIA, for example). In two sectors—rail passenger service and ferry operations—it has eliminated subsidies and replaced them with contract payments, reinforcing the image of CN as a profit-oriented business rather than a public works program. But actual changes in outputs have lagged behind what a true market-oriented policy would produce, as Ottawa has stepped in to preserve services, investments, and jobs that Canadian National proposed to eliminate.

Perhaps most important, Canadian National has gradually altered the climate of expectations and its bargaining positions with the federal government. By no means completely independent of Ottawa, CN has managed, nevertheless, to attain substantial autonomy from its political masters. As an aide to former Transport Minister Otto Lang noted in 1979:

> There are a lot of "potential" areas for intervention, but they are likely to remain "potential" because it is politically impossible to use them. You could put pressure on Bandeen or [Air Canada President] Claude Taylor to do something, but they would probably quit, and it wouldn't be worth it.

As this comment shows, Canadian National's autonomy is by no means secure: its continuation depends on the calculation by CN's owner that giving the company substantial autonomy is in the federal government's policy and political interests. Many of the financial and structural constraints that were relaxed by the federal government have been institutionalized in statutory form (for example, the National Transportation Act subsidies and 1978 recapitalization). But many CN actions (notably acquiescence in work force reductions) require that the government directly absorb short-term political losses.

Showing that changes in CN's strategy and outputs are consistent with changing government constraints does not necessarily mean that the former were caused by the latter. Many officials in both CN and the federal government favor an alternative hypothesis, attributing the firm's increased autonomy and profitability solely to the Bandeen-era management. Such an argument is overly simplistic. The change in management in 1974 coincided with CN's improvements in employee productivity relative to that of CP, but occurred after CN had begun to reduce passenger train service. And while new management may have been necessary for many of the company's changes, it was by no means sufficient. CN has enjoyed substantial success primarily because the federal government has been willing to forgo many of its controls, making an autonomy orientation feasible. The company has been able to win most autonomy in areas where its goals coincide with the federal government's goals (for example, rail improvements in the Prairie provinces). Where their interests have clashed, notably over branch-line abandonments, much less progress has been made. Canadian National has not risked open confrontation with Ottawa—witness its refusal to put the Newfoundland rail line up for abandonment.

A second explanation of changes in CN policy and outputs is almost the opposite of the first: the changes are attributed not to a shift in management goals, but to implementation of new public service objectives of the federal government. The independent role of management in promoting industrial adjustment is thus mistakenly denied. While this argument is supported by the provisions of the National Transportation Act, it drastically oversimplifies both the decisionmaking process and the policy outcomes achieved. Most transport policy decisions involve complex trade-offs among a variety of competing goals: limiting federal expenditures, promoting regional economic development, preserving and creating jobs, and maintaining an economically viable railway system. The incentives are strong for government to delay hard choices among goals and to shift emphasis between goals in response to short-term political pressures. In practice, governments almost invariably decide what is in the public interest as they go along, mingling policy and political principles. Ottawa has been no exception.

Moreover, Ottawa rarely proclaims the public interest with a single voice: Transport Canada generally supports cuts in unprofitable rail services, while the Canadian Transport Commission emphasizes the concerns of rail users. If CN were to rely on signals from Ottawa for its policy direction, the company would often find itself either paralyzed or splitting the difference between opposing policy principles. Thus one of CN management's major tasks has been to prompt Ottawa to finalize trade-offs among its goals. In trying to shape the federal response to the problems of the Newfoundland Railway, for example, CN proposed a commission of inquiry to support its complaints, created a separate profit center (TerraTransport) to highlight losses, threatened abandonments and layoffs of railway personnel, and proposed containerization of freight traffic. The decisionmaking process—from appointment of the commission to announcement of federal aid for containerization and labor protection—took almost four years. Far from being a passive implementer of the public interest, CN actively helped to form federal policy. Without CN's pressure to substitute commercial criteria for vague and conflicting notions of the public interest, it is doubtful whether a federal program would have been developed. In its final form, the Newfoundland containerization program typifies the outcome of CN strategy: the railway accepts a second-best partial cutback of services, federal policies are clarified, and the federal government assumes some of the costs.

As the case of Canadian National Railways makes clear, the policies of public enterprises are the product of multisided bargaining by the enterprise, federal and provincial agencies, and other parties rather than the simple result of federal initiatives or corporate goals. Neither totally passive nor totally autonomous, Canadian National pursued an autonomy strategy when federal constraints made such a strategy seem attainable. The 1974 change in management consolidated and strengthened strategic trends that were already under way.

Ottawa and Canadian National often have opposing interests, with Ottawa wanting to delay politically costly decisions and CN seeking to force them. In this context, corporate pressure on the government to develop consistent public service goals represents an attempt to avoid ad hoc political interventions that disrupt corporate planning, drain resources, and hurt management morale. CN has incorporated public service into its goals to avoid intervention in the implementation of its policies and to improve its relations with the government. But the company is also attempting to convince Ottawa that it should not be forced to conduct uneconomic operations unless it is compensated.

The existence of a private sector rival of comparable size has been a valuable tool for CN in its quest for autonomy and compensation for unprofitable operations. CP has faced many of the same problems as CN (notably grain and intercity passenger commuter deficits). Thus simply letting CN absorb the cost of its own deficit-producing services will not make the problem "disappear."[61] CN has been able to let CP take the lead in lobbying for relief on most sensitive issues—while making it clear that it shares CP's views. And the company has generally fared better in eliminating its losses entirely in sectors where CP also has a heavy stake than in areas where it does not (for example, TerraTransport, CN Express, the Hudson Bay Railway).

If CP is a valuable asset to CN in attaining its goals, the devolution of power and legitimacy to the provinces is an extraordinary liability. It is not merely that Canadian National must be responsive to many masters with conflicting interests. The problem is the absence of definitive channels for resolving disputes between levels of government, which is the special plague of the Canadian system. The extraordinary regionalization of Canadian politics has made regional development issues—and consequently transportation issues—both highly visible and highly salient in federal-provincial conflict. The conflict is not only a substantive dispute over allocation of powers and benefits but also a symbolic one. There are real political gains to be won in the provinces by showing that the federal government and its agents have malevolent intentions, as disputes over the Anzac coal line, grain-dependent branch lines, and the Newfoundland Railway show. In such situations, there is little incentive for the provinces to moderate their demands, and the political pressures on Ottawa to take over the financial burden of protectionist solutions, rather than imposing or permitting industrial adjustment, are enormous.

Consolidated Rail Corporation

The Consolidated Rail Corporation (Conrail) has been operating less than a decade, compared with more than sixty years for Canadian National. Thus any evaluation of performance must necessarily be more tentative, based on a more limited set of data. Despite its shorter history, Conrail also illuminates the impact of changing government constraints

---

61. Another possible solution is to transfer money losing services from CP to CN, using it as a dumping ground (for example, the St. John-Digby ferry service and corridor passenger services). But CP would not be willing to give up some of these operations (for example, its Prairie rail network).

210 POLITICS OF INDUSTRIAL CHANGE

on public enterprise behavior, while highlighting the role of differing national political environments.

Both Conrail and CN are primarily freight railways, but there are important differences between the two companies. CN has substantial interests outside of transportation; Conrail is forbidden by statute from such activities so long as more than 50 percent of its debt is owed by or guaranteed to the federal government.[62] Canadian National operates throughout Canada, while Conrail is concentrated in the northeastern United States. Canadian National's takeover by Ottawa was fairly straightforward, while Washington's role in the financing of Conrail evolved gradually. Federal financing was supposed to be temporary and was ostensibly an alternative to nationalization. But in the first years after Conrail began operation in 1976, hope that Conrail could be returned to the private sector faded. A report by the United States Railway Association (USRA), the independent government-owned corporation set up to plan and monitor Conrail, gloomily concluded in December 1980 that "continuing Conrail in its present form would probably impose a burden on the public treasury for the indefinite future."[63] Incremental changes in Conrail productivity would not be enough to make the company profitable, the association argued; fundamental changes in its cost structure were required.

By April 1983, however, Conrail was able to obtain a $100 million unsecured line of credit from a group of major banks, signifying its reacceptance by the financial community. In mid-1984 the federal government began the process of returning Conrail to the private sector, with more than a dozen bids received. What changes in government constraints and corporate strategy made this amazing turnaround possible? As in the case of Canadian National, changes in both constraints and strategy interacted to make the turnaround possible. It was a change in government constraints, however—notably, in this case, a more market-oriented regulatory philosophy by the Interstate Commerce Commission and a hard-line position by the Reagan administration against continuation of support to Conrail—that was the sine qua non for improving Conrail's financial performance. Conrail had shown strong elements of an autonomy orientation in its early years, but had not had

62. Regional Rail Reorganization Act of 1973, 87 Stat. 1005, sec. 302, January 2, 1974.
63. United States Railway Association, *Federal Funding of Conrail: Rail Service Objectives and Economic Realities* (Washington, D.C.: USRA, 1980), p. 19.

Table 7-4. *Railway Operating Expenses as a Percentage of Operating Revenue, 1979–80*[a]

Year	Conrail	Chesapeake and Ohio	Norfolk and Western	All Class I
1979	112.9	91.8	78.6	95.1
1980	109.2	87.5	77.9	93.4

Source: Interstate Commerce Commission, *Transport Statistics in the United States,* various years.
a. The operating ratios are calculated on an ICC accounting basis.

the freedom to implement it. Only when government constraints were loosened could that orientation become dominant and industrial change take place.

Government Constraints

FINANCIAL CONSTRAINTS. Conrail's first five years of operations offered little hope that it could ever become financially self-sufficient. As table 7-4 shows, the corporation's cost-to-revenue ratio was seriously out of line with those of other carriers. Moreover, freight traffic in the Northeast did not rebound as the United States Railway Association's *Final System Plan* had forecast, but continued to decline. Through the end of 1980, Conrail lost $1.55 billion compared with the *Final System Plan* projection of $0.2 billion. Conrail continued to have a negative cash flow from operations through 1980, instead of the turnaround forecast by the plan for 1978. Conrail could not afford to pay interest on its debentures held by the United States Railway Association and was forced to issue additional shares in lieu of interest. In 1978, with the $2.1 billion in capital assistance it had authorized for Conrail running out, Congress anted up an additional $1.2 billion.[64]

The outlook for Conrail is now considerably brighter due to a loosening of government-imposed financial constraints. The Staggers Rail Act of 1980 and its implementation by the Interstate Commerce Commission (ICC) eased a number of regulatory burdens on Conrail. The act allowed the corporation to lower prices selectively to capture traffic while raising rates that were noncompensatory. The act also permitted Conrail to close selected gateways (interchange points with other railways), forcing shippers to give Conrail rather than parallel railroads the long-haul on

64. United States Railway Association Amendments Act of 1978, 92 Stat. 2397, sec. 2, November 1, 1978.

traffic movements Conrail shared with those carriers. Finally, Conrail was permitted to impose surcharges on movements shared with other carriers when its return on that traffic was inadequate.[65]

The Northeast Rail Service Act of 1981, passed in the wake of USRA's gloomy projections and renewed efforts by the U.S. Department of Transportation (DOT) to sell Conrail in pieces to private sector carriers, directly attacked the problems of Conrail's cost structure.[66] The act provided an expedited procedure for abandoning Conrail lines, required a transfer of money losing commuter operations to local transit authorities or to Amtrak by the end of 1982, and set up a new (and less generous) federally funded Conrail employee protection plan to replace the plan established by the Regional Rail Reorganization (3R) Act of 1973. Perhaps most important, the 1981 act provided a strong incentive to Conrail managers, shippers, and labor to work together to produce additional savings: if the corporation did not become profitable by 1983, the secretary of transportation would have authority to begin selling Conrail in pieces beginning in 1984.

COMMAND STRUCTURE CONSTRAINTS. Conrail's governmental command structure is simple in theory but complicated in practice. Under the 3R act, the corporation's direct interactions with the federal government were to be limited to the regulatory mechanisms of the Interstate Commerce Commission. Federal aid to and monitoring of Conrail were to be funneled through the United States Railway Association.[67] The

65. *Staggers Rail Act of 1980*, 94 Stat. 1895, October 14, 1980.
66. On negotiation of the Northeast Rail Service Act of 1981, see Henry H. Perritt, Jr., "Ask and Ye Shall Receive: The Legislative Response to the Northeast Rail Crisis," *Villanova Law Review*, vol. 28 (January 1983), pp. 271–375, especially pp. 332–50. The act also made available to Conrail an additional $262 million in preferred stock funding and eliminated the shareholdings (Series B stock) held by the estates of Conrail's bankrupt predecessors. Northeast Rail Service Act of 1981, 95 Stat. 357,653, secs. 1140 and 1167, August 13, 1981.
67. The Regional Rail Reorganization Act provided for an eleven-member USRA board, consisting of a chairman nominated by the president of the United States, three government members (the secretary of transportation, the chairman of the Interstate Commerce Commission, and the secretary of the treasury, or their appointed representatives), and seven members recommended by organizations of large shippers, small shippers, state and local governments, the rail industry, organized labor, and the financial community. The Northeast Rail Service Act of 1981 removed the interest group representatives from the USRA board. In addition, the comptroller general replaced the secretary of the treasury, and Conrail's board chairman was added. They joined the USRA chairman, the secretary of transportation, and the ICC chairman, for a total of five members. The 1981 act also made the USRA chairman an appointee of the USRA board rather than of the president of the United States (95 Stat. 357,673, sec. 1147).

USRA appoints six of thirteen members of the Conrail board in its capacity as owner of the company's debentures and Series A preferred stock. Five additional members were originally selected by the special court in charge of Conrail litigation as representatives of the estates of Conrail's bankrupt predecessors, who held the rest of the company's stock. Conrail's chief executive officer and chief operating officer (selected by the other Conrail board members) complete its membership.[68]

The United States Railway Association and the Department of Transportation have repeatedly clashed over their respective roles in monitoring and guiding Conrail and in their views of what the future of the railroad should be. In 1980 the department sought to dismantle USRA by assuming some of its functions and by transferring others to a variety of government agencies. The move was rejected by Congress.[69] And when DOT began settling lawsuits brought by the estates of Conrail's predecessor railroads, paying them cash for their Conrail securities, the department retained control of the stock (and hence board appointments) rather than transferred it to USRA.

The dispute between USRA and DOT concerned policy as well as turf. When it appeared after 1980 that Conrail could not become profitable, the department revived its mid-1970s proposal of "controlled transfer" of Conrail lines to private sector carriers, while the association favored giving Conrail one more chance.[70]

The third major actor in Conrail's governmental command structure

68. Railroad Revitalization and Regulatory Reform Act of 1976, 90 Stat. 31,106, sec. 611, February 5, 1976. This section modified section 301(d) of the Regional Rail Reorganization Act, which had provided for direct representation on a fifteen-member Conrail board of the secretary of transportation and of the chairman and president of the USRA, plus five other individuals named by the president of the United States and approved by the Senate.

69. See *Reauthorization of the U.S. Railway Association for Fiscal Year 1981*, Hearings before the Subcommittee on Transportation and Commerce of the Senate Committee on Interstate and Foreign Commerce, 96 Cong. 2 sess. (GPO, 1980). See also *Traffic World*, February 18, 1980, p. 19; April 28, 1980, pp. 15–16; May 5, 1980, p. 31.

70. See United States Railway Association, *Conrail at the Crossroads: The Future of Rail Service in the Northeast*, April 1981; and U.S. Department of Transportation, Federal Railroad Administration, *Recommendations for Northeast Rail Service* (DOT, 1981). See also the statements by DOT Secretary Drew Lewis and USRA Chairman Stephen Berger in *Northeast Rail Service Act of 1981*, Hearings before the Subcommittee on Surface Transportation of the Senate Committee on Commerce, Science and Transportation, 97 Cong. 1 sess. (GPO, 1981), pp. 8–12, 19–24.

is Congress. The United States Railway Association, originally established by Congress to provide a buffer between Conrail and the Department of Transportation, actually helped to shield Conrail from district-specific, protectionist demands by legislators. USRA had extraordinary leeway in funding Conrail in the late 1970s: capital assistance was authorized in huge blocks—$2.1 billion and $1.2 billion—and Congress even permitted multiyear appropriations, something it is generally reluctant to do. The rationale for USRA's freedom was outlined by Congressman Joe Skubitz in debate over additional Conrail funding in 1978: Congress "should give Conrail the money that was needed for them to achieve their goals rather than dish it out on a piecemeal basis . . . [to] make it possible for Conrail to behave like a business rather than like a political ward heeler."[71] Yet others in Congress felt very uneasy about Conrail's autonomy. Congressman Toby Moffett complained:

> We are voting to spend taxpayers' dollars on things over which we have very little control. It is not as though it is a federal agency. I feel that we get the worst of both worlds. On the one hand, this is supposed to be a profitmaking corporation, and we spend this money; on the other hand, I cannot go to my constituents, nor can many of the other Members, and say that we paid this money but we do have this control. I think we have neither. I think that we have to get a lot shorter leash on these projects.[72]

A "shorter leash" almost inevitably translates into political resource allocation, however. Although Conrail was not able to entirely avoid congressional pressures or direct commands (for example, earmarking funds for specific projects), it did manage to do so to a remarkable degree, especially as compared with Amtrak.

Corporate Strategy

At the outset in 1976, Conrail's management outlined the corporation's objectives in autonomy-oriented terms: "profitability and economic self-sustainability in the private sector . . . at the least cost to the taxpayer."[73] This goal was to be obtained through rapid rehabilitation of its major

---

71. At the time Skubitz was ranking minority member of the Subcommittee on Transportation and Commerce of the House Interstate and Foreign Commerce Committee. *Congressional Record*, daily edition, October 11, 1978, p. H12263.

72. Ibid.

73. Edward Jordan, "Chairman's Message," in Consolidated Rail Corporation, *Annual Report, 1976*, p. 3.

routes, yards, and rolling stock. As the company began to fall short of *Final System Plan* traffic and revenue projections, Conrail began to justify its existence in somewhat different terms. The new "line" had more of a public service tone, although it was a response to security concerns: Congress had established Conrail "to provide adequate and efficient rail service in the Northeast at the least cost to taxpayers." Despite setbacks, management believed that "the Conrail structure still appears to present the 'best opportunity' to attain the stated goals."[74] But Conrail management never moved to define trade-offs between service adequacy and efficiency; instead it cautiously sought to alter its constraints.

Conrail's constraint pattern made that a very delicate task; much more difficult, for example, than for Canadian National Railways. CN needed to win the support of top officials in the Ministry of Transport; if the minister was persuaded, the cabinet was likely to follow, and Parliament was certain to go along as well. Moreover, on deregulation legislation, CN could generally rely on support from Canadian Pacific. Conrail, on the other hand, would need friends in Congress to win changes in its constraints. If the company moved too quickly to use its limited power to promote adjustment (and hence to increase its viability), legislators might attach protectionist restrictions on continued USRA funding to Conrail. Although many of Conrail's railway competitors had an interest in keeping Conrail in business (because they interchanged a large amount of traffic), some of Conrail's proposed solutions—notably branch line surcharges and closing of gateways—would help Conrail at the competitors' expense. If, on the other hand, Conrail attempted to buy political support by providing selective benefits, it would move further from the goal of financial autonomy and create an "open season" of demands on the enterprise.

Even if Conrail had followed a clear-cut political support-building strategy, it might not have been able to maintain majority support in Congress over the long term. Unlike Amtrak, Conrail does not provide nationwide service. It primarily serves the area east of the Mississippi and north of the Ohio and Potomac rivers. A stable support coalition in Congress probably would have required the development of log-rolling coalitions with region-specific programs in other areas (as the various agricultural commodity programs have done), but there were few obvious

74. Edward Jordan and Richard Spence, "Chairman's and President's Message," in Consolidated Rail Corporation, *Annual Report, 1977*, p. 3.

log-rolling candidates in Conrail's case. Thus legislators from other regions might in the future support a breakup of Conrail if it seemed possible to do so without greatly disrupting commerce in their own regions.[75]

To maintain political support for the corporation and win changes in its constraints, Conrail had to construct an amalgamation of the security and autonomy strategies. This strategy had three features: (1) rejection of politically motivated *positive* actions (for example, allocating capital projects to the districts of powerful legislators); (2) restraint in exercising its limited discretion to cut unprofitable operations—that is, it engaged in *nonactions* to avoid losing supporters; and (3) lobbying for changes in its constraints. Conrail management first focused on obtaining meaningful rate deregulation, which had been promised by the Railroad Revitalization and Regulatory Reform (4R) Act of 1976, but which Conrail's leaders felt had been stymied by restrictive ICC implementation. Indeed, as Conrail chairman Stanley Crane argued, the company was "the strongest advocate of this [Staggers Act deregulation] legislation, [and] it has moved more aggressively than other railroads in using the Act's provisions to determine the market-driven demand for rail service."[76]

Conrail's corporate strategy underwent an important shift in 1981 coinciding with the replacement of Ed Jordan by Stanley Crane as Conrail chairman. Fundamentally this change reflected management's recognition that deregulation alone would not make Conrail self-sufficient (since it did not address Conrail's cost structure). It also reflected the new political balance of forces that resulted from the hard line on "controlled transfer" taken by the new Reagan administration. Now Conrail could realize its security objectives only by achieving financial autonomy as well; if it did not, it was to be dismantled. As a result, Conrail pursued a more clearly autonomy-oriented set of policies and increased its pressure for changes in financial constraints. This strategy

75. Conrail faces the additional problem that one of its primary oversight committees, the Senate Committee on Commerce, Science and Transportation, is dominated by senators from outside Conrail's service region. In 1981, for example, fifteen of seventeen senators were from states outside Conrail's service region; another, Danforth of Missouri, was from a state bordering on Conrail's service region. Northeasterners were much more heavily represented on the House Energy and Commerce Committee, and in 1981 they dominated (eight of ten members) its Subcommittee on Commerce, Transportation and Tourism.

76. L. Stanley Crane and Stuart M. Reed, "A New Era for Conrail," in Consolidated Rail Corporation, *Annual Report, 1981*, p. 4.

has continued as Conrail has sought to meet the tests of profitability that would allow it to remain as a single unit.

Policies and Outcomes

Conrail's shift from a cautious amalgam of the autonomy and security strategies to a more straightforward autonomy orientation is evident in its policies toward unprofitable operations, capital expenditures, and employment.

UNPROFITABLE OPERATIONS. While Canadian National by the mid-1970s had a substantial core of profitable operations accompanied by a limited number of identifiable money losers, Conrail had an overall cost structure that was out of line with revenues. Clearly, if Conrail was to become viable, broad action was necessary on both the revenue side (through adjustment of rate structures) and on the cost side.

Conrail did identify several areas as especially burdensome, notably commuter operations, relations with Amtrak on the latter's Northeast Corridor, and low-traffic-density branch lines. Conrail was obligated by the Regional Rail Reorganization Act of 1973 to continue running commuter services as long as regional transit authorities designated Conrail as contractor and fully reimbursed it for costs incurred. In addition, it was to provide train and engine crews to Amtrak passenger trains on the Northeast Corridor, while paying Amtrak rent for running its freight trains on the corridor. As a result of what Conrail felt to be unfair allocation of shared right-of-way costs for the corridor and chronic late and disputed payments by commuter authorities, Conrail estimated in 1981 that it was losing between $50 million and $100 million annually on commuter and corridor operations.[77] The Northeast Rail Service Act of 1981 responded to these corporate complaints by removing Conrail's obligation to provide commuter services and Amtrak train and engine crews, by requiring USRA to purchase Conrail's commuter agency accounts receivable, and by establishing a mechanism for resolving Northeast Corridor cost allocation disputes.

Branch lines offered much more discretion to Conrail in cutting losses than the other two areas, and thus reveal more about its corporate strategy. Conrail was forbidden to discontinue branch lines included in

77. See *Consolidated Rail Corporation,* Hearings before the Subcommittee on Commerce, Transportation and Tourism of the House Committee on Energy and Commerce, 97 Cong. 1 sess. (GPO, 1981), pp. 22–24.

the *Final System Plan* for its first two years (until April 1978), but after that time it could use standard ICC procedures for seeking abandonments. In 1978 Conrail announced that it would seek to abandon about one hundred branch lines over the next four years, but the company later decided to defer all abandonment applications for a year.[78] Ostensibly, the delay was to give Congress time to consider deregulation legislation so that Conrail would know how much rate flexibility it might have as an alternative to abandonments. But the decision to delay all abandonments signals a deeper motivation. As one top Conrail official put it in 1984: "It was political. We had too many other fish to fry—deregulation, etc.—to do that [abandon branch lines]." In short, Conrail managers feared upsetting the prospects for deregulation by taking controversial moves that would provide a rallying point for shippers and antagonize legislators.

Not until the Northeast Rail Service Act of 1981 gave Conrail unprecedented authority to abandon lines free from regulatory restraints did the company begin to trim its physical plant. Under the act the Interstate Commerce Commission was required to grant all Conrail abandonment requests made before December 1, 1981, within ninety days, unless an offer was received to purchase the line within ninety days at 75 percent of net liquidation value. The usual ICC trade-offs of "public convenience and necessity" versus carrier financial needs were forgone. Financial considerations alone determined what lines would be abandoned, and Conrail enjoyed complete autonomy in making these decisions. This "easy abandonment" procedure, it should be noted, was not granted to any other railroad.[79] Conrail made extensive use of this procedure. In a dramatic shift from its earlier reluctance to abandon, Conrail cut its route mileage by about 25 percent, from almost 18,000 miles to about 14,000 miles, between 1981 and 1983.

CAPITAL EXPENDITURES. Discontinuance of unprofitable operations, a key feature of an autonomy strategy, requires positive actions to change the status quo (for example, changing rates or abandoning lines). Firms pursuing a security strategy in most cases need only maintain the status quo to protect their political support. In capital allocation, on the other hand, a security strategy requires positive decisions to spend money to maintain or upgrade investments. This is particularly true in the railroad

78. General Accounting Office, *Information on Questions about Conrail's Track Abandonment Program*, Report CED-79-45 (GAO, 1979).
79. Northeast Rail Service Act of 1981, sec. 1156.

industry, where heavy ongoing investment is needed to maintain right-of-way to high service standards. Thus an autonomy strategy can be implemented in part through inaction—noninvestment in unprofitable fixed plant. When a public enterprise such as Conrail pursues a mixture of the autonomy and security strategies, the former should be particularly noticeable in capital allocations, where inaction can accomplish much of what is needed.

The case of Conrail appears to support this argument. Conrail has concentrated its capital spending in areas that would maximize return on investment—notably in main-line track and yard improvements and in rolling stock purchases. Further evidence for Conrail's autonomy orientation is furnished by its behavior in 1979, when it appeared that the firm's federal funding of $3.3 billion would soon be exhausted. Conrail management decided to defer many planned investments, gambling that Congress would soon pass deregulation legislation that would improve its internal cash flow. Conrail took this gamble despite the serious concern expressed by both the United States Railway Association and the General Accounting Office that those deferrals might lower service quality and raise operating costs.[80] A public service–oriented firm presumably would have requested additional federal funding to meet the goals of an "adequate and efficient rail service in the Northeast," as would have a security-oriented firm, but Conrail refused to do so.

Conrail has had success in pursuing an autonomy strategy in capital allocations largely because of congressional restraint in mandating specific (usually protectionist) investments. With one exception—a congressional order in 1978 that Conrail repair and reopen the Poughkeepsie Bridge across the Hudson River (a long-standing request of shippers and legislators in southern New England and New York City)—Congress and the executive branch have given Conrail freedom to renovate its system as the USRA and Conrail see fit.[81] Even in the Poughkeepsie Bridge case, Congress authorized the bridge repair as a separate category from Conrail's normal capital funding process. Moreover, the funds were never appropriated and the bridge remains closed.

80. United States Railway Association, *Annual Report, 1979*, p. 4; and General Accounting Office, *Conrail's Reduced Capital Program Could Jeopardize the Northeast Rail Freight System*, Report CED-80-56 (GAO, 1980).

81. The Poughkeepsie Bridge order is given in United States Railway Association Amendments Act of 1978, sec. 6.

Table 7-5. *Railroad Labor Costs as a Percentage of Operating Revenues, 1978*

Labor Costs	Conrail	All Class I	Differ-ence
Track maintenance	9.5	7.3	2.2
Equipment maintenance	6.1	5.7	0.4
Transportation			
Road train and engine	9.3	9.1	0.2
Yard train and engine	7.5	5.4	2.1
All other transportation	10.4	9.0	1.4
Passenger operations	5.1	1.5	3.6
General and administrative	3.5	3.8	(0.3)
Total wages and salary	**51.4**	**41.8**	**9.6**
Health and welfare cost	3.0	2.6	0.4
Payroll tax	8.4	6.9	1.5
Total labor cost	**62.8**	**51.3**	**11.5**

Source: General Accounting Office, *Contrail's Attempts to Control Labor Costs and Improve Its Labor Productivity*, Report CED-80-61 (GAO, 1980), p. 7.

EMPLOYMENT. Compared with other large U.S. railways, Conrail was created with several major labor productivity handicaps. Table 7-5 shows the ratio of labor costs to revenues for Conrail and other Class I railways in 1978.

There are a number of reasons for this labor productivity gap. Conrail terminates a large portion of traffic, requiring many labor intensive switching movements. The deteriorated condition of Conrail's physical plant at conveyance also lowered labor productivity by slowing down train movements, increasing derailments and equipment failures, and requiring additional employees for capital improvements. Differing collective bargaining agreements—more than 270 separate contracts when Conrail began operation—also inhibited productivity improvement, especially in Conrail's early years.[82] Title V of the 3R act (the labor protection section) also prevented the company from contracting out work where active or furloughed Conrail employees were available to do it. Finally, the labor protection provisions of the act made it difficult for Conrail to adjust its wage bill. The statute mandated separation allowances, moving expenses for relocated employees, and continuation of fringe benefits for current and furloughed employees. Conrail employees with more than five years of service at the time the 3R act was passed

82. See General Accounting Office, *Conrail's Attempt to Control Labor Costs and Improve Its Labor Productivity*, Report CED-80-61 (GAO, 1980).

were given "monthly displacement allowances" (MDAs) that essentially guaranteed their 1974 earnings (adjusted for general wage increases) until age sixty-five. Nor could Conrail shift excess personnel across craft lines to fill available vacancies without their consent.

Congress originally authorized $250 million to pay for Title V benefits, recognizing that Conrail could not hope to fund them in its precarious financial state. But federal funding ran out much earlier than anticipated, in February 1980, in large measure because far fewer employees chose to take separation allowances than had been anticipated.[83] Thus Conrail was stuck temporarily with the remaining labor protection bill, which was estimated to reach between $884 million and $1.7 billion before the last payments were made in the year 2021.[84]

To improve its labor cost–revenue ratio, Conrail had three basic options: it could impose unilateral changes in work rules or compensation, arguing that drastic measures were needed to keep the company afloat; it could seek concessions through collective bargaining; or it could seek legislative relief through Congress. The first of these options was very high-risk because it would almost certainly provoke a strike and lawsuits that Conrail probably would lose. It would also poison relations with the unions and might undercut political support by making Conrail appear highhanded. Not even the Rock Island Railroad attempted such provocative measures until it was on its deathbed, and then its effort failed. Continental Airlines successfully used a claim of impending bankruptcy to break its union contracts, but that bold move did not occur until 1983, several years after the main Conrail battles.

The legislative route also risked alienating Conrail's work force, for it essentially was asking Congress to give legislative sanction to breaking Conrail's contracts. Thus Conrail was reluctant to pursue this option until Title V funding ran out in 1980.

Conrail first attempted to win changes in work rules and train-manning provisions through the collective bargaining process. Although it succeeded in easing freight crew manning rules in 1978, savings proved to be less than had been anticipated.[85] The company also instituted pro-

83. In the program's first three years, more than 67 percent of Title V payments were for MDAs for active and furloughed Conrail employees. General Accounting Office, *Employee Protection Provisions of the Rail Act Need Change*, Report CED-80-16 (GAO, 1979), pp. 8–11.

84. Ibid., pp. 13–16.

85. GAO, *Conrail's Attempt to Control Labor Costs*, pp. 27–29.

grams to improve productivity, but a General Accounting Office report on one of those programs found that Conrail used it to increase the amount of work done rather than to reduce the number of employees "because labor is sensitive to productivity improvement efforts."[86]

Conrail made its first bid for legislative intervention when federal Title V funding ran out in 1980. The Staggers Rail Act of 1980, which authorized another $235 million for Title V, made it clear that Congress was unlikely to provide additional funding when that was used up.[87]

Several changes in Conrail's political environment made the legislative solutions easier to pursue in 1981, however. Legislation in 1979 and 1980 to deal with the collapse of the Milwaukee Road and Rock Island set a precedent for the easing of labor protection accords by Congress. In addition, the Chrysler loan guarantee program of 1979 set a precedent for wage concessions as a condition for federal assistance. Most important, the new administration's push for "controlled transfer" of Conrail to the private sector made the company's survival as an entity dependent upon achieving further autonomy. This, in turn, made labor amenable to concessions. (Conrail estimated that 20,000 of Conrail's freight employees would lose their jobs under a "controlled transfer" and about 40,000 if Conrail were liquidated.)[88]

In response to the Reagan administration's transfer proposal, Conrail presented a major set of labor initiatives to Congress early in 1981.[89] Most of these initiatives were incorporated in the Northeast Rail Service Act, which transferred Northeast Corridor and commuter personnel to Amtrak and regional transit authorities; repealed Title V (including monthly displacement allowances); and replaced it with a labor protection program providing benefits substantially less generous than the rail industry norm (total benefits were capped at $20,000 per employee). The act also created a separate federally funded program to terminate 4,600 Conrail firemen and brakemen and exempted Conrail and Amtrak from state "full crew laws" requiring a minimum number of crew members on trains (usually in excess of what railroads considered necessary for their safe operation). An additional $385 million in federal funding was authorized to fund the new program.[90] In addition, the act contained a

86. Ibid., p. 31.
87. Staggers Rail Act of 1980, sec. 504; and *Staggers Rail Act of 1980*, H. Rept. 96-1430, 96 Cong. 2 sess. (GPO, 1980), p. 133.
88. *Consolidated Rail Corporation*, Hearings, p. 410.
89. Ibid., pp. 399–411.
90. Northeast Rail Service Act of 1981, secs. 1142, 1143. See also Perritt, "Ask and Ye Shall Receive," pp. 359–72.

Table 7-6. *Conrail Employment, 1976–84*

Year	Average number of total employees	Percent change from previous year	Average number of freight service employees	Percent change from previous year
1976	99,827	. . .	n.a.	. . .
1977	94,605	−5.2	81,905	n.a.
1978	91,318	−3.5	78,383	−4.3
1979	87,511	−4.2	74,435	−5.0
1980	79,574	−9.1	65,704	−11.7
1981	70,264	−11.7	56,287	−14.3
1982	57,704	−17.9	45,295	−19.5
1983	39,820	−31.0	38,409	−15.2
1984	39,044	−1.9	n.a.	n.a.

Source: Consolidated Rail Corporation, *Annual Report, 1981*, p. 39; *1982*, p. 5; *1983*, pp. 1, 4; and *1984*, p. 1.
n.a. not available

statutory "goal" that Conrail employees sacrifice $200 million per year over the next three years from the compensation they would have received by applying the national collective bargaining agreement: a more direct command was unnecessary since most of Conrail's unions, anxious to avoid "controlled transfer," had already agreed to the pay cuts in May.[91]

The impact of the Northeast Rail Service Act of 1981 on Conrail employment is clearly evident in table 7-6. The transfer of commuter service employees and Northeast Corridor train and engine crews helped Conrail to cut nonfreight service employment by about 13,000 between 1981 and 1983. The changes in freight service employment were even more striking: a drop of almost 50 percent from 1979 to 1983, with the acceleration of employment decline beginning in the recession year of 1980 and continuing after the passage of the act. Conrail's freight service employment continued its steady decline even in 1983, when traffic rose slightly. Labor productivity also began to show significant improvements despite a secular decline in traffic. The evidence shows, in short, that a determined and powerful administration (as the Reagan administration was in the spring of 1981) and an autonomy-oriented management can impose substantial losses on public enterprise employees, placing them in a worse position with respect to wage levels and protection against income loss than their counterparts in the private sector.

91. Northeast Rail Service Act of 1981, sec. 1134(4). The act called for proportionately equivalent sacrifices by nonagreement personnel. See also *Traffic World,* May 11, 1981, pp. 20–21. Labor agreed to the wage cuts on the condition that Conrail legislation passed by Congress not mandate the dissolution of Conrail. On the role of rail labor in the development of the act, see *Northeast Rail Service Act of 1981,* Hearings, pp. 34–44.

Conclusions

After a very inauspicious beginning, Conrail has freed itself from dependence on federal funds. It almost certainly will be returned to private sector ownership. Many of the same elements that contributed to Canadian National's turnaround are also present in the Conrail case: a transfer of unprofitable operations to other entities, successful enterprise lobbying for regulatory reform, and government payment of "social costs" that the firm could not afford (for example, the revised labor protection accord of the Northeast Rail Service Act).

To explain how such a change could occur, it is not sufficient to look at Conrail's official status as a private, profit-seeking firm. Amtrak had a very similar status when it was created in 1970, but it evolved in a very different direction, as chapter 8 will discuss. Conrail's unique governmental command structure—in particular the buffering effect of having the United States Railroad Association as its primary "monitor"—largely explains the quite remarkable success of this public enterprise. Unlike Amtrak, Conrail did not have to choose to ally itself with either the U.S. Department of Transportation or Congress. Certainly Conrail did display elements of a security strategy in its early reluctance to cut unprofitable operations and to press for work-force reduction. But these were largely status quo–preserving actions rather than the provision of new benefits to build support. Conrail thus avoided being seen as primarily a purveyor of selective benefits, which would have opened floodgates to a torrent of congressional demands.

Conrail could not have shifted to a strategy strongly oriented toward autonomy after 1980 had it not been for the Reagan administration's hard line (and its perceived ability to enforce that hard line) against long-term federal funding. In Rousseauian fashion, the Northeast Rail Service Act "forced Conrail to be free": the probable alternative was dissolution. As with CN, managerial objectives and governmental constraints interacted to produce a new strategic thrust by Conrail. But it was the relaxation of government constraints that was the dominant element in the equation.

Public Enterprise and Industrial Adjustment

The adjustment tasks in the North American rail industry are extraordinarily complex. Technological change and competition from other modes have left firms with excessive physical plants and work forces. Political pressure is strong to retain unprofitable operations on "public needs" grounds. At the same time, there are specific sectors of the industry that offer opportunities for profitable growth in the future. Canadian National Railways and Conrail have attempted to promote industrial adjustment in their respective markets, retrenching in some areas (passenger service and little-used branch lines, for example), while increasing investment in others. The adjustment goals of both enterprises have not been "accelerationist," however. Instead, they have been market-oriented, based not on government objectives but on the objectives of the firm—notably the desire to win increased financial and decisionmaking autonomy. Although the formation of Conrail had accelerationist consequences by merging a number of failing firms, most of the adjustment consequences of that change were not realized until after Conrail's constraints were radically altered in 1981. And both Canadian National and Conrail have tempered their autonomy-oriented behavior (and hence their efforts to promote adjustment) to avoid alienating their owner governments.

For the most part, the owner governments have not pressed the two enterprises to pursue accelerationist behavior (for example, by providing incentives for shared use of fixed plant by multiple carriers and helping to arrange work-force reduction programs with adequate but not extravagant compensation levels). Although both governments have lessened protectionist constraints on their enterprises in recent years, the Canadian government in particular has intervened to force protectionist outcomes when the political costs to Ottawa of adjustment would be high.

The CN and Conrail cases suggest two conclusions. First, governments may have to choose between corporate efficiency and accountability for a public enterprise with relatively weak financial constraints. Enterprise managers will seek to preserve the firm's autonomy, while governments attempt to enlist its efforts on behalf of political and social goals. Giving managers more freedom is likely to increase industrial adjustment. Second, market-oriented behavior by a public enterprise will inevitably rest on a fragile foundation. Regardless of the enterprise's command structure and financial constraints, implementation of market-oriented policies ultimately depends on the owner government's willingness to avoid using the firm for political gain.

Given the strong incentives for governments to force protectionist outcomes on public enterprises, Conrail and CN have had considerable success in implementing market-oriented policies. But this raises another question: if public enterprises act in a way indistinguishable from private sector companies, and if governments seek to modify that behavior only with financial incentives (contracts and subsidies), why should they be in the public sector at all? Why not simply sell them off? A first reason is that privatization may not be a realistic option, either because of public disapproval or because there are no politically acceptable (for example, nonforeign) purchasers. Second, the costs of negotiating contracts are likely to be higher with a private firm, particularly where that firm has a monopoly; if government has the power to compel a public enterprise to undertake certain actions, the firm is likely to negotiate an acceptable compensation arrangement in good faith. Transaction costs are particularly important where quick responsiveness to government policy is required. Finally, public ownership may be valuable as a means of gaining information and expertise that private sector firms in an industry are unwilling to share.

Of course, efficient use of public enterprise to achieve a mixture of industrial adjustment and "public needs" objectives assumes that adjustment goals can be protected from encroachment by public needs goals. The cases of CN and Conrail suggest that public enterprises can have a strong, if incomplete, market orientation given the right set of financial constraints and a "hands off" policy by government. But it is doubtful whether government-owned firms can stress adjustment goals as much as their private sector counterparts can over the long term. Thus if industrial adjustment is a government's dominant goal in a sector, and the distinctive attributes of public enterprise are no longer required to promote public needs objectives, then privatization may indeed be desirable.

In the case of Conrail, the U.S. government has decided that public ownership—which it sought to avoid in the first place—is no longer either desirable or necessary. Whether the Canadian government is willing to pay the political and social costs that privatization of CN might bring (for example, a decline in investment in the railway) to win further gains in efficiency remains to be seen.

Privatization will not end protectionist pressures. At most, it can eliminate one channel through which those pressures are expressed. Governments still must confront the fact that industrial change inevitably imposes concentrated losses. Affected interests will try to gain relief and protection from the state. The electoral incentives of government to respond to those pressures in a protectionist manner remain strong.

CHAPTER EIGHT

Public Enterprise in the Rail Passenger Industry

INTERCITY rail passenger service poses the conflict between enterprise financial viability and "public needs" goals in particularly stark terms. With a few exceptions, rail passenger service loses money everywhere in the world. It faces particularly severe problems in the United States and Canada. The long distances between cities make rail service less competitive with air service than in Europe and Japan. The U.S. and Canadian governments have not kept domestic air fares high to divert passengers to the railways—a common practice of many European governments. And on most routes, passenger trains must share tracks with freight trains, which inhibits high-speed service. Major investment in grade-separated rights-of-way is needed if rail passenger service is to reach its full potential.[1] In both countries, subsidies to rail passenger service are much higher than subsidies to other modes on a per-passenger-mile basis because rail constitutes such a small portion of intercity travel.[2] These subsidies may also undermine the viability of

1. Almost all Amtrak and VIA Rail Canada trains run on tracks owned by freight railways. Amtrak's Northeast Corridor is the main exception. Freight traffic requires a roadbed with less banking in curves and lower maintenance standards than what is optimal for high-speed passenger service. Running fast passenger trains on the same lines as slower freight trains may also pose major scheduling problems, especially on congested or single-track lines.

2. In 1980 rail travel comprised only 0.29 percent of intercity passenger miles in the United States, while auto travel accounted for 83.97 percent; commercial aviation, 13.0 percent; bus, 1.77 percent; and general aviation, 0.96 percent. If federal subsidies are offset by user fees, rail passengers received a subsidy of 23.6 cents per passenger mile in 1980, compared with only 0.1 cents for car and bus passengers and 0.2 cents for users of commercial aviation. Congressional Budget Office, *Federal Subsidies for Rail Passenger Service: An Assessment of Amtrak* (CBO, 1982), pp. 11, 13.

Statistics for all (that is, both intercity and local) passenger travel in Canada in 1979 show auto travel again with the largest share (82 percent), followed by air (15 percent), bus and urban transit (2 percent), and rail (1 percent). Canadian Transport Commission,

227

other common carriers, notably in the bus industry, by diverting passengers and by forcing those carriers to lower fares.

Energy efficiency is one of a number of public needs justifications often cited for preserving and upgrading rail passenger services. But market size and route length determine whether rail travel saves energy. Rail is indeed the most energy efficient form of passenger transportation in its "best case"—high-capacity trains (for example, fifteen cars) with most seats filled, traveling medium-distance routes requiring a minimum of nonrevenue or high weight-per-passenger (dining car, sleeping car) space. But such conditions apply only for travel between very large markets (New York to Washington, for example) and for moderate trip lengths (about 150 to 400 miles). Neither VIA Rail Canada nor the National Railroad Passenger Corporation (Amtrak) approximates these conditions over most of its route system. In 1982 Amtrak averaged only 146 passenger miles per train mile and VIA only 127—about two rail car loads. For low-density markets, buses are far more energy efficient than trains. According to a 1978 General Accounting Office study of eleven poorly performing Amtrak routes, less energy would have been consumed if all passengers on those routes had traveled by car.[3] Several government studies have concluded that Amtrak is a net energy waster outside of the Northeast Corridor.[4] And in the event of an energy emergency that curtailed auto and airplane usage, VIA and Amtrak do not have adequate equipment capacity to be of much assistance.

Other potential advantages of intercity passenger trains—such as their ability to relieve highway and airport congestion, promote tourism, continue operation when other transport modes are disrupted by severe weather, and, in Canada, serve isolated communities and symbolize

---

Transport Review: Trends and Selected Issues (Ottawa: CTC, 1981), p. 20. VIA rail passengers in 1980 were subsidized an average of 11.1 cents per passenger kilometer; air passengers, 2.1 cents; bus passengers, 0.6–0.8 cents; and auto passengers, 0.6–1.0 cents. David McQueen, Aspects of Rail Passenger Policy in Canada, Working Paper 10-84-09 (Ottawa: CTC, Research Branch, 1984).

3. This finding was based on standard assumptions of auto fuel efficiency and ridership per auto. General Accounting Office, Should Amtrak's Highly Unprofitable Routes Be Discontinued? Report CED-79-3 (GAO, 1978), pp. 6–8. See also U.S. Department of Transportation, A Reexamination of the Amtrak Route Structure (DOT, 1978), pp. 3-18 to 3-24.

4. Congressional Budget Office, The Current and Future Savings of Energy Attributable to Amtrak (CBO, 1979); and CBO, Federal Subsidies for Rail Passenger Service, pp. 13–15.

national unity—are more difficult to assess quantitatively. Many, if not most, rail passenger services to low-density markets do not appear to produce social benefits that justify their subsidy costs. Eliminating those services is likely to be perceived by the public as inequitable, however. Thus policymakers and enterprise managers are reluctant to concentrate their efforts on high-density corridor-type operations.

Executive branch policymakers in the United States and Canada saw establishment of a separate public enterprise (or, in the case of Amtrak, a quasi-public enterprise) devoted to rail passenger service as a means to improve the quality of service while lowering costs and cutting the quantity of service offered. Efforts to cut service have been largely unsuccessful: the location-specific nature of passenger train benefits makes them difficult to eliminate in any case. But a public enterprise that specializes in providing those region-specific benefits exacerbates the problem of dropping services. Amtrak and VIA Rail Canada have a very different set of incentives from those of Canadian National Railways (CN) and Conrail, which have a large base of profitable operations. Eliminating passenger trains can help CN and Conrail lower their financial dependence on government. But when Amtrak and VIA cut services, their overall size and base of political support decline as well. Thus executive branch decisionmakers in the two countries will achieve their cost-cutting goals only by imposing those goals over the security interests of the firms.

Amtrak

As chapter 4 pointed out, Amtrak was created in 1970 as the result of a policy impasse between executive branch officials determined to avoid long-term federal expenditures for intercity rail passenger service and legislators who sought to avoid the elimination of that service. The establishment of Amtrak resolved none of these conflicts. Instead, it began a struggle for control of the corporation and its funding level that continues today. The corporation has gone through a cycle from experiment (roughly 1971–73), to institutionalization and expansion (1974–78), back to uncertainty about the corporation's future (1979–81), to relative stability and limited expansion since 1982.

The Rail Passenger Service Act of 1970 did not make Amtrak a true railroad: Amtrak was to run its trains over the tracks of the private sector railroads and contract with those carriers for most aspects of train operations.[5] Amtrak was to operate along designated routes for twenty-six months, after which it could drop those that were unprofitable. But what was intended to be a temporary test of the viability of rail passenger service under new management soon fell by the wayside. Congress directed Amtrak to take over on-train services in 1972 and maintenance operations in 1974.[6] The transfer of the Northeast Corridor from the bankrupt Penn Central to Amtrak in 1976 made Amtrak an operating railroad for the first time, while adding an estimated $68 million to its annual costs.[7] Increasing concern over Amtrak's deficits led to a series of controversial restructuring proposals in the late 1970s and to a Reagan administration budget proposal in 1981 that Amtrak's supporters feared would cause the corporation's demise.

Tremendous conflict over the scope of Amtrak's operations and disadvantageous governmental constraints have forced Amtrak's managers to pursue a security strategy through most of the company's history. To ensure Amtrak's continued existence, they have attempted to build a coalition of support among rail labor, rail passenger groups, state governments, and federal legislators who have Amtrak trains running through their districts. Only very recently has substantial agreement evolved on the scope of Amtrak service.

Government Constraints on Corporate Strategy

FINANCIAL CONSTRAINTS. Because of its virtually complete concentration in the rail passenger business, Amtrak is highly dependent on federal largesse for operating and capital expenditures. (Some state governments have also contracted with Amtrak to share the deficit for specific trains.) Table 8-1 shows Amtrak's revenue shortfalls from 1971 to 1984. Even with interest expenses excluded, revenues have covered less than 50

5. Rail Passenger Service Act of 1970, 84 Stat. 1327, 1332, sec. 305, October 30, 1970.

6. Amtrak Financial Assistance, 86 Stat. 227, 228, sec. 2, June 22, 1972; and Amtrak Improvement Act of 1974, 88 Stat. 1526, 1527, sec. 3, October 28, 1974.

7. The Northeast Corridor (621 miles) consists of the former Penn Central mainline from Washington, D.C., to Boston, with spurs from Philadelphia to Harrisburg and from New Haven to Springfield, Massachusetts. Eighty-three miles of track from Kalamazoo, Michigan, to Michigan City, Indiana, were acquired at the same time. Both were conveyed to Amtrak as a result of the United States Railway Association's *Final System Plan*. The association based its recommendation on the principle that the major user of rail properties should own them.

Table 8-1. *Amtrak Revenue Shortfalls, 1971–84*
Thousands of dollars

Fiscal year	Operating revenue[a]	Operating expense[b]	Deficit	Revenue as percent of expense
1971	22,645	45,301	22,656	50.0
1972	152,709	306,179	153,470	49.9
1973	177,303	319,151	141,848	55.6
1974	240,071	437,932	197,861	54.8
1975	246,549	559,807	313,348	44.0
1976	268,038	674,307	406,269	39.8
Transition quarter	77,167	176,298	99,131	43.7
1977	311,272	832,850	521,578	37.4
1978	313,002	856,598	543,596	36.5
1979	375,120	966,765	591,645	38.8
1980	428,682	1,121,945	693,263	38.2
1981	506,287	1,276,852	770,565	39.7
1982	557,812	1,208,269	650,457	46.2
1983	664,422	1,375,895	711,473	48.3
1984	758,782	1,516,063	757,281	50.0

Sources: George Hilton, *Amtrak: The National Railroad Passenger Corporation* (American Enterprise Institute for Public Policy Research, 1980), p. 58; and Amtrak, *Annual Report*, various years.
a. Includes funds provided by the states for shared-cost routes except for 1979 and 1980.
b. Excludes interest expenses but includes depreciation and general and administrative expenses.

percent of expenses each year since 1975.[8] Moreover, the corporation's funding has been intensely political and highly discretionary; Congress usually approved Amtrak's funding authorization on an annual basis until 1979. Appropriated funds have often been less than those Congress had authorized earlier, forcing Amtrak to choose between cutting its system or returning for a supplemental appropriation. The funding process has made capital planning particularly difficult because Amtrak cannot be sure what its equipment and fixed plant needs will be.

COMMAND STRUCTURE CONSTRAINTS. The impact of Amtrak's financial dependence on the federal government is compounded by its government command structure. What is most striking about that command structure is not merely the strength and dispersion of controls, but their instability. Each Amtrak authorizing act has imposed changes in Amtrak's mandate and in the relation between the corporation and the major agents of control—the Department of Transportation (DOT), the Office of Management and Budget, and Congress. Nor have the changes in Amtrak's

8. Amtrak reports its revenue-expense ratio as greater than 50 percent, but it excludes capital costs from those calculations.

charter been mere bureaucratic shuffles. They reflect important attempts to control Amtrak's direction and policies.

Although the Department of Transportation is the federal funding and supervisory agency for Amtrak, it has few effective levers of control to apply to the corporation on a regular basis. The department can recommend a budget to Congress, but there is no certainty that it will be adopted. Before 1981 only one of the seats on the Amtrak board of directors was reserved for a representative of the department. Department officials generally profess a lack of interest in the Amtrak route structure, the perennial focus of conflict within Congress. They see route selection as the corporation's responsibility rather than their own or Congress's. But they do resent having a substantial portion of the department's budget taken up by an agency over which they have very little control.

Congress has been unwilling to provide the Department of Transportation with more leverage over the corporation, fearing that DOT would make major cuts in the system, as it did when Amtrak was established. Relations deteriorated further during the Ford administration, when Transportation Secretary William Coleman openly expressed his desire to shut Amtrak down. With weak direct controls, the department has had to lobby within Congress for spending limitations and other restrictions on Amtrak.

Many of the changing command structure relationships are reflected in the appointments procedure for Amtrak's board of directors. The Rail Passenger Service Act of 1970 mandated a fifteen-member board, including the secretary of transportation and seven others (one of whom was to be a consumer representative) nominated by the president and confirmed by the Senate; three named by railroads holding common stock in Amtrak; and four named by preferred stockholders, if such stock was ever sold.[9] The Amtrak Improvement Act of 1973 added two more seats for consumer representatives.[10] Revisions in 1976 replaced one presidential nominee with the president of Amtrak as an ex officio member.[11] The thrust of these changes was to undercut executive control over Amtrak.

9. Rail Passenger Service Act of 1970, 84 Stat. 1327, 1330, sec. 303, October 30, 1970.

10. 87 Stat. 548, sec. 3. The same section added the requirement that of the nine members nominated by the president, no more than five could be members of a single political party.

11. Amtrak Improvement Act of 1976, 90 Stat. 2613, 2615, sec. 103, October 19, 1976.

The presidential nomination process has also undercut attempts by the Department of Transportation to control Amtrak. Nominees have tended to be party loyalists appointed by the White House on a patronage basis rather than on the basis of policy expertise or loyalty to administration policy. As one DOT official interviewed in 1980 put it: "There is only one director among those we appoint to whom we can say, 'This is the policy of the Administration.' The easiest way to get the others to vote the way we want is to tell them to vote the opposite." As in the case of Canadian National Railways, the appointment of individuals with little expertise led to deference to management and weak board input into corporate policy. Finally, it also led to the isolation of DOT on the board, particularly during the Coleman years. As one former Amtrak official said, "We had a lot of 11 to 1 votes on the Board."

Changes in the Amtrak board enacted by the Amtrak Improvement Act of 1981 reflect weakening political support for Amtrak's independence. The board was cut to nine members, including the Amtrak president (who now serves as board chairman) and the secretary of transportation ex officio. The secretary appoints an additional two members (without Senate confirmation) in his or her capacity as holder of Amtrak preferred stock. Three others are nominated by the president from specific interests (one suggested by the Railway Labor Executives' Association, one state governor, and one "representative of business with an interest in rail transportation"), all subject to Senate confirmation. Two others represent commuter authorities doing business with Amtrak.[12] The net impact has been to strengthen the position of the Department of Transportation on the Amtrak board, but still leave it in the minority.

The Office of Management and Budget, the executive branch's spending watchdog, has been the most persistent government critic of Amtrak. The corporation's budgetary process, in turn, clearly reveals the divisions and shifts within Amtrak's governmental command structure. Normally, government agencies submit their budgets and five-year financial projections to their respective departments and then to the Office of Management and Budget before presentation to Congress. From 1973 to 1978, however, Amtrak was forbidden by statute from submitting "any legislative recommendation, proposed testimony, or

12. Representation of common stockholders (that is, the three railroads that "purchased" Amtrak stock in 1970) and consumer representatives was eliminated by the 1981 act. Omnibus Reconciliation Act of 1981, Title XI, Subtitle F (Amtrak Improvement Act of 1981), 95 Stat. 357, 689, sec. 1170, August 13, 1981.

comments on legislation" to the president, DOT, or OMB without concurrently giving a copy to Congress.[13] This weakened OMB control over Amtrak's budget, since Amtrak's supporters in Congress were able to draw on Amtrak's own budget proposals when criticizing those of the administration.[14] The Nixon and Ford administrations retaliated by impounding Amtrak grant funds on several occasions. Although Amtrak has been required since 1978 to follow the same budgetary procedures as other federal agencies, DOT officials interviewed for this study complained in strong terms that Amtrak has ignored that requirement.

Congress has been the major arena for conflict over Amtrak and an independent source of commands as well. Annual Amtrak funding requests have provided legislators a vehicle for exercising their power to curry favor with executive agencies and with Amtrak. The power of individual legislators and committees to direct Amtrak's future became evident even before Amtrak began operations on May 1, 1971. Senate Majority Leader Mike Mansfield threatened to hold up indefinitely Senate confirmation of Amtrak's board of directors unless a train running through his home state of Montana was restored. It was.[15] Other trains were added by both Amtrak and the administration as a means of winning the support of individual legislators. The Committee on Commerce, Science and Transportation, particularly its Subcommittee on Surface Transportation, has jurisdiction over Amtrak in the Senate; while in the House, the Committee on Energy and Commerce, particularly its Subcommittee on Transportation and Commerce, has jurisdiction.[16] The transportation subcommittees of the House and Senate appropriations committees also influence Amtrak's fate.

To gain funding, Amtrak must win overall legislative majorities as well as placate specialized committees. It has drawn strong lobbying support from the National Association of Railroad Passengers, a highly organized group of rail enthusiasts, and from the railroad brotherhoods.

13. Amtrak Improvement Act of 1973, 87 Stat. 548, sec. 12, November 3, 1973. The measure was repealed by the Amtrak Improvement Act of 1978, 92 Stat. 923, sec. 3, October 5, 1978.

14. See DOT, *A Reexamination of the Amtrak Route Structure*, pp. 7-41 to 7-46.

15. *National Railroad Passenger Corporation*, Hearings before the Subcommittee on Surface Transportation of the Senate Committee on Commerce, 92 Cong. 1 sess. (Government Printing Office, 1971), pp. 17–18. Senator Mansfield retired in 1976. The train, the North Coast Hiawatha, was eliminated in the 1979 Amtrak route restructuring.

16. Until the 97th Congress, the Energy and Commerce Committee was called the Committee on Interstate and Foreign Commerce.

Critics include the National Taxpayers' Union and the American Bus Association, which charges that subsidized competition is disrupting the intercity bus industry.[17]

Amtrak's rising deficits and inability to capture an increasing share of the intercity passenger market made Amtrak funding increasingly contentious in the late 1970s. The Department of Transportation, in particular, favored concentrating Amtrak's resources on corridors of high population density.[18] Yet service cutbacks would undercut the congressional support Amtrak needed to meet its high fixed costs, notably in the Northeast Corridor. As Ohio Congressman Donald J. Pease remarked in 1979 hearings on DOT's proposed cuts in Amtrak service:

> If you cut the Amtrak route structure by 43 percent, to a large extent you are also cutting support in Congress for Amtrak by 43 percent. . . . And to the extent that this [restructured] system saves a relatively small amount of money by cutting out service to a great many States and to a great many Congressional districts, it undercuts the entire support in Congress in the future of Amtrak.[19]

Once cuts start being made in the Amtrak system, declining political support can threaten its very survival. For Amtrak, unlike Conrail and CN, maximizing political support must be the paramount concern in corporate strategy and policy.

The conflicting goals of Amtrak's various political masters and the corporation's own changing political fortunes are evident in the content of policy guidelines set for Amtrak. Congress did not modify Amtrak's status as a "for profit" corporation until 1978, but long before then other requirements, notably that Amtrak operate a "national system" (necessitating operation of high-cost, long-distance trains), made the profitability objective impossible to achieve. Additional legislative provisions

17. A study by the General Accounting Office found that the bus industry has been declining for a number of reasons. The establishment of Amtrak hurt the bus industry in selected markets (for example, through the elimination of differentials between bus and rail fares in the Northeast Corridor). General Accounting Office, *Amtrak's Economic Impact on the Intercity Bus Industry,* Report PAD-79-32 (GAO, 1979).

18. See, for example, the statement of the deputy secretary of the Department of Transportation, John Barnum, in *Criteria and Procedures for Making Route and Service Decisions by Amtrak,* Hearings before the Subcommittee on Surface Transportation of the Senate Committee on Commerce, Science and Transportation, 94 Cong. 2 sess. (GPO, 1976), pp. 48–49.

19. *Amtrak Fiscal Year 1980 Authorization and Amtrak Route Restructuring,* Hearings before the Subcommittee on Transportation and Commerce of the House Committee on Interstate and Foreign Commerce, 96 Cong. 1 sess. (GPO, 1979), p. 90.

added in the 1970s further undermined the possibility of Amtrak becoming self-sufficient. In 1974, for example, legislators from rural states had a provision inserted in the Rail Passenger Service Act stating that Amtrak "should give priority to experimental routes designed to extend intercity rail passenger service to the major population center of each of the contiguous 48 states which does not have such service to any large population area."[20] Equality of access was thus added to efficiency considerations as the legislative criterion for expanding the Amtrak system.

By the late 1970s, the pendulum began to swing back, as minimum performance criteria were enacted for the corporation as a whole and for individual Amtrak trains. Most notably, the Amtrak Reorganization Act of 1979 set a goal of 44 percent cost recovery (excluding depreciation) by 1982 and 50 percent by 1985.[21] The Passenger Railroad Rebuilding Act of 1980 added a goal of full cost recovery for Northeast Corridor passenger operations by 1987.[22] Finally, the Amtrak Improvement Act of 1981, at the request of the Reagan administration, advanced the 50 percent system-wide cost recovery goal to 1982 and made it a statutory requirement.[23]

In the case of Amtrak, Congress has not been content to set broad policy guidelines, even conflicting ones. Many of the commands imbedded in Amtrak legislation concern matters over which firms normally have discretion. Congress has dictated specific train routes, limited the Amtrak president's salary, subjected Amtrak to Freedom of Information Act requests, required Amtrak to develop a special fare program for elderly and handicapped passengers, and limited the company's expenditures on food and beverage service aboard Amtrak trains. Some legislative provisions have been trivial to the point of inanity—for example, prohibiting the use of federal funds to lease cars for Amtrak officers other than the president.[24] In short, efforts by Amtrak's government masters to impose conflicting goals on the corporation have led to an escalating battle to lessen Amtrak's discretion. As a result, Amtrak

20. Amtrak Improvement Act of 1974, 88 Stat. 1526, 1527, sec. 5.
21. 93 Stat. 537, 538, sec. 103, September 29, 1979.
22. Title II, 94 Stat. 399, 412, sec. 205, May 30, 1980.
23. 95 Stat. 357, 695, sec. 1183, August 13, 1981. Capital costs were excluded from the total, and Amtrak was allowed to include subsidies from states and transit authorities as revenue.
24. Department of Transportation and Related Agencies Appropriations Act, 91 Stat. 402, 410, August 2, 1977.

has been saddled with an overly detailed and contradictory mandate that has shifted as political support for the corporation changed.

Corporate Strategy

Gaining a more stable operating environment and political support for the corporation's survival have been very real concerns for Amtrak management. These concerns were stated clearly by Amtrak President Alan Boyd in 1979:

> Amtrak started off, I thought, as a brave new idea in 1971 and we have now arrived back at ground zero. The issues which were debated at the time Amtrak was created are being debated again today and in the same context. Why an Amtrak? How big should it be? How much money should the public put in it? . . . I need some stability. Either please make up your mind to support a rail passenger service or put us out of our misery.[25]

Amtrak's high dependence on federal funds and its divided command structure make an autonomy-oriented strategy impractical for achieving these goals. But what of the other two strategies, public service and security? Public service–oriented companies develop or follow externally imposed trade-offs among financial and social objectives. Political alliances are pursued for policy ends. Security-oriented companies emphasize survival and growth over policy goals. In practice, the two strategies may overlap significantly. Managers of state enterprises are likely to see a close connection between an organization's welfare and the public interest, and alliances that serve policy ends may be helpful in building political support. Distinguishing strategies in the case of Amtrak is also made more difficult by the fact that legislation determines many corporate decisions such as route structure. Although Amtrak may have little discretion once Congress has acted, its influence and strategy may have played a major role in shaping that legislation. Hence the formation of federal policy must be considered in addition to its implementation by the corporation.

In attempting to distinguish between public service and security strategies, it is helpful to concentrate first on situations in which the two strategies dictate differing behavior. In these situations, does Amtrak act in ways that advance its policy interests, or is it more interested in building a stable coalition of support and "base" of operations?

25. *Amtrak Fiscal Year 1980 Authorization and Amtrak Route Restructuring,* Hearings, p. 149.

Second, how much emphasis is given to each of the goals in its mandate when they come in conflict with one another? If Amtrak consistently stresses the parts of its mandate that solidify and build the firm's coalition of support while sacrificing those that do not, a security strategy is indicated. Finally, does Amtrak change its policy goals as the political winds shift? This again indicates a security strategy. When those tests are used, Amtrak's actions appear most consistent with a security strategy.

The development of a public service strategy for Amtrak has been hindered by internal instability. Since 1971 Amtrak has had four presidents: Roger Lewis (1971–75), Paul Reistrup (1975–78), Alan Boyd (1978–82), and Graham Claytor (1982–). Lewis stressed Amtrak's experimental nature and looked to the Department of Transportation for policy direction.[26] As DOT concern over budget deficits grew, his successors began to place more emphasis on maintaining political support in Congress.

In 1976 Amtrak's board of directors listed five goals for the corporation: (1) provide modern, safe, intercity rail passenger service, (2) develop and maintain an integrated national rail passenger system, (3) operate efficiently on a "for profit" basis, (4) reduce congestion, conserve energy, and preserve the environment, and (5) serve the public convenience and necessity.[27] Through most of the 1970s, Amtrak emphasized route and ridership growth and its mandate to provide a nationwide passenger service over the goal of profitability. The impact of the 1979 requirement that Amtrak eventually meet 50 percent of its operating costs through revenues was thus summarized by one Amtrak planner: "Decision-making has become very clear. If a project meets over 50 percent of its costs then it is considered to contribute to earnings, so you go ahead." In short, revenue goals were to be minimally satisfied, while growth was pursued. Differences in the institutional perspectives of Amtrak and the Department of Transportation were succinctly stated by one DOT official in a 1980 interview: "One Amtrak officer told us that their strategy could be summed up in one word: 'grow.' I told him that our strategy is one three letter word: 'why?' "

26. See, for example, Lewis's statement in *Amtrak Oversight and Authorization,* Hearings before the Subcommittee on Surface Transportation of the Senate Committee on Commerce, 93 Cong. 1 sess. (GPO, 1973), p. 153.

27. *Criteria and Procedures for Making Route and Service Decisions by Amtrak,* Hearings, pp. 44–45.

The corporation has interpreted other goals in such a manner as to maintain or expand its current size. For example, Amtrak officials repeatedly stress that in the "best case," rail travel is the most energy efficient means of transportation, neglecting to add that few of Amtrak's operations outside of the Northeast Corridor could ever approximate the best case.[28] Amtrak has resisted efforts to reduce its service to a few corridors of high population density, believing, as Congressman Pease stated, that this would fatally undercut the corporation's support.[29]

Amtrak's growth strategy culminated in a "mission statement" issued by the corporation's board in December 1978.[30] The statement did not really outline a clear mission or set of trade-offs among the corporation's conflicting objectives, but it did suggest a new command structure that would have strengthened Amtrak's ties to Congress, the institution that had shown the greatest support for Amtrak's growth, while minimizing the power of the more hostile Department of Transportation and Office of Management and Budget.[31] In large measure, the mission statement was a response to the extensive Amtrak route cuts (to be discussed in the next section) recommended by the Department of Transportation. It was never seriously considered by Congress, and when the Reagan administration moved to tighten DOT control over Amtrak in 1981, the mission statement became a dead letter.

The bruising political battles of 1979 and 1981 led Amtrak to modify its growth orientation. Under president Graham Claytor, Amtrak has focused its attention on stabilizing support for the current system while

28. See the conflicting statements by Secretary of Transportation Brock Adams and Amtrak President Alan Boyd in *Amtrak Fiscal Year 1980 Authorization and Amtrak Route Restructuring,* Hearings, pp. 124–25, 151–53. Department officials stressed that because rail passenger service constitutes only about 1 percent of intercity passenger miles, the best hope for improving transportation energy efficiency lies in improving auto gasoline mileage.

29. General Accounting Office, *Amtrak's Subsidy Needs Cannot Be Reduced without Reducing Service,* Report CED-78-86 (GAO, 1978), p. 49.

30. See *Railway Age,* January 8, 1979, pp. 18–19; and *New York Times,* December 14, 1978.

31. The mission statement recommended the establishment of a contractual relationship between Amtrak and Congress. Congress would set a basic system with Amtrak's advice. Amtrak would be given a fixed level of funding to operate this system. The statement also recommended that Amtrak be given authority to add or delete routes from its network; Amtrak could apply for funding for supplementary appropriations for specific additional routes if they could not be funded within the basic congressional grant. Finally, the mission statement proposed that the secretary of transportation be eliminated from the Amtrak board.

meeting its legislative mandate to reduce subsidies: in Claytor's words, "to take what we've got and make it work."[32] In short, throughout its history, Amtrak has interpreted its mandate in ways most consistent with its security interests. It has shifted its emphasis as its political support has waxed and waned.

Policies and Outcomes

The argument that Amtrak has subordinated public service to security objectives whenever the two strategies have conflicted will be examined for three specific policy areas: unprofitable operations, capital expenditures, and employment.

UNPROFITABLE OPERATIONS. Amtrak has vacillated between an overall policy of favoring growth and temporary support for cutbacks. The corporation has tried to adjust to the prevailing political climate, but this is difficult to do when it is receiving concurrent contradictory orders and its political support is changing rapidly.

Amtrak's route mileage, train mileage, and number of passengers carried increased substantially through the early 1970s, as shown in table 8-2. During the 1973–74 and 1979 gasoline shortages, the corporation scored major traffic gains that it was unable to maintain. Nor was it able to increase significantly its minute share of the intercity passenger market. Moreover, the crucial statistic of passenger miles per train mile fell during most of Amtrak's growth phase, in large measure because new routes added to the Amtrak system were poor performers.

For much of its brief existence, Amtrak has had little control over the extent of its service. The original "basic system" was frozen until 1976, and experimental routes added by Congress were frozen until early in 1977. In 1975 Amtrak adopted a set of criteria for deleting and adding routes, once the route freeze expired. Following the criteria raised a political problem, however. The worst performing trains in the Amtrak system were generally trains with backing from powerful legislators. Not until March 1977 was Amtrak's first study of a low-performance train completed. Rather than dropping that train, Amtrak shortened and rerouted it, while preserving the most politically volatile portion of its run, the section through West Virginia—home of the new Senate majority leader, Robert Byrd, and of the chairman of the House Interstate and

32. McQueen, *Aspects of Rail Passenger Policy*, p. 83.

Table 8-2. *Amtrak Operating Statistics, 1972–84*

Fiscal year	System route miles (thousands)	Stations served	Passengers carried (millions)	Passenger miles (millions)	Train miles (millions)	Passenger miles per train mile
1972	23	440	16.6[a]	3,038[a]	26	117
1973	22	451	16.9[a]	3,806[a]	27	141
1974	24	473	18.7	4,484	29	155
1975	26	484	17.4	3,956	30	132
1976	26	495	18.2	4,155	30.98	134.1
1977	26	524	19.2	4,333	32.97	131.4
1978	26	543	18.9	4,029	32.37	124.5
1979	27	571	21.4	4,915	32.38	151.8
1980	24	525	21.2	4,582	29.43	155.7
1981	24	525	20.6	4,762	30.97	153.8
1982	23	506	19.0	4,172	28.66	145.6
1983	24	497	19.0	4,246	29.12	145.8
1984	24	510	19.0	4,552	28.97	157.1

Sources: For 1972–75, National Railroad Passenger Corporation, *Background on Amtrak,* September 1978; for 1976–84, Amtrak, *Annual Report,* various years.
a. Calendar year.

Foreign Commerce Committee, Harley Staggers. (Staggers was so successful in gaining Amtrak service for his home state that the various trains running through West Virginia were known among Amtrak senior managers as "Harley Staggers Mark I," "Harley Staggers Mark II," and so on. He retired from the House in 1980.) The second route study was not completed until October 1977, two years after the criteria were adopted.[33]

It seems clear that Amtrak was, if not actively stalling on route reductions, at the very least reluctant to offend its supporters by cutting routes hastily. A former top Amtrak officer bluntly confirmed this interpretation: "We feared a DOT plan to gut Amtrak. In that situation, we knew we would need the support of all congressmen." Cutting routes would eat into that base of political support.

Amtrak could not maintain the support of all legislators, however. Congressional critics accused the corporation of living beyond its budget and then threatening massive route cuts if Congress did not approve

33. For a summary of the route criteria and Amtrak's implementation of those criteria, see GAO, *Should Amtrak's Highly Unprofitable Routes Be Discontinued?* chap. 3.

Figure 8-1. *Amtrak Route Structure*

A. Structure before the 1979 changes

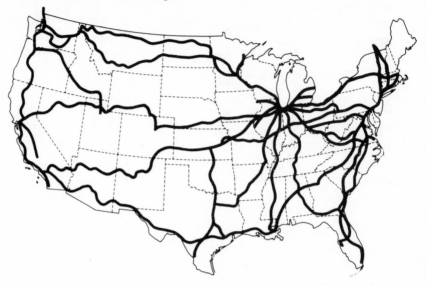

B. Structure proposed by the Department of Transportation, 1979 [a]

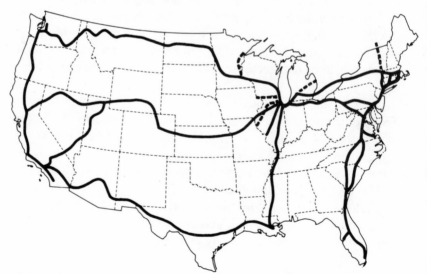

Source: U.S. Department of Transportation, *Final Report to Congress on the Amtrak Route System* (DOT, 1979), pp. 2-4, 4-4.

a. Dashed lines indicate state-assisted services to be retained if states continue subsidies.

supplemental appropriations.[34] In November 1977 the House and Senate appropriations committees ordered a new study of the Amtrak route structure by the only body that was willing to take responsibility for cuts in service, the Department of Transportation.[35] The request for a new DOT route study was later incorporated into the Amtrak Improvement Act of 1978, which required that Amtrak implement the DOT rate proposal once it was approved by Congress.

The method of congressional approval became an important source of conflict between Amtrak's proponents and critics. Chairman Staggers proposed that both the House and Senate approve the DOT recommendations before they went into effect; Russell Long, chairman of the Senate Subcommittee on Surface Transportation, proposed that they go into effect immediately unless one house vetoed the proposal within sixty days of receiving it. Significantly, Amtrak favored the Staggers proposal, which would have provided greater protection against cuts than the Senate proposal.[36] The act followed the Senate version, although it extended the deadline for a disapproval resolution to ninety days. Service cutbacks were delayed until after October 1, 1979. This gave Congress an opportunity to review the route structure as it authorized Amtrak's fiscal 1980 budget.

The final DOT plan, issued in January 1979, called for cutting 43 percent of Amtrak's total route miles (see figure 8-1). The plan was estimated to reduce deficits 23 percent over those in the existing system.[37]

34. Ann Cooper, "Congress Forbids Amtrak to Cut Train Service," *Congressional Quarterly Weekly Report*, November 12, 1977, pp. 2403–04.

35. See H. Rept. 95-812, 95 Cong. 1 sess. (GPO, 1977); and H. Rept. 95-829, 95 Cong. 1 sess. (GPO, 1977).

36. *National Railroad Passenger Corporation Authorization Act of 1978*, Hearings before the Subcommittee on Surface Transportation of the Senate Committee on Commerce, Science and Transportation, 95 Cong. 2 sess. (GPO, 1978), p. 9; and *Amtrak Authorization*, Hearings before the Subcommittee on Transportation and Commerce of the House Committee on Interstate and Foreign Commerce, 95 Cong. 2 sess. (GPO, 1978), pp. 9, 163.

37. The preliminary DOT plan issued in May 1978 called for cutbacks of about 30 percent in the Amtrak route structure, while retaining a limited national system. Public hearings were then held by the Interstate Commerce Commission's Rail Services Planning Office, which recommended a larger system. Meanwhile, the Office of Management and Budget imposed a ceiling of $450 million on Amtrak operating grants. Although this ceiling was lifted after an appeal by Secretary of Transportation Brock Adams to the White House, the final DOT plan made further cuts to fit within the revised OMB ceiling of $550 million. See U.S. Department of Transportation, *A Reexamination of the Amtrak Route Structure* (DOT, 1978); and *Final Report to the*

At first it appeared that Congress would agree to the department's plan. Amtrak's president publicly supported the proposal, and neither house passed a resolution of disapproval by the legislative deadline. Then the gasoline shortage of spring and early summer 1979 caused Amtrak ridership to rise significantly, placing severe pressure on Congress to preserve more trains. Amtrak management changed its position as well. Feeling that the DOT plan was politically dead, Amtrak representatives worked behind the scenes with congressional staff and legislators to develop a plan that would provide more service than the DOT plan, while stabilizing political support for the corporation. This did not sit well with the department. As one DOT official put it: "They walked out from under us. Boyd said okay to the plan in the hearings but he had his people all over the Hill trying to change it. That is the source of a lot of the current tension between Amtrak and DOT."

Both the House and Senate passed bills that added significantly to the DOT route proposal. The Amtrak Reorganization Act of 1979 cut only the worst performing trains, reducing Amtrak route mileage by 14 percent. The act appears on superficial examination to create an objective formula for train retention, but there were in fact no fewer than nine separate sets of criteria under which service could be retained, with many of the categories designed around specific trains.[38]

Congress on the Amtrak Route System (DOT, 1979). See also Interstate Commerce Commission, *Evaluation Report of the Secretary of Transportation's Preliminary Recommendations on Amtrak's Route Structure* (ICC, 1978). For a discussion of the OMB ceiling, see *New York Times,* December 5, 1978.

Because many of the routes scheduled for elimination under the DOT final plan were lightly patronized or long-haul trains, there would have been only about a 20 percent reduction in the number of passenger miles and a 10 percent reduction in passenger trips.

38. The following trains were to be retained under the act. (1) All trains recommended in the secretary's final report (sec. 104). (2) All long-distance trains meeting specified criteria (150 passenger miles per train mile and short-term avoidable loss of no more than 7 cents per passenger mile, both projected for fiscal 1980) (sec. 119). (3) All short-distance trains meeting specified criteria (80 passenger miles per train mile and short-term avoidable loss no greater than 9 cents per passenger mile, both projected for fiscal 1980) (sec. 119). (4) An additional long-distance train in each quadrant of the country, if one had not been added back under the second criterion. This provision saved the *Inter-American* from Chicago to Houston and Laredo (sec. 119). (5) Services that states, groups of states, or regional authorities were willing to partially subsidize at a lower percentage rate than had been required previously (sec. 115). (6) Trains recommended in the secretary's report for restructuring, until such time as equal or better track facilities were available (sec. 127). This provision saved two of three trains through West Virginia. (7) Additional short-distance "demonstration" routes. Queries placed in

Conflict over the Amtrak route structure recurred in 1981. After the inauguration of President Reagan, the Office of Management and Budget sought to impose a $613 million ceiling on federal subsidies to the corporation in fiscal 1982—$380 million less than what President Jimmy Carter had proposed. The funding would be further reduced the following year and gradually phased out. Rather than mandating specific route cuts, as in 1979, Amtrak would be given discretion to cut routes to fit the budget figure. Amtrak's management immediately criticized the administration's proposal. Amtrak charged that because of labor protection payments, fixed operating costs, and contractually obligated capital expenditures, Reagan's budget ceiling would force the shutdown of all routes outside the Northeast Corridor.[39] Although the Department of Transportation disputed that claim, it proved to be an effective strategy. The Republican-controlled Senate agreed to the administration's budget ceiling, but the House did not. After Amtrak announced a series of economy moves, the Senate Commerce Committee agreed to increase funding. The final reconciliation bill followed the House provisions. It provided for a ceiling of $735 million in fiscal 1982 and $788 million in fiscal 1983. In addition, the bill deferred interest payments from Amtrak totaling $182 million over the two years. This funding allowed Amtrak to continue more than 90 percent of the system then in operation.[40] The power of West Virginians in Amtrak politics was reconfirmed once again in November as Senate Majority Leader Robert Byrd forced reinstitution of a route through his state.[41]

Following the 1981 budget battle, Amtrak enjoyed a three-year respite. The Reagan administration was unwilling to expend the political capital

the *Congressional Record* (August 1, 1979, pp. 11115–16) by Senators Bayh of Indiana and Magnuson of Washington directed service from Seattle to Vancouver and from Chicago to Indianapolis under this section (sec. 119). Senator Magnuson was chairman of the Senate Appropriations Committee, and Senator Bayh chaired its Subcommittee on Transportation. (8) Commuter trains operated by Amtrak were protected until April 1, 1981 (sec. 115). (9) A Conrail-operated Chicago–Valparaiso commuter route threatened with discontinuance was converted into an Amtrak train and protected until April 1, 1981 (sec. 115). For those categories involving performance criteria (loss per passenger mile, passenger miles per train mile), Amtrak was directed to use ridership data artificially inflated by the gasoline shortage of spring–summer 1979.

39. See the statements of Amtrak President Alan Boyd and Federal Railroad Administrator Robert Blanchette in *Amtrak Reauthorization,* Hearings before the Subcommittee on Surface Transportation of the Senate Committee on Commerce, Science and Transportation, 97 Cong. 1 sess. (GPO, 1981).

40. For details on the route cuts, see *New York Times,* August 27, 1981.

41. *New York Times,* December 28, 1981.

needed to press a major cutback initiative since it had enjoyed so little success in its first attempt. After Reagan's reelection, however, the administration made an even more dramatic proposal: a complete end to Amtrak subsidies at the end of fiscal 1985, which would have shut down service even on the Northeast Corridor. Again it was the Office of Management and Budget, Amtrak's perennial adversary, that led the attack. OMB overruled a Department of Transportation budget request that would have left Amtrak untouched.[42]

As in 1981, Amtrak management criticized the administration's plan, arguing that it would result in the waste of more than $3 billion (after depreciation) of federal investment in the corporation and drastically increase costs for freight railways and commuter agencies that use Amtrak's Northeast Corridor. President Claytor suggested that the company's budget be frozen at the previous year's level of $684 million rather than eliminated altogether.[43] Congress rejected the administration's request to kill Amtrak, but it did agree in its fiscal 1986 budget resolution to trim Amtrak funding by 15 percent.[44]

Amtrak's overall record in cutting unprofitable operations is poor. On those occasions when it has had flexibility to cut operations that have performed poorly by both economic and social criteria, the corporation has generally been unwilling to use it. The objective criteria specified in the Amtrak Reorganization Act of 1979 have been interpreted by the corporation in such a way as to maximize service retention.[45] Amtrak

42. The department's first request for $765 million for Amtrak was rejected by OMB, as was its later request of $608 million. Reginald Stuart, "Stockman Presses Senators to End Amtrak Subsidy," *New York Times,* April 30, 1985.

43. Testimony of Graham Claytor before the Subcommittee on Commerce, Transportation and Tourism of the House Committee on Energy, Commerce and Tourism, March 14, 1985. Claytor estimated the total increased costs to other carriers to continue their operations on the Washington–New York section of the corridor at $164 million, of which the greatest shares would be borne by Conrail ($82 million) and New Jersey Transit ($47 million).

44. Robert Pear, "Compromise Avoids Major Cuts in Benefits," *New York Times,* August 2, 1985. The final budget resolution was a compromise between the Senate's proposal, which had called for phased cuts in Amtrak subsidies of 12 percent, 25 percent, and 40 percent in fiscal 1986, 1987, and 1988, respectively, and the House plan, which had proposed only a one-year 10 percent funding cut for Amtrak.

45. An example of Amtrak's interpretation of statutory criteria to maximize service retention is the Salt Lake City–Portland–Seattle *Pioneer,* which goes through Oregon, home state of Bob Packwood, the former chairman of the Senate Commerce Committee. The *Pioneer* carried 78 passengers per train mile in 1980, far below the legislative criterion of 150. Beginning in 1981, *Pioneer* cars were added to the Chicago–Ogden

has not developed clear trade-offs between goals, because they might threaten operations needed to maintain the corporation's coalition of political support. Nor has Amtrak pressed strongly for increased discretion in making service cutbacks, preferring that someone else take the political heat. It has favored cutbacks only when waning political support appeared to dictate such a strategy, and it has sought to minimize those cutbacks. In short, when public service considerations have conflicted with security considerations, Amtrak management has almost always chosen the latter.

In recent years Amtrak's system has reflected swings in the electoral cycle. The effect appears surprising at first glance, however. As table 8-2 shows, cutbacks have occurred in even-numbered (election) years. Why this unexpected correlation? Debates over Amtrak cutbacks generally occur in the spring after congressional elections, when the executive branch is more willing to press for cuts, and Congress is more willing to grant them. The cuts take effect at the beginning of Amtrak's next fiscal year (even-numbered), which coincides with the beginning of the federal fiscal year on October 1 (of the odd-numbered year). Thus debate and cutbacks are completed more than thirteen months before the next congressional election.

CAPITAL EXPENDITURES. A security-oriented public enterprise will allocate capital on the basis of political returns; a public service–oriented enterprise will allocate capital based on specific trade-offs among goals in the firm's mandate. These two criteria may overlap.[46] But when they conflict, Amtrak has interpreted its mandate in such a way as to maximize its security.

The obvious sorts of patronage associated with political support building, such as "pork barrel" projects in powerful legislators' districts, are generally not available to Amtrak because it owns track only in the

portion of the San Francisco *Zephyr*. By counting all traffic on the through (Chicago–Seattle) cars as "incremental passenger miles" per "incremental (Salt Lake City–Seattle) train mile," traffic statistics on the *Pioneer* were projected to rise to 164 passenger miles per train mile in 1982, higher than that of the *Zephyr* itself, but allowing both trains to be retained. *Amtrak Reauthorization*, Hearings, p. 44.

46. For example, Amtrak's emphasis on modernization of equipment on all routes is consistent with its statutory mandate to provide "modern, safe service" over a national system. Modernization also has the political advantages of justifying budget increases and excusing Amtrak's past deficits as the result of insufficient government support. It follows directly from the "discouragement hypothesis" that the intercity rail passenger industry declined primarily because of bad service rather than because of any inability to compete for the transportation dollar.

Northeast Corridor and a short segment in Michigan and Indiana. Moreover, the massive Northeast Corridor Improvement Project (NECIP) has been managed by DOT rather than Amtrak.[47] But this has not stopped Amtrak from playing politics. The corporation has occasionally allocated new equipment to the districts of powerful legislators, even where the equipment was clearly ill-suited.[48]

More important is the corporation's attempt to build a political base of support in Congress. Amtrak has also backed programs that spread benefits widely, first through equipment modernization, and later through "emerging corridors." Equipment modernization was the first priority. Virtually the entire Amtrak fleet had been replaced or rebuilt by 1981. While the new equipment was sorely needed to improve the quality of service and to lower operating costs, its political dividends were unmistakable. When Amtrak managers were fighting the Reagan administration's proposed budget cuts in 1981, they stressed repeatedly that if Amtrak were reduced to serving only the Northeast Corridor, its 284 new bilevel cars, which were built for western routes at a cost of $313 million, could not meet tunnel clearances on the corridor and would be useless.

The arrival of new equipment did not substantially improve Amtrak's financial performance, however. After the passage of the Amtrak Improvement Act of 1978, it became obvious that the corporation's nationwide system of conventional services (that is, one or two trains per day on a route) was likely to shrink rather than grow. Amtrak thus began to seek funding for investment in corridor operations. These frequent, high-speed operations over relatively short distances (generally 100 to 300 miles) offer the greatest potential energy benefits because they minimize requirements for lounge, dining, and sleeping car space. But corridors also pose operating and financial problems: the more trains the more interference with freight operations. The railroads over which Amtrak operates have been reluctant to grant rights for more frequent service.[49] Corridor service works best on a "dedicated" right-of-way

47. See General Accounting Office, *Problems in the Northeast Corridor Railway Improvement Project*, Report CED-79-38 (GAO, 1979).

48. The major example is use of a Turbotrain on a route from Washington, D.C., to Parkersburg, West Virginia, in Congressman Staggers's district. The Turbotrain was built for high-speed corridor service on level track. The substantial gradients and curvature of the Washington–Parkersburg line led to frequent breakdowns of the Turbotrain.

49. See, for example, the statement of Larry Cena, president of the Atchison,

(that is, one that excludes freight and commuter traffic). Service is also improved if the corridor is grade-separated from highway traffic. These improvements are enormously expensive, as the Northeast Corridor Improvement Project has demonstrated. Although the project took over a route that was already largely grade-separated, improvements had cost $2.2 billion by 1984.

Corridor projects create political problems for Amtrak by concentrating benefits in a few regions. Only areas of very high population density can support corridor operations, and since they are so expensive, only a few can be built. Indeed, the large share of Amtrak's costs spent on the Northeast Corridor has long been a source of political embarrassment to the corporation. Amtrak's managers view the Southwest Corridor (Los Angeles to San Diego) as the most promising area for further development. But the corporation has supported a program of more than a dozen scaled-down corridors, geographically dispersed throughout the country, as a way of building political support for corridor development.[50] The Department of Transportation has been very skeptical about corridor development, and Congress has been unwilling to provide funds.[51]

Topeka, and Santa Fe Railway, in *Railroad Corridors*, Hearings before the Subcommittee on Transportation and Commerce of the House Committee on Interstate and Foreign Commerce, 96 Cong. 2 sess. (GPO, 1980), pp. 537–43. The Santa Fe Railway owns the Southwest Corridor, from Los Angeles to San Diego.

50. "As Amtrak Sees It," *NARP News*, vol. 13 (October 1979), p. 3. See also the testimony by Boyd and Gilson in *Railroad Corridors*, Hearings, pp. 442–60. For critical evaluations of the corridor concept, see General Accounting Office, *Should Amtrak Develop High-Speed Corridor Service Outside the Northeast?* Report CED-78-67 (GAO, 1978); and U.S. Congress, Office of Technology Assessment, *U.S. Passenger Rail Technologies*, Report OTA-STI-222 (GPO, 1983).

51. The scope of disagreement between DOT and Amtrak on corridor development was underscored in a series of jointly prepared reports on the subject. Their final report, issued in 1981, carried no recommendations because the two organizations could not agree. Transportation Secretary Drew Lewis argued that "few, if any, of the markets have any potential to support cost effective rail corridor service." In his opinion, "energy impacts of rail corridor development are at best insignificant and at worst wasteful." Amtrak President Alan Boyd, on the other hand, questioned the methodology used to calculate energy savings. Many proposed corridor trains would have better revenue-to-cost ratios than current Amtrak routes, he claimed. Boyd recommended broader evaluation criteria, including urban revitalization, improved traveler safety, and reduction of highway and airport congestion. U.S. Department of Transportation, Federal Railroad Administration and National Railroad Passenger Corporation, *Rail Passenger Corridors: Final Evaluation* (DOT, 1981).

Amtrak came closest to winning funding for a series of corridors in 1980, when Amtrak's allies on the House Interstate and Foreign Commerce Committee won approval of a plan to set aside $955 million from the Windfall Profits Tax account to evaluate,

Amtrak's corridor strategy took an unusual twist in 1982. Federal support for corridor development appeared unlikely in the aftermath of Reagan's budget cuts of the previous year. To recruit allies in the private sector, Amtrak President Alan Boyd announced in April 1982 the formation of the American High Speed Rail Corporation (AHSR), with himself as chairman and Larry Gilson, Amtrak's corporate development vice-president, as president. (Boyd left Amtrak a few months later to go to AHSR.) The new company attempted to raise private capital of more than $3.1 billion to construct a Southwest Corridor using Japanese "bullet train" technology. Additional routes from Amtrak's list of emerging corridors were to be considered for future development. Initial studies were financed in part by a loan from Amtrak (since repaid). Amtrak holds the exclusive operating rights for most potential intercity routes under the Rail Passenger Service Act. It concluded an agreement with American High Speed Rail under which the latter agreed to pay Amtrak an annual license fee and a share of any profits if AHSR began operating San Diego–Los Angeles trains.[52]

By building close links with American High Speed Rail, Amtrak managers attempted to keep open the option of growth during a period of limited capital funding from the federal government. The effort failed, however: AHSR was unable to secure needed funding in the private sector and, in November 1984, was forced to cancel its construction plans in the corridor. The AHSR experience illustrates how unlikely it is that rail passenger corridors can be built without some form of government assistance. Indeed, support could take the same form as aid to Amtrak: a progression from small grants and loan guarantees to direct assistance and finally a government takeover.

---

plan, and begin construction on a series of rail corridors. Construction funds ($850 million of the $955 million) would require further authorization of specific projects. The secretary of transportation threatened a veto recommendation, and the Senate balked as well. Conferees authorized only $63.2 million for corridor evaluation and equipment purchases. See *Passenger Railroad Rebuilding Act—Rock Island Employee Assistance Act,* H. Rept. 96-839 (GPO, 1980), p. 31; and *Providing for an Extension of Directed Service on the Rock Island Railroad,* H. Rept. 96-1041 (GPO, 1980). The corridor provisions are Title II of the reported bill.

52. Under the agreement, Amtrak also became a preferred shareholder in AHSR, with representation on its board of directors. See the statement by Amtrak President Claytor in *Reauthorization of Amtrak,* Hearings before the Senate Committee on Commerce, Science and Transportation, 98 Cong. 1 sess. (GPO, 1983), pp. 24–25; and *Railway Age,* January 1984, pp. 46–54. In 1982 the California legislature authorized up to $1.25 billion in tax-free bonds for rail passenger firms, which must apply to state agencies for the funds.

In the short term, however, no new funding for corridors appears likely. Indeed, Amtrak management announced in 1985 that it might defer planned capital and maintenance expenditures if its budget was cut.[53] This response—preserving current service levels at the risk of damaging long-term service quality—appears to be an attempt to maintain Amtrak's political base. But if carried very far, it may damage the long-term viability of the system and place Amtrak in the 1990s in the same position it was in when it began operations in 1971: plagued by undermaintained equipment and facilities, low service quality, and low staff morale.

As noted at the beginning of this section, Amtrak's pattern of capital allocation has been consistent, for the most part, with both the public service and security strategies. Amtrak's policy of spreading capital investment widely throughout the country is consistent with its mandate to provide a national system as well as with its need to maximize political support. When public service and security goals have conflicted, however, Amtrak has emphasized survival first and foremost, as the timing of its shifts from equipment modernization, to corridor operations, to partnership with private capital indicate. Amtrak moved toward "emerging corridors" as political support for a national system eroded. The movement toward partnership with private capital in corridor development was a further effort to maintain corporate growth and perhaps repeat the cycle of gradually increasing government involvement that led to the establishment of Amtrak. In short, Amtrak has changed its notion of public service in capital allocations to accommodate corporate maintenance and growth.[54]

EMPLOYMENT. Labor policy has been an area of persistent problems and limited discretion for Amtrak. When the company first began operating in 1971, it performed only marketing functions; all direct train operations were performed by railroads under contract. Thus its direct

53. Reginald Stuart, "Panel Votes to Continue U.S. Subsidy for Amtrak," *New York Times,* May 3, 1985.

54. Budget cuts have also stimulated efforts by Amtrak to expand corporate activities outside the rail passenger arena. Diversification opportunities have been limited by Amtrak's total dependence on the federal government for capital funding. But Amtrak does have substantial assets, notably an unbroken right-of-way in the Northeast Corridor and real estate holdings in major northeastern cities. Not until 1981 did Amtrak establish a Corporate Development Department to pursue opportunities arising from those resources, including real estate development and use of right-of-way for a fiber optics communications system.

employment was very small. These arrangements did not allow Amtrak sufficient control over employees dealing with the public. In 1972 it successfully petitioned Congress to be allowed to employ these workers directly.[55] Amtrak's work force almost doubled with the acquisition of the Northeast Corridor in 1976. (Train and engine crews on the corridor remained Conrail employees.) By the beginning of 1978, Amtrak employed more than 21,000 people; employment fell slightly in later years but was back to that level by 1985.

Direct and indirect labor costs account for about 60 percent of Amtrak's total costs. These high labor costs, in part a result of the rail industry's antiquated work and payment rules, have hurt Amtrak's efforts to compete with other modes of passenger transportation. For example, an engineer on a Metroliner who made one New York–Washington round trip in a day received pay for 4.2 days under union contracts.[56] Persistent productivity problems not caused by work rules have also plagued the corporation.[57]

Not only are Amtrak's labor costs high, but they are also uncontrollable to a substantial degree. Train and engine crews (engineers, firemen, conductors, brakemen) and many nonoperating employees (for example, track maintenance workers) outside the Northeast Corridor are employed by contracting railroads and therefore do not negotiate directly with Amtrak. The same was true of Northeast Corridor train and engine crews until 1983. In addition, Amtrak's bargaining power with nonoperating unions on the corridor is weak. Under the Regional Rail Reorganization Act, the bargaining agreement in effect when employees were transferred to Amtrak goes into effect automatically unless Amtrak and the unions reach agreement within sixty days.[58] This provision gave railway brotherhoods little incentive to negotiate work rule concessions with Amtrak.

Labor protection agreements mandated by the Rail Passenger Service

55. Amtrak, *Annual Report, 1972*, pp. 19–23.

56. GAO, *Should Amtrak Develop High-Speed Corridor Service Outside the Northeast?* p. 21.

57. In three common maintenance-of-way functions, Amtrak's labor productivity lagged far behind that of other railroads—less than half of Conrail's in some cases. General Accounting Office, *Amtrak's Productivity on Track Rehabilitation Is Lower Than Other Railroads': Precise Comparison Not Feasible*, Report CED-81-60 (GAO, 1981).

58. Section 504(f)(2) was added as an amendment to the Railroad Revitalization and Regulatory Reform Act of 1976, sec. 615, February 5, 1976.

Act of 1970 also limited Amtrak's discretion by guaranteeing employees with five or more years seniority up to six years' salary when they are laid off. Until 1981 Amtrak was prohibited from contracting out any work if it would result in any employees being laid off.

Because Amtrak has such limited discretion in employment, its strategic preferences should be manifested primarily in federal policy formation and adoption. Job preservation is not part of Amtrak's explicit mandate. If Amtrak is a public service–oriented corporation, it should press Congress for relief from legislatively imposed burdens, requesting a freer bargaining environment with Northeast Corridor employees and eased labor protection conditions similar to those imposed in the Milwaukee Road and Rock Island cases. On the other hand, if Amtrak is following a security strategy, it would be reluctant to offend its most important political ally in Congress, rail labor. Indeed, it might argue that because protective agreements make labor a fixed cost, it makes more sense to retain services than to pay furloughed workers who are not providing a service.

Amtrak's strategy appears much closer to the security approach. Amtrak did not request a change in the 3R act bargaining conditions until its survival was threatened in 1981. Then, instead of advocating changes in its labor protection agreements,[59] Amtrak used labor protection costs with devastating effect to resist the Reagan administration's efforts to impose cutbacks. Amtrak President Boyd argued that the Reagan budget ceiling for Amtrak would require a shutdown of all Amtrak routes outside the Northeast Corridor. Department of Transportation officials countered with estimates that labor protection costs might be no more than $125 million. The two estimates were never reconciled, but Amtrak's claim that discontinuing service might be much more expensive in the short term than maintaining service was a powerful argument against the administration's proposals. The same arguments were used in 1985. Amtrak's supporters claimed that a shutdown of the corporation would trigger $2.1 billion in labor protection claims, with a higher outlay in the first year ($800 million) than it would cost to keep the entire Amtrak system running. Amtrak's president warned that any attempt to weaken those protections legislatively would probably be overturned by the courts.[60]

59. *Amtrak Reauthorization*, Hearings, p. 50.
60. Stephen Gettinger, "Amtrak Survival without Subsidies Debated," *Congres-*

At the height of the congressional conflict over Amtrak budget cuts in 1981, Amtrak did announce a 25 percent cut in its headquarters' staff. Amtrak also used the budget crisis to win work rule concessions from nonoperating employees in the Northeast Corridor in 1981 and from operating employees late in 1982. Nevertheless, the timing of these changes once again suggests Amtrak's political dilemma and its underlying political strategy: the corporation is reluctant to offend its political supporters and is likely to make cutbacks only when forced to do so by a strong countervailing political force.

Conclusions

Since its creation, Amtrak has operated in an environment of financial uncertainty and dependence, conflicting mandates and controls, and limited discretion. It is not surprising, therefore, that the corporation's managers have been preoccupied with obtaining a more secure environment. With the autonomy strategy foreclosed, and facing continuing challenges from the Department of Transportation and Office of Management and Budget, Amtrak's managers placed primary emphasis on building support for the firm within Congress. This strategy sometimes took the form of placating individual legislators, but more often it has focused on a broader attempt at support-building, with benefits spread widely to maintain congressional majorities.

In defending itself against cutbacks, Amtrak has used public interest arguments (for example, energy conservation) to great effect. But its notion of public service has been both selective and malleable, and its claims—notably with regard to energy efficiency—have often been overstated. Amtrak has emphasized its mandate to provide a national system over financial objectives (that is, minimizing losses). Financial targets have been regarded as a minimum to be met rather than as an objective to be surpassed. Corporate growth became a goal in itself. Beginning in the late 1970s, the goal shifted toward preservation of the status quo.

Amtrak's choice of a security strategy was not simply the personal choice of top executives. Instead, it was a necessity dictated by the corporation's environment. Amtrak needed political allies, and Congress

sional Quarterly Weekly Report, February 16, 1985, p. 295; and testimony of Graham Claytor before the Subcommittee on Commerce, Transportation and Tourism of the House Committee on Energy and Commerce, March 14, 1985, pp. 4–5.

was the place to look. Given the structure of Congress, a price had to be paid in terms of district-specific and majority-building benefits. A public service strategy, in which the corporation developed its own clearly stated policy goals, or adopted those of one of its political masters, would almost certainly require sacrificing some of that political support. Thus the corporation has been forced to respond to multiple conflicting objectives, using its limited discretion to apply those objectives in ways consistent with political survival and growth. The lesson that emerges from the Amtrak experience is that governments cannot expect a state-owned enterprise to develop a consistent public service mission out of unclear mandates and conflicting commands.

Amtrak legislation enacted in 1979, 1981, and 1985 did not resolve the fundamental policy disputes between the Department of Transportation, the Office of Management and Budget, Congress, and Amtrak. Nor did this legislation eliminate Amtrak's need to retain political support in Congress by preserving its nationwide route structure. Indeed, there are many parallels between the newborn Amtrak of 1971 and the restructured Amtrak of 1985. In both cases Amtrak was underfunded relative to what was required over the long term to preserve its political base and to build (or maintain) service quality. And in both cases the corporation was supposedly being subjected to a limited-term test, with cutbacks intended for operations failing that test. Whether the corporation has entered a new era, or is simply repeating an old cycle, remains to be seen.

VIA Rail Canada

Like Amtrak, VIA Rail Canada grew out of a long conflict over the proper scope and method for providing rail passenger service. VIA gained several benefits from the experience of its southern neighbor— for example, passenger services were assumed over a two-year period rather than overnight, easing the burden on the new company's managers. The changeover, ending in 1979, was less complex than Amtrak's in any case; VIA received equipment and employees and contracted for services with only two railways (Canadian National Railways and Canadian Pacific Railway), and the overwhelming majority of these dealings were with its temporary parent, CN. Moreover, VIA's takeover was not accompanied by the massive route cuts that left Amtrak's political masters mistrusting one another.

Despite these advantages, VIA is a textbook case of what can go wrong with a public enterprise: huge deficits, antiquated equipment operating on an overextended system, politically motivated investment decisions, complaints by competitors of unfair competition, and service cuts and restorations that have created ill will among the public and lowered corporate morale.

Little of this can be blamed on the corporation's managers. The blame rests with the Canadian government, which has failed to give the corporation a coherent mandate and resources with which to achieve it.

Government Constraints on Corporate Strategy

FINANCIAL CONSTRAINTS. Many of the operating problems besetting Amtrak are evident in even starker form in the case of VIA Rail Canada. VIA operates in a country of vast distances. Its route system is about half as long as Amtrak's, serving 50 percent more stations than its southern counterpart, although Canada's population is only one-tenth that of the United States. While some of Canada's population centers are quite large, they are far apart, making rail passenger service less competitive with airlines. Only the Quebec City–Montreal–Ottawa–Toronto–Windsor and possibly the Calgary–Edmonton routes offer anything approaching the combinations of medium distance and high population density that might support frequent, high-speed corridor service—the only kind of rail passenger service that can come close to being self-supporting.[61] Efforts to concentrate rail passenger operations where they can be most efficient have been hampered by pervasive interregional conflict. Peripheral regions complain that once again the interests of Ontario and Quebec have been put before their own.

Most of VIA's equipment is antiquated, raising operating and maintenance costs. VIA must also deal with severe winters that further increase its operating costs and create political demands for ostensibly "all weather" rail service. And VIA, unlike Amtrak, must serve small

---

61. Even on the Montreal–Toronto corridor, however, population per linear route mile is only one-fifth that of the Northeast Corridor in the United States and similar corridors in Japan and the United Kingdom. A 1970 CTC study cited the following figures for corridor length and population per linear mile: Windsor–Quebec City, 715, 14,000; Montreal–Toronto only, 325, 18,000; Washington, D.C.–Boston, 450, 100,000; Tokyo–Osaka, 370, 95,000; London–Liverpool/Leeds, 200, 100,000. Canadian Transport Commission, Research Branch, *Intercity Passenger Transport Study* (Ottawa: Information Canada, 1970).

remote communities that have no road access for part or all of the year. VIA also lacks substantial control over its operations and costs. In 1983, 61 percent of the company's expenses were paid to Canadian National and Canadian Pacific for operating VIA trains, following a costing order established by the Canadian Transport Commission (CTC) for use in train discontinuance decisions.[62] VIA management has repeatedly criticized this arrangement on a number of grounds: it raises VIA's costs while giving CN and CP little incentive to improve their efficiency; it gives VIA little access to cost information; and VIA's total expenses cannot be known until several months after the end of the fiscal year, when the railways present their final bill to VIA.[63]

Given these constraints, it is not surprising that VIA's losses have been even higher on a per passenger basis than Amtrak's, and its dependence on federal subsidies has been greater as well. While Amtrak earned 50 percent of its operating expenses from fares in 1984, VIA earned only about 30 percent.[64]

COMMAND STRUCTURE CONSTRAINTS. Perhaps the most unusual aspect of VIA's command structure—and a particularly vivid contrast with Amtrak's—is its frail legislative basis. VIA has existed since 1977 on the basis of a $1 appropriation and a brief cabinet order outlining regulations for contracts between the transport minister, VIA, and the railways.[65] The federal government has repeatedly promised to bring a VIA Rail act before Parliament, but it has not done so for several reasons. A full-scale parliamentary debate would provide a ready forum for opponents of cutbacks in VIA service—a very contentious political issue. Moreover, the House of Commons has a crowded agenda, and so long as VIA does not have a governance crisis, it is easy to put off consideration of a VIA

62. VIA Rail Canada, *Annual Report, 1983*, p. 6.

63. Reimbursement is based on system-average, fully allocated costs (that is, including a portion of shared costs, such as track maintenance, on track used primarily by freight trains). This is unlike Amtrak's short-term avoidable costs system.

64. Amtrak figures include state subsidies as revenues. Nevertheless, VIA has managed to earn a small "profit" in each year of its existence, but only in a nominal sense. Originally, federal subsidies were negotiated in advance every year for VIA's overall management of rail passenger service and for specific routes: if the corporation managed to provide its service at lower cost or to attract higher ridership and thus higher revenues, it could keep the difference. This system was intended to provide incentives for corporate efficiency. But because costs billed by the railways proved to be less predictable than anticipated, contract payments from Transport Canada to VIA are now adjusted in line with VIA's actual costs, allowing a small "profit."

65. P. C. 1978-952, March 23, 1978.

Rail act in favor of more pressing matters. Finally, there is conflict over what such an act should say. In 1979 the Department of Transport proposed reducing the Canadian Transport Commission's jurisdiction over route discontinuances to advisory status, but the commission strongly objected to such a change.[66]

Conflicts among VIA's governmental masters (Transport Canada, the Canadian Transport Commission, the Ministry of Finance, and Treasury Board) are an even more serious problem for VIA than its lack of a firm legislative basis. Federal subsidies are channeled to VIA through contracts with Transport Canada. The transport minister also has authority to approve VIA's fares. Transport Canada has stressed the goal of obtaining value for money in its outlays to VIA. To lower subsidies, Transport Canada has pushed for cuts in service and higher fares. It has also advocated concentrating VIA's services on high-capacity corridors. In interviews for this study, VIA managers repeatedly objected to departmental "meddling" in details of the company's operations—for example, the number of trains on specific routes, marketing, and fare discount plans.

The Canadian Transport Commission sets minimum frequencies and levels of service for VIA's routes, but the federal cabinet can overturn or change its decisions. The CTC has stressed preservation of service to current customers.

The Treasury Board and Ministry of Finance must approve Transport Canada's budget requests for VIA. The primary objectives of these agencies have been to hold down VIA's spending. They have objected both to the size of the corporation's budget requests and to their unpredictability, manifest in repeated requests for supplemental appropriations when the original budget request proved inadequate.[67]

The House of Commons holds yearly hearings on VIA, but its power over the company is negligible. VIA, like Amtrak, has vocal opponents outside of government. Foremost among them is the bus industry, which accuses VIA of predatory pricing. Advocates include passenger groups (notably Transport 2000), rail labor, and provincial and community governments concerned about service cutbacks.

66. Transport Canada, *VIA Rail Canada,* Cabinet discussion paper, July 26, 1979, point 112; Canadian Transport Commission, "The Ministry of Transport's Proposed VIA Rail Canada Legislation: A Response by the Commission," undated.

67. See the *Report of the Auditor General to the House of Commons, Fiscal Year Ending 31 March 1982* (Ottawa: Supply and Services, 1982), p. 42.

VIA's board of directors, like Canadian National's, is appointed by the cabinet on the recommendation of the minister of transport. The board has evolved toward the CN pattern of regional representation.[68] As with CN, political considerations have been important in selecting board members. The Conservative government elected in 1984 fired all of VIA's (mostly Liberal) private sector members and replaced them with nominees of their own political persuasion.[69] VIA management officials echo the complaints of their CN counterparts about the lack of expertise and passivity of most board members.

Both Amtrak and VIA have divided command structures, but there are important differences between the two. Amtrak's conflicting masters in the executive branch and Congress share jurisdiction over all aspects of the company and therefore must compromise. Amtrak's budget must be cleared by the Department of Transportation and the Office of Management and Budget and then passed by Congress. It may be vetoed by the president. These arrangements have given Amtrak leeway to pursue a support-maximizing security strategy in Congress. Equally important, it has led to a situation in which Amtrak's route and capital allocations are reasonably compatible. VIA's governmental masters, on the other hand, have had more autonomy in specific decision areas. The Canadian Transport Commission has jurisdiction over route discontinuances; it need not compromise with the Department of Transport. If the cabinet overrides CTC decisions, the commission has no recourse. The Department of Transport and Treasury Board have effective control over VIA's capital budget, subject to cabinet approval; the CTC plays no role in the process. Thus VIA, unlike Amtrak, can do little to forge compromises favorable to the company's own interests. A helpless bystander, VIA watches government agencies pursue their own agendas.

VIA is also vulnerable to shifts in power among its controlling agencies. After the Conservatives won office in 1984, for example, the

68. The original ten-member VIA board was composed of three federal civil servants and several other members who had expertise relevant to VIA (one from labor unions, two from the travel industry, one from Canadian National Railways). The CN representative was President Robert Bandeen, who served as VIA's board chairman while VIA was a CN subsidiary. After VIA became an independent Crown corporation, VIA's president, Frank Roberts, assumed the post of board chairman as well. The posts of chairman and president were separated after Roberts resigned in 1982.

69. *Globe and Mail* (Toronto), January 11, 1985, and March 27, 1985. The informal practice of reserving a board seat for a senior official of Transport Canada was also ended at this time.

Ministry of Finance was given broad discretion to make major cuts in the federal budget. VIA's budget was slashed $93 million immediately, with further cuts of $200 million to be made by the end of the decade.[70] It remains doubtful that all of these cuts will be implemented. Nevertheless, agencies' conflicting agendas for VIA have made planning very difficult and have led to service and capital allocation decisions that are often inconsistent.

VIA is also vulnerable to goal changes by its controlling agencies. As one VIA official said after Lloyd Axworthy succeeded Jean-Luc Pepin as transport minister, "Our mandate changes from year to year. Pepin stressed economy and efficiency; Axworthy asked to take a look at restoring services that had been cut. The policy ground is so shaky that Ministers can change priorities completely. . . . Crown corporations are being used to get them re-elected."

Corporate Strategy

VIA's heavy dependence on federal subsidies makes an autonomy strategy untenable. And like Amtrak, VIA has little discretion over many of the most important decisions affecting the corporation. Three strategic options remain, however: (1) it can attempt to fashion and implement its own public service priorities, (2) it can adopt the priorities of one of its controlling agencies, or (3) it can attempt to build a base of political support by preserving the status quo and responding sequentially to conflicting demands (the security strategy). Each of these strategies depends upon the acquiescence of government actors with a different set of goals and with veto power over VIA's attempts to implement at least part of any one of these strategies.

Under its first president, Frank Roberts, VIA tentatively developed a public service strategy of its own.[71] VIA stressed that other modes of transport were indirectly subsidized through government provision of infrastructure. Statements of profit and loss by carriers, VIA claimed, did not reflect indirect public subsidies received by other modes of

70. Ibid., May 24, 1985.
71. The company also sought a clearer and more stable mandate through a VIA Rail Act and changes in the CTC costing order under which VIA paid CN and CP for services rendered by them. See VIA Rail Canada, *Annual Report, 1979*, p. 5.

transport.[72] Moreover, the potential of the rail mode could not be fairly evaluated until substantial investments were made to compensate for twenty years of neglect by the railways. VIA further argued that bus, air, and rail services had distinctive (although partially overlapping) travel ranges where they were most effective and that "Canada's public transportation policy should be designed to take advantage of these inherent capabilities and benefits."[73] Roberts suggested that the different modes of transport cooperate—through intermodal terminals, for example—rather than compete. VIA's role was to be primarily in corridor-type operations in the 100-to-500 mile range.

The split in modal responsibilities that he envisioned would clearly be in VIA's interests, for it would effectively guarantee VIA a sizable share of Canada's public transportation market, despite growing losses. But it was not in the best interest of the other modes—especially the bus industry. More important, it clashed with the department's determination to contain and cut rail passenger subsidies. Roberts's strategy had made little headway by the time he left VIA in 1982.

His successor, Pierre Franche, who had reorganized the National Harbours Board, was brought in from outside to improve management. Franche has articulated a somewhat different mission for VIA. He has argued that different standards must be used to evaluate services that can come close to being profitable (corridor trains) and those requiring social justifications (transcontinental, regional intercity, and remote services). VIA claims that upgrading the central Canadian corridor— which would include electrification of a passenger-only Montreal–Ottawa–Toronto segment to allow operation of 180-mile-per-hour trains— could become profitable and repay the investment.[74] At the same time, VIA would manage other services (which VIA argues could be provided more efficiently with new equipment) according to standards set by the government. The hope is that management of the corridor service on a "bottom line" basis would increase concern for efficiency throughout the company. This, in turn, would cut down on the Department of

72. See the statement by J. Frank Roberts before the House of Commons, Standing Committee on Transport and Communications, *Minutes of Proceedings and Evidence,* 30 Parl. 3 sess., issue 1, November 15, 1977, p. 17.

73. See J. Frank Roberts, "VIA and the Future," address to the Board of Trade Club of Metropolitan Toronto, March 19, 1979, p. 19.

74. VIA Rail Canada, *High Speed Passenger Rail in Canada* (Montreal: VIA, 1984), chap. 1. The Calgary–Edmonton could not repay its investment, according to VIA projections.

Transport's alleged meddling by strengthening its confidence in VIA management. This strategy also justifies major capital investments in the company.

In the present budgetary climate, however, the chance of such a major investment being approved is virtually nonexistent. A more realistic concern has been whether the corporation would survive at all: the Conservative government elected in 1984 considered re-merging VIA into Canadian National Railways. This idea was strongly opposed by VIA management. President Franche argued that "a totally independent rail corporation, committed to rebuilding and renaissance, is preferable to a CN preoccupied by many and sometimes conflicting profit-centres, where passenger rail would be merely a poor cousin to freight."[75] The merger idea has apparently been dropped. But the fact that it was considered at all shows how weak the "independence" of VIA is and makes clear that VIA once again has failed to articulate a public service mission acceptable to its disparate government masters.

Policies and Outcomes

With VIA unable to implement a corporate strategy of its own, rail policy outcomes have reflected the policy preferences of government agencies with direct control over various aspects of VIA operations.

UNPROFITABLE OPERATIONS. Changes in the scope of VIA's operations have been much more sporadic than the almost continuous sparring over the Amtrak route system. In 1977 and in 1979 the Canadian Transport Commission announced plans to restructure the Canadian rail system. But service was not reduced as much as the Department of Transport had hoped. Responding to rapid growth in federal subsidies, the cabinet in 1981 ordered a major cut in aid to the firm. VIA was instructed to come up quickly with cuts in service to fit a lower budget; routes composing about 20 percent of the VIA system were then canceled by cabinet order, bypassing the Canadian Transport Commission entirely.[76] Money saved on service reductions was to be put in a VIA funding

75. *Globe and Mail* (Toronto), January 9, 1985; and *Toronto Star,* December 8, 1984.
76. P. C. 1981-2171, August 6, 1981, in *Canada Gazette,* pt. II, November 6, 1981. Most of the routes were terminated effective November 15, 1981, but several commuter-type trains were continued through September 7, 1982, to allow provincial governments time to take over those services if they wished.

"envelope" to be made available for capital expenditures. Cuts were based on various criteria including ridership, the level of losses, and regional balance (for example, one of each of the two western and eastern transcontinentals was eliminated).[77] Although the Canadian Senate held hearings and there were protests nationwide, opponents were powerless to prevent the cuts from taking effect; the contrast with the prolonged conflict and eventual compromise over the Amtrak route cuts of 1979 and 1981 is clear. The successful termination of many unprofitable routes in the VIA system was aided by strong pressure from central budgetary agencies. The fact that the secure Liberal government did not have to face the electorate for three years and had its electoral base in the region of Canada least affected by route cuts was equally important.

VIA's vulnerability to the vagaries of the electoral cycle and to changes in transport ministers' priorities was reemphasized two years later. Prior to the 1984 election, Axworthy reversed several of the 1981 route cutbacks and offered to consider restoring additional routes (preferably with financial assistance from affected provinces). The rival Conservatives also promised to restore services cut by the Liberals. Service restorations were indeed made in 1985, including the costly second eastern and western transcontinental trains. These changes further stretched VIA's limited financial resources and equipment.

CAPITAL EXPENDITURES. Nowhere are the conflicting controls over VIA more evident than in capital allocations. In this area the minister of transport and his department need not contend with CTC restrictions. But Transport Canada does have to contend with the budget cutters on the Treasury Board and the Ministry of Finance. For these agencies, capital expenditures are a relatively easy place to cut budget requests since they do not impose visible short-term costs on the public. (They do, of course, raise operating costs and discourage ridership, but these consequences are less visible.) As a result, VIA has had constant difficulty obtaining capital funds, and its investment planning has been frequently disrupted by the electoral cycle, regional politics, and bureaucratic infighting within the federal government. Expenditures have generally reflected Transport Canada's belief that the Quebec–Windsor corridor should be the focus of improvements in rail passenger service.

While Amtrak has been successful in funding new equipment for all

77. Unlike the fixed legislative criteria used for the 1979 Amtrak cuts, however, the criteria used in the VIA cuts were informal.

of its services (corridor, western transcontinental, and intercity),[78] to date VIA has obtained new equipment only for corridor services. Federal support for VIA's new equipment—the Light, Rapid, Comfortable (LRC) trains manufactured by the Montreal Locomotive Works (now a subsidiary of Bombardier)—antedates the establishment of VIA. Moreover, this support reflects Ottawa's desire to bail out the manufacturer more than it does support for VIA.

Development of these trains took place in the early 1970s with partial financing by the federal Department of Industry, Trade and Commerce.[79] The most distinctive feature of the LRC is a "banking" system intended to allow it to reach very high speeds on roadbeds used primarily by slower freights—the prevailing conditions in North America. But CN and CP were uninterested in purchasing new passenger equipment, and foreign markets were limited by nationalized railways' propensity to buy from domestic producers. The LRC program thus nearly collapsed.

In November 1977 Transport Minister Otto Lang announced that Ottawa would buy ten LRC trains for VIA. Bowing to regional pressure, he agreed to disperse the LRCs throughout the VIA system, even though they were designed for high-density corridor service and required sophisticated maintenance facilities (then available only in the Montreal area).[80] The decision to disperse the LRCs was later reversed. They are currently in service only in the Quebec–Windsor corridor. The LRCs have had persistent maintenance problems, and their key feature, the banking system, still was not operational in 1985. Despite these problems, Transport Minister Pepin ordered ten more LRC trains at the time of the 1981 VIA service cutbacks as part of an effort to soften political opposition to those cuts.

VIA's efforts to replace its aging equipment used on transcontinental and regional services—almost all of it more than thirty years old—met with more resistance despite evidence that modern equipment could pay for itself in reduced operating costs. (Most existing equipment has been refurbished, but it remains expensive to operate and prone to break-

78. Two-thirds of Amtrak's active passenger cars in 1983 had been built after 1975. Amtrak, *Annual Report, 1982*, p. 6. Amtrak had ordered new regional and transcontinental equipment by 1975, four years after it began operation.

79. See Julius Lukasiewicz, *The Railway Game* (Toronto: McClelland and Stewart, 1976), pp. 155–56.

80. On allocation of the LRC trains, see Roberts's testimony, Commons, Standing Committee on Transport and Communications, *Minutes of Proceedings and Evidence*, 30 Parl. 3 sess., issue 1, November 15, 1977, pp. 32–33.

downs.) As noted earlier, Transport Canada has expressed strong doubts about the desirability of noncorridor services. While in opposition, the Conservative party, which has its political base outside the central Canadian corridor, strongly criticized the concentration of VIA investments in the corridor. After winning power in the 1984 election, the Conservatives gained an opportunity to change VIA's investment priorities, and they appear to be doing so: VIA's proposal for a massive upgrading of the corridor has been shelved indefinitely, and in 1985 the government announced tentative plans to purchase new transcontinental equipment.[81]

EMPLOYMENT. VIA has limited autonomy in employment because most of its work (including train operations, road maintenance, and equipment maintenance) is performed under contract by CN and CP employees. Thus VIA employs only about one-sixth as many people as Amtrak. Under Pierre Franche, VIA has pushed very hard for transfer of the CN and CP employees who work entirely for VIA, believing that having direct control over them would result in significant savings for the company. These moves have been resisted by the unions, which fear that working for VIA would not be as secure as working for the major railways.[82] VIA has attempted to allay these fears by negotiating agreements that exchange increased job security for union concessions on work rules.[83] Negotiations concluded or under way in 1985 may result in a doubling of VIA employment. Improving employee productivity has been an important part of Franche's efforts to improve VIA's image with Transport Canada, but a realistic evaluation of these efforts can be made only after VIA's employee base has stabilized.

Conclusions

Like Amtrak, VIA Rail Canada has operated within an environment of tremendous uncertainty and conflict. VIA has attempted to develop

81. *Railway Age,* July 1985, p. 86. Political jockeying and the electoral cycle have also been evident in VIA's efforts to obtain modern maintenance facilities. In December 1983, with new federal elections expected within a year, Ottawa approved $306 million for four major new VIA maintenance facilities strategically distributed throughout Canada, in Halifax, Montreal, Toronto, and Winnipeg. The Conservative government elected in 1984 first put a hold on these facilities and approved them on a scaled-down basis.
82. *Gazette* (Montreal), April 6, 1985.
83. *Gazette* (Montreal), July 16, 1985.

public service strategies defining the company's place in the Canadian transportation marketplace, but it has had limited success in implementing those strategies.

VIA has less leverage than Amtrak to develop policy compromises in its own interest because the federal agencies that determine its fate (primarily Transport Canada, the Canadian Transport Commission, and the budgetary agencies) do not have to forge a consensus as Congress and the executive branch do in the United States. Unlike Amtrak, VIA cannot appeal directly to the legislators to increase its government support. It must rely on informal and indirect pressures on the government—notably the political popularity of passenger trains and the deep regional feelings they evoke. But this way of operating is far more effective in preventing changes that may or may not be favored by VIA management (route cuts, for example) than in bringing about changes that might help the corporation. Thus VIA has been unable to win a permanent statutory framework or revisions in the costing system under which VIA reimburses the railways for services they provide to VIA. Nor has VIA been able to modernize equipment as quickly as Amtrak did in its early years. There is little doubt that such changes would have occurred in the United States as a result of coalition building between the public enterprise and legislators, but legislators in the Canadian House of Commons do not have the independent power needed to build such coalitions. Equally important, the federal executive's reluctance to provide a parliamentary forum for critics of VIA cutbacks has prevented changes in the haphazardly evolved constraints on VIA that are regarded by all sides as unsatisfactory.

Public Enterprise and Industrial Adjustment

In both the Amtrak and VIA Rail Canada cases, the executive branch viewed the establishment of public enterprise as a mechanism for promoting adjustment in the rail passenger industry by taking control of the industry away from service-oriented regulatory commissions. This effort was successful at the outset in the United States; about half of the remaining intercity trains were eliminated in DOT's 1971 planning process for Amtrak. The restructuring that coincided with the establishment of VIA was done by the CTC and resulted in cuts of only about 10 percent of remaining trains.

Over the long term, the national patterns differ somewhat, but in both countries the rapid elimination of rail passenger services that character-ized the 1950s and 1960s has been stopped. After growth in the early 1970s, Amtrak's route structure now covers approximately 24,000 miles, slightly more than when the corporation began operations in 1971. VIA shrunk an additional 20 percent in 1981, but many of these trains were placed back in service in 1985. And VIA still operates more than four times as many train miles per capita of national population as Amtrak, and its per capita subsidy level is also more than four times as high as Amtrak's.

Thus if industrial adjustment is defined as the elimination of and disinvestment in economic activities that are not financially self-suffi-cient, both VIA and Amtrak clearly have served protectionist rather than market-oriented or accelerationist ends. If broader criteria are used to evaluate industrial adjustment—notably energy conservation—the record is little better: neither country has fundamentally realigned rail passenger service toward corridor-type operations that offer maximum energy savings.

Adjustment goals were a major objective of the U.S. and Canadian governments in establishing Amtrak and VIA. Why then have they not been attained? The core answer is that both governments were unable or unwilling to impose concentrated, visible losses on groups and localities. Nor could executive branch officials rely on enterprise man-agers to cut services for them: VIA's managers lacked the authority to cut routes, while Amtrak's managers have pursued expansion or stability in operations throughout most of Amtrak's history. Executive branch efforts to increase control over the corporations stem in large measure from their inability to use the firms to control expenditure growth, as originally planned.

Once government begins financial assistance to a declining industry, or operates all or part of it as a public enterprise, the policymaking dynamic shifts. Corporate managers develop a stake in the continuation of government assistance (unless, of course, the supported activity is a small segment of their overall business). The stakes become more visible for those who depend on continuation of the activity (consumers and workers). Most important, if government lowers its support, it is not merely *allowing* these groups to suffer losses, but *imposing* losses. In democratic societies, even governments that have the power to impose visible losses are reluctant to do so. If these governments lack allies in enterprise management who are willing to take the lead in proposing cutbacks, the task becomes nearly impossible.

CHAPTER NINE

Comparative Advantage in Policy Choice

POLITICAL as well as economic attributes give nations distinctive comparative advantages in choosing public policies. In the United States, for example, the system of checks and balances between the executive, legislative, and judicial branches of the federal government and the fragmentation of power within these branches (notably within Congress) make it especially difficult to impose losses on well-organized and powerful groups. Thus policies that work well in Japan might not work in the United States and Canada. It makes no more sense for those governments to attempt to imitate Japanese industrial policy than for Floridians to imitate Coloradoans in building ski resorts. In seeking to build on the strengths of their economic systems, the United States and Canada should make use of the strengths of their political systems and concentrate on those policies that are best suited to their own governments.[1] This final chapter outlines some of the comparative policy advantages and disadvantages that constrain sectoral policy choice by the U.S. and Canadian governments. Industrial policy choice, instrument choice, and the determinants of public enterprise behavior will be reviewed in turn. Each discussion draws upon the findings of this study to suggest lessons for policymakers.

---

1. Political comparative advantages, like economic advantages, are not absolute. Just as sectors within an industry may find market niches long after most of the industry has been wiped out by foreign competition, so an unusual conjunction of political and industrial events may contribute to successful policy choices in national environments where those choices generally have not flourished. The United States and Canada will not always fail in efforts to promote adjustment. But public policy cannot be built upon anomalous cases, unless the environment can be changed to make the anomalous circumstances more commonplace.

Promoting Industrial Change

Government responses to industrial adjustment crises can take three broad forms. Market-oriented policies eschew sector-specific solutions, relying instead on market processes and general macroeconomic and social policies. Protectionist policies attempt to prevent exit by the less competitive segments of the industry, diffusing the costs of propping up the industry among a broader population (generally consumers or taxpayers). Accelerationist policies, on the other hand, attempt to lower political and economic barriers to industrial adjustment by picking winners and, where necessary, by compensating losers.

Agreement is generally easiest to reach on protectionist policies, because they spread costs among unorganized interests and benefit groups that would be hurt by market solutions. Accelerationist policies almost always impose concentrated costs on some groups despite compensation schemes. For this reason, accelerationist policies are most likely to be implemented successfully by governments with (1) few veto points at which losers can block or subvert accelerationist initiatives; (2) bureaucrats that have substantial autonomy and expertise in decisionmaking; and (3) strong mechanisms to enforce compliance by recalcitrant groups—for example, control over credit. Governments do not easily acquire these characteristics through a political learning process. They grow out of a very long period of historical development. Thus governments that do not possess these characteristics are likely to be at a permanent comparative disadvantage in designing and implementing accelerationist policies.

National industrial policies inevitably reflect, and will have to adapt themselves to, existing institutional arrangements and behavior patterns. In the United States this means, above all, fragmented political power within the federal government. In Canada it means strong interregional conflict and competition between the federal and provincial governments. The institutional patterns in both countries greatly impede the successful development of accelerationist industrial policy.

The rail industry clearly exemplifies the difficulties in imposing an accelerationist industrial policy in the United States. The federal government has seldom been granted authority to restructure the rail industry, despite the industry's repeated economic crises, and it has not used that authority when it has had it. In merger and abandonment cases, the Interstate Commerce Commission until recently moved very slowly. It was reluctant to impose losses on communities and carriers except where necessary to preserve the financial viability of the industry. Instead the commission erected a vast administrative artifice intended to balance the needs of the transport modes, communities, and employees under its jurisdiction.

The reorganization of the northeastern railroads in the United States into the Consolidated Rail Corporation (Conrail)—the major case of government promotion of industrial adjustment examined in this book— can be considered a success in many ways. Fixed plant has been trimmed and that which remains has been rehabilitated, responsibility for money-losing passenger services has been transferred to various levels of government, a vestige of rail competition has been preserved in the Northeast, and Conrail has become profitable enough that its return to the private sector now seems assured. The United States Railway Association creditably performed its planning and monitoring task and minimized direct congressional intervention in capital allocation decisions, although its financial projections for Conrail proved to be over-optimistic.

But the federally sponsored reorganization in the Northeast was hardly a model of prompt, efficient action. After the collapse of the Penn Central in mid-1970, three and one-half years elapsed before passage of the Regional Reorganization Act of 1973, which even then was passed only when a shutdown was threatened. It was another two years before Conrail began operating. A total of eleven years elapsed before enactment of the Northeast Rail Service Act of 1981, which lifted many of the burdens imposed on Conrail—and this legislation won passage in a period of unusual presidential dominance, as part of the Reagan budget cuts. Fourteen years elapsed between the Penn Central bankruptcy and the closing of bids on offers to buy Conrail. Clearly, the reorganization was not swift. Nor were industrial adjustment goals paramount in federal policy. Congress mandated a variety of "public needs" goals (continued freight service, upgraded passenger service, preservation of employment) that led to policy compromise and a sacrificing of adjustment goals.

This is not to imply that public needs goals are illegitimate and the creation of Conrail a mistake. On the contrary, Conrail is probably the best that could be expected given the strong political constraints and the disastrous financial condition of the rail industry (which the federal government had helped to create through misguided regulation). Conrail is not, however, a model to be emulated for promoting industrial adjustment. The Conrail experience should serve as a warning against the dangers of protectionist policies, for it is those policies that made Conrail necessary in the first place.

The Canadian government faces fewer internal obstacles to imposing concentrated losses than the U.S. government. Nevertheless, Ottawa fears the political consequences of doing so, especially where they are strong and region-specific. The Canadian rail industry is a classic example of how government efforts to promote industrial adjustment can go astray: subsidies for rail passenger services and branch lines, originally intended to slow down the pace of change to make it less painful for affected communities, turned into long-term support to preserve those services.

The federal government has advantages in promoting rail industry adjustment that it lacks in other sectors: almost exclusive constitutional jurisdiction vis-à-vis the provinces, little foreign ownership or competition, and a strong federal ownership role through Canadian National Railways and VIA Rail Canada. In most industries successful accelerationist policies would require a consensus among Ottawa, affected provincial governments, and corporations that are often foreign-controlled.[2] These political and economic constraints have led the federal government to concentrate most of its sectoral policy efforts on subsidizing industries locating in disadvantaged regions. In short, federal industrial policy has been a form of social policy rather than adjustment policy. Meanwhile, several activist provincial governments have adopted policies with "an inevitable beggar-thy-neighbor quality which renders them more competitive than complementary."[3]

Proponents of accelerationist policies argue that governments need to adopt such policies to preempt protectionist policies. But successful pursuit of an accelerationist industrial policy—especially the delicate task of picking winners and losers—requires a degree of bureaucratic autonomy and internal cohesion within government that is rarely present in the United States or Canada. In a political environment where

2. On these constraints, see Science Council of Canada, *The Politics of an Industrial Strategy: A Seminar* (Ottawa: Science Council of Canada, 1979).
3. Richard D. French, *How Ottawa Decides: Planning and Industrial Policy-Making, 1968–1980* (Toronto: James Lorimer and Co., 1980), p. 90.

accelerationist policies are unlikely to succeed and where market mechanisms are reasonably efficient, it is wiser to develop market-oriented policies that preempt straightforwardly protectionist policies and accelerationist policies that decay into protectionist policies.

But are policies designed to pick winners and speed change doomed to failure in the United States? Proponents of an activist industrial policy argue that the United States has successfully promoted industrial change in the past as a byproduct of other policies. The U.S. civilian airliner industry, for example, became the world's dominant producer largely because of research and development funding by the Pentagon.[4] All that is needed to carry out successful accelerationist policies, they suggest, is to make sectoral viability objectives explicit.

To do so, however, changes the policymaking dynamic and the logic of congressional decisionmaking. When a government program—military aircraft procurement, for example—produces general benefits (that is, benefits not limited to specific interest groups or localities), constituency benefits are likely to be secondary in legislators' minds; when benefits are primarily local, the scramble to ensure constituency benefits will be intense.[5] The difficulty with an activist industrial policy is that policymakers must focus on the financial viability of specific firms and from there on the effects on specific plants and communities. The general benefits of an accelerationist industrial policy, such as increased productivity and lower consumer prices, may take a long time to occur, while transitional costs are immediate and substantial. The short-term costs and benefits are likely to be geographically specific, as some firms are encouraged to expand production and employment, and others are encouraged to do the opposite. To expect Congress to stay aloof from these allocational struggles or to choose loss-imposing accelerationist solutions over loss-diffusing protectionist ones is naive at best.

This argument raises serious questions about one of the most promi-

---

4. Industrial proponents also cite the housing and farm industries as cases of successful sectoral policies. But the growth of the home building industry is a byproduct of extremely popular policies designed to encourage homeownership, not efforts to increase efficiency in the industry. Agricultural loan programs are not intended to pick winners and losers in accelerationist fashion, but rather to sustain weak producers. By diverting resources to these sectors, federal policies impose losses on other sectors of the economy, a fact generally ignored by the proponents of industrial policy.

5. R. Douglas Arnold, "The Local Roots of Domestic Policy," in Thomas Mann and Norman Ornstein, eds., *The New Congress* (Washington, D.C.: American Enterprise Institute for Public Policy Research, 1981), pp. 250–87.

nent industrial policy proposals being considered today: the creation of pools of capital to revive declining industries and speed the development of new ones. This would be accomplished through a latter-day Reconstruction Finance Corporation (RFC) that would make loans and, in some cases, take equity positions in companies. Its objective would be to pick "winners" that eventually would be able to repay RFC-type investments but were of sufficient size or risk that they could not attract adequate private capital. In some versions of this proposal, federal assistance would be offered only when the private sector provided an equal or greater contribution.[6]

What are some of the problems a new RFC would face or create? First, because it would operate in many sectors, it would be unlikely to have the expertise and managerial focus on industry-specific problems that characterized the United States Railway Association in its planning process for Conrail. This expertise would be essential if substantial sectoral reorganization as well as financial assistance was required to make the industry viable (as in the rail industry case).

Second, a new RFC would face serious challenges to its autonomy in dispensing funds. The redeemable preference share program established under Section 505 of the Railroad Revitalization and Regulatory Reform (4R) Act of 1976 offers some indication of what can happen to bureaucratic discretion: despite the free rein supposedly given to the secretary of transportation in dispersing preference share funds, of $128.9 million available for obligation in fiscal 1982, only $900,000 was not already earmarked by statute or legislative report.[7] Moreover, some of the funds originally intended in the 4R act for rail rehabilitation were diverted by Congress to other purposes, such as providing continued service on bankrupt railroads.

Third, the RFC would find itself on a slippery slope by providing assistance to firms. Assistance once given becomes a sunk cost and often is used to justify even more funds if the initial commitment proves inadequate. Government must "protect its investment" in failing companies by anteing up even more. Thus far the U.S. government has been

6. This proposal is most often associated with Felix Rohatyn. See Center for National Policy, *Restoring American Competitiveness: Proposals for an Industry Policy* (Washington, D.C.: CNP, 1984).

7. See the testimony by Federal Railroad Administrator Robert Blanchette in *Reauthorization of the Railroad Financial Assistance Programs,* Hearings before the Subcommittee on Surface Transportation of the Senate Committee on Commerce, Science and Transportation, 97 Cong. 2 sess. (Government Printing Office, 1982), p. 11.

relatively lucky in its ad hoc industrial policies: the Chrysler and Lockheed corporations never forced the federal government to confront the question "How much money must we lose before we give up and pull the plug?" Amtrak and Conrail did pose this question, although Conrail's situation has improved. The answer in both cases was that additional support would be provided to save the sunk investments. Canada's support for its deficit-ridden aircraft manufacturers Canadair and DeHavilland of Canada shows that the same answer is likely to be given north of the Forty-ninth Parallel. Any RFC-type company would have a heavy stake in defending its investments; and even if it wished to cut off aid and let a firm go belly-up, the government almost certainly would pressure it not to do so.

Fourth, the RFC-type corporation would weaken the institutional barriers to corporate bail-outs by providing a permanent mechanism to aid failing firms. But bail-outs should be difficult to obtain. They should be publicly debated and the public interest benefits fully presented. The obstacle course on Capitol Hill may not be well adapted to making accelerationist decisions, but it can act as a barrier to preservationist policy, and a politically responsive RFC would undermine that barrier.

Linking federal financial assistance to private sector contributions would eliminate some of the weakest firms from consideration for assistance, but it would create other problems. Most important, it would widen the class of potential claimants to those who were able to raise capital on their own, but at too high a price or in too small amounts. Who then would define what price is too high or what amount is too small? Once again the problems of government earmarking are likely to be considerable.

These problems of government intervention might not be serious ones if the RFC were to have autonomy and an effective screening device for claims on its resources, and were to operate according to accelerationist principles. But these conditions are unlikely to be simultaneously fulfilled in practice, especially in the United States. To understand why, it is helpful to remember that a new RFC would be, in essence, a public enterprise. How the RFC would behave would depend on the pattern of constraints operating on the firm. If the RFC had weak financial and command structure constraints, it would want to protect those attributes—probably by making safe investments, almost indistinguishable from those in the private sector. Indeed, the Canada Development Corporation, a mixed public-private corporation established to encourage investment in Canada, has been criticized on precisely these grounds. On the other hand, if the RFC was very financially dependent on government and had a divided command structure, it would find it difficult to resist pressure from powerful clientele groups exercised through its government masters.

For an RFC to carry out what its proponents have claimed, it must pursue a public service strategy guided by accelerationist principles. And such a strategy will be adopted only under one of two conditions: (1) if a government agency holds accelerationist values and is able to develop an exclusive tutelary relationship with the corporation, or (2) if the managers of the RFC enjoy autonomy and choose to press accelerationist principles.[8] The first condition is unlikely in the United States because of divided government and in Canada because of regional pressures. The second condition is unlikely to persist in either country because the incentives are so strong for managers to pursue safe, profitable investments if they wish to maintain their autonomy.

The constraints on accelerationist industrial policy in the United States and Canada cannot be removed simply by both governments learning a better way to conduct their business. Fundamental changes would be required in the way that governments and societal interests are organized and function. There is little reason to believe that these deeply ingrained characteristics can be changed in the near future.

Choosing Policy Instruments

Governments can choose from among many policy instruments—for example, public enterprise, subsidies, tax incentives, loans, and regulation—to carry out an industrial policy. National differences in instrument choice are particularly evident in a comparison of public enterprise in the United States and Canada. U.S. public enterprise at the federal level has been limited primarily to narrow segments of the credit and insurance sector. Public enterprise also has been employed in the infrastructure industries mainly at the state and local levels. Canadian governments have used public enterprise in infrastructure industries (railways, airlines, broadcasting, telecommunications, electricity), as

8. In addition, a firm might press accelerationist principles if all of its several governmental masters could agree on those principles. But this is even more unlikely than a single government agency being able to do so.

well as in manufacturing, energy, and natural resources sectors where public enterprise is virtually nonexistent in the United States.

Whether a government chooses public enterprise is heavily influenced by its political system. First, political factors influence policymakers' preferences for specific attributes of instruments. Socialist governments, for example, will probably prefer instruments that give them substantial control over implementation, such as public enterprise or direct administration by a government agency. Governments that are concerned with limiting government spending may prefer to use regulation or loan guarantees. (The U.S. and Canadian governments' reliance on regulation-imposed cross-subsidies to preserve money-losing rail passenger services is a classic example.) In Canada, intense rivalry in state building between the federal and provincial governments reinforces the preference of political leaders at both levels for instruments that offer maximum control over policy implementation. Canada's industrial structure further reinforces this preference for instruments that offer substantial control. The Canadian market's small size and dependence on foreign investment have led to a high degree of corporate concentration (as in the case of railways) and often a real or imagined threat of foreign control.[9] Public attitudes toward corporate power are thus very different from those in the United States, where regulation and antitrust enforcement are seen as sufficient checks on corporate power because the number of competitors in most key industries is relatively large and most are domestically controlled.

Second, political system constraints influence the extent to which the economic advantages of a particular policy instrument can be realized in practice. For example, an internally divided government is less likely to be able to exercise firm control over a public enterprise, undercutting one of that instrument's major advantages. Thus Canada's parliamentary system increases the probability that government-owned firms will be able to achieve their potential for enterprise flexibility and control because the legislature and executive are less likely to issue conflicting commands to the enterprise. Governments also differ in the limitations that civil service, budget controls, and other restrictions place on the flexibility of government agencies.

Finally, political system constraints affect the barriers to adoption of specific instruments. Executive dominance in Canada's parliamentary

9. See Royal Commission on Corporate Concentration (Bryce Commission), *Report* (Ottawa: Supply and Services, 1978).

system has lowered the barriers to adoption of public enterprise because the executive can generally force a nationalization if it wishes to do so. In the United States, multiple veto points make a broad consensus of groups and government actors necessary for nationalization: this consensus is rarely attainable. Moreover, the Government Corporation Control Act requires that all U.S. public enterprises be created by statute, which has further institutionalized limits on the power of the federal executive to create government-owned firms.

In selecting policy instruments, policymakers need to be aware of their distinctive attributes and avoid choosing instruments that are clearly inappropriate. This seemingly elementary precaution is often ignored, however. For example, the U.S. government has used loan guarantees to finance the operating expenses of failing railroads, and both the U.S. and Canadian governments have used cross-subsidies to support money-losing rail operations when carriers could no longer afford them. The economic attributes of these two instruments—contingency of liabilities rather than direct outlays for loan guarantees and shifting of costs to the private sector for regulation—have a strong appeal to governments concerned with limiting spending. These instruments provide a low immediate-cost mechanism for allocating, diffusing, or delaying the costs incurred in an industrial adjustment crisis. But when they are used to impose protectionist solutions rather than to deal with the root causes of a crisis, that crisis will simply fester over time.

It is equally important to remember that political environments greatly influence how instruments function. For example, a government should choose public enterprise as a policy instrument because one or more of the specific attributes of public enterprise—commitment, information and expertise, control and flexibility—is required. But if political system constraints undermine the desired attribute, another instrument choice may be more appropriate. The dispersion of power within the U.S. federal government makes it particularly difficult for that government to employ public enterprise effectively. Both the model of public enterprise behavior developed in chapter 6 and the case of Amtrak suggest that fragmentation of power tends to lead a public enterprise to adopt a security strategy, particularly if the enterprise's financial dependence on government is great. Economic efficiency then becomes a secondary goal. In other words, Washington has a comparative disadvantage in use of the public enterprise instrument. Thus the relatively greater reliance of the U.S. federal government on regulatory and incentive instruments is perhaps good public policy—or at least more desirable than a plethora of security-oriented public enterprises.

Public Enterprise as a Policy Instrument

Public enterprise behavior cannot be explained as pursuit of any single goal, whether it be maximizing political support, maximizing profits, or serving the public interest. Public enterprises have incentives to pursue each of these goals. The goals (and consequent strategies and policies) chosen by individual firms will vary substantially across companies depending upon their pattern of financial and command structure constraints.[10]

Although weak environmental constraints, such as low levels of stockholder control and imperfectly competitive markets, appear to lower stress on profits by firms in the private sector, the opposite seems to be true in the public sector. Weakly constrained public firms are most likely to emphasize profits—not for their own sake, but to preserve their autonomy from government. Canadian National, for example, has enjoyed considerable success in its efforts to institute a strategy oriented toward corporate autonomy and profitability. In those segments of its operations where that has not been possible, CN has attempted to establish a stable, compensatory relationship with government agencies as a second-best strategy. Like CN, Conrail has increasingly favored an autonomy strategy. But autonomy is likely to be an attainable goal only for firms with a strong base of profitable operations. For firms like Amtrak, a cutback in unprofitable operations means a cutback in the overall size of the enterprise and potentially a threat to the organization's survival.

Government financial assistance to an enterprise—particularly when that support is direct, substantial, and subject to government discretion— weakens the enterprise's autonomy and increases its need to build a

---

10. Government influences on public enterprise decisions are not limited to constraining choice of overall strategy. Governments often intervene to modify or overturn specific enterprise decisions. Although government-owned firms adapt their strategies in response to government constraints, complete adaptation may be neither desirable nor possible: managers may choose policies in some areas that conflict with government policy and, as noted earlier, governments themselves often act inconsistently.

coalition of political support through a security strategy.[11] Government assistance for specific services (rather than simply to meet deficits) clarifies an enterprise's mandate and simultaneously limits claims on its resources. Thus service-specific funding is likely to increase the enterprise's public service orientation in that particular sector, but increase its autonomy orientation overall.

The difficulty of getting government-owned firms to pursue a public service strategy primarily stems from governments' inability to define and compel adherence to a realistic mandate for the firms they own. In pluralist societies, governments usually build policies from discrete, often conflicting demands (for example, make profits, add services, retain workers) rather than from preconceived priorities. Demands may be channeled through several agencies with differing goals.[12] It is unrealistic to expect public enterprises to convert such a jumble of demands into consistent policy priorities, particularly when they risk needed political support by doing so. Moreover, failure on one of those conflicting criteria is almost inevitable, and attacks on the enterprise and its managers are certain to follow. On the other hand, if public enterprise managers are able to define a limited and feasible set of goals centering on self-sufficiency for the firm, they can hope to attain them and be rewarded for doing so.

As a result, enterprise managers are likely to pursue an autonomy strategy whenever success in that strategy seems attainable. Enterprise

11. See Yair Aharoni, "Managerial Discretion," in Raymond Vernon and Yair Aharoni, eds., *State-Owned Enterprise in the Western Economies* (St. Martin's Press, 1981), p. 190. Aharoni asserts that multiple conflicting commands may increase managerial discretion by allowing management to choose which commands will be followed and which will be ignored. This may be true in situations where the outcomes desired by government entities are incompatible (for example, building a plant in Province A or not doing so). Usually, however, the conflicts between commands, although real (for example, making profits and keeping redundant workers on the payroll) are "at the margin." In this more normal case, whether an enterprise will be forced to comply with (and presumably fail to accomplish) multiple sets of commands depends upon the strength of the agencies' controls and the enterprise's resource dependence. If control by all government bodies over the enterprise is weak, and they are unable to compel compliance, managerial discretion may be quite high. But if one agency has much stronger authority than the others in a particular decision area, as in the case of VIA Rail Canada, its commands will be followed to the exclusion of all others. And if several agencies are able to force compliance, the public enterprise will have to respond to all of their commands.

12. The cause of conflicting demands on government-owned firms is not always multiple sources of commands. As the case of Amtrak shows, a single government entity (notably Congress) may give a public enterprise inconsistent directives.

managers also may try to alter government constraints. In the cases of CN, VIA, Amtrak, and Conrail, managers attempted to convince government policymakers to provide them with a more consistent mandate and more stable financing. But they were not always successful; government always retains the upper hand.

An enterprise's formal command structure is less important in determining enterprise strategy than how that structure is used. If a government agency has strong formal authority over a publicly owned firm but fails to exercise it, the firm may begin to move toward an autonomy strategy. The changes in Canadian National's strategy under Robert Bandeen, for example, were aided enormously by the cooperation of the Transport Ministry, which did not use its powers to push CN into projects (for example, the Anzac coal line) that might have increased its dependence on Ottawa. Conversely, agencies that lack formal authority over a public enterprise may exercise strong indirect influence. The role of provincial governments in placing demands on Canadian National is particularly striking. While very few of CN's operations come directly under provincial jurisdiction, these governments have been able to bring pressure to bear through federal entities (the Canadian Transport Commission and the cabinet) that are generally responsive to provincial concerns.

The cases examined here show that there are no immutable national patterns of public enterprise behavior: Canadian National Railways acts differently from VIA Rail Canada, and Amtrak from Conrail. Both CN and Conrail changed their strategies considerably over time. These within-nation variations in enterprise behavior reflect parallel differences in constraints on the firms. Within-nation differences are especially likely with regard to financial constraints: a nationalized oil company, for example, has a better chance of being profitable than a shipyard. A freight railway is more likely to be profitable than a passenger railway. Distinctive national patterns occur more often in command structure, however. These patterns may be intentional and codified in legislation (for example, the Government Corporation Control Act in the United States, the Financial Administration Act in Canada) or unintended consequences of the political system.

The unintended but endemic characteristics of political systems appear to be more important influences on enterprise behavior than statutory guidelines. Fragmentation within the U.S. federal government makes it difficult for executive branch policymakers to control public enterprises. Conflicting controls and mandates are by no means unknown in Canada (for example, Transport Canada and the Canadian Transport Commission have tried to steer VIA in different directions), but they are structural anomalies rather than structural imperatives. In comparison with Ottawa, the federal government in the United States has greater structural obstacles to public enterprise autonomy and to the development of a tutelary relationship between an agency and a firm.

The obstacles to an autonomy strategy are by no means insuperable, however. Conrail has moved toward an autonomy strategy as the government has relaxed financial and command structure constraints. The obstacles a public enterprise faces if it wants to pursue a public service mission are even greater, as the case of Amtrak illustrates. Once again the problem lies in giving the enterprise consistent incentives and commands. Indeed, governments often intervene in specific enterprise decisions—usually for protectionist ends—overruling the firm's strategic preferences.

The history of public enterprise in the North American railroad industry suggests several lessons for policymakers. First, the traditional mechanisms of enterprise accountability (adequate flow of information from enterprise to government, careful monitoring of management compliance with government directives) are inadequate to ensure that enterprises follow their mandates. It is more important that governments establish clear goals and then provide incentives to the enterprise that are consistent with them. It makes no sense to give an enterprise a mandate to be self-sustaining accompanied by command and financial controls that push it toward a security strategy.

Second, since the strategies of public enterprises depend on government constraints, governments should resist the temptation to set up uniform command structures and financial controls applicable to all public enterprises. Such rules (for example, all enterprises must obtain their capital by borrowing from the Treasury) ignore the diversity of purposes for which public enterprise can be used. Instead, governments must tailor their controls to the individual enterprise and to the goals they have established for it.

Enterprise constraints can be designed to enhance or minimize the impact of the broader political system on public enterprise strategy and performance. The firm's command structure can be manipulated: more or fewer government bodies can be given stronger or weaker mechanisms for controlling the enterprise. Substantial leeway may also be available in designing financial constraints. Creating an enterprise that requires minimal financial support from government gives enterprise managers increased leverage to defend and strengthen their independence by pursuing an autonomy strategy, while weakening the enterprise's need to build political support coalitions.[13]

Third, both the Canadian and U.S. governments should rethink the criteria they use to make appointments to the boards of public enterprises. The appointment of individuals on the basis of political service rather than business or policy expertise tends to make board members defer to senior management. Thus the board's proper function in setting overall corporate priorities is lost. This leads to direct intervention by agencies that feel they cannot have an impact in any other way. On the other hand, direct agency representation on public enterprise boards often creates the kind of friction evident on the boards of the United States Railway Association and Amtrak. In short, the appointments process should be custom-designed to fit the strategy that government wants the enterprise to pursue; "independent and expert" is an appropriate starting point in framing that process.

Fourth, major changes in the strategy and outputs of public enterprises should not be expected without changes in government-imposed constraints. Enterprise strategies and policies are not set by inertia or muddling through, but by positive and negative incentives. The changes in Amtrak's policy toward labor and service cutbacks in 1981 reflect management's awareness of the changed constraints imposed by "Reagan's reconciliation revolution." And the relaxation of financial and command constraints on Canadian National Railways and Conrail have encouraged those firms to adopt a more autonomy-oriented strategy.

---

13. Minimizing a firm's financial dependence on government may require creating a larger public enterprise than would otherwise be the case. If a government nationalizes only the unprofitable operations within an industry, the resulting firm will certainly be dependent on government. A larger firm with a substantial base of profitable operations might be less dependent and hence more capable of pursuing an autonomy strategy and more interested in promoting industrial adjustment.

Autonomy-oriented behavior on the part of public enterprises, which mirrors the behavior of private firms in similar markets, may be undesirable in some cases. Most notably, autonomy-oriented public enterprises in monopoly markets would behave like private sector monopolists. Conrail, for example, has moved aggressively to close freight interchange "gateways" that gave its competitors the long haul on shared freight movements. On the impact of market structure on public enterprise performance, see Michael Denning, "The Structure and Performance of Government Enterprise" (Ph.D. dissertation, University of Washington, 1984).

Fifth, if governments wish an enterprise to follow a public-service strategy, they must put their own houses in order first. It is not enough to provide an enterprise with a mandate, even one that is clear and without unmanageable internal conflicts. There must be accompanying commands and financial controls that reinforce the mandate. Generally this will mean control by a single agency and compensation for specific services and for high-risk or low-return investments.

Sixth, use of service-specific subsidies and contracts can help governments to identify the costs of their policies and can help enterprises to become more efficiency-oriented.[14] The contracting approach is not without problems of its own, however, notably the incentives it creates for the enterprise and the responsibility it places on a politically sensitive government. The case of Canadian National Railways is instructive. Many of the losses formerly absorbed by CN are now financed directly by the federal government through subsidies, contracts, and capital grants. With costs evident to both sides, more rational choices presumably will be made than under a system of subsidies to meet deficits. Once costs are clearly identified and paid for directly, Ottawa may eventually realize that some programs are not effective uses of resources and allow them to be phased out.

While the pedagogical value of service-specific subsidies and contracts may be real, they remove much of the financial incentive for the railways to eliminate uneconomic operations (although not necessarily the incentive to operate them efficiently). Only government retains the incentive to cut inefficient programs. The contract system has improved CN's income statement, but it has not been successful in eliminating inefficient operations. It places pressure directly on government to make decisions about service cuts, decisions that few governments have the political courage to make. Faced with extreme regional discontent and electoral insecurity, Ottawa has not been very courageous. Indeed, one of the major justifications for using public enterprise is to take the onus for such decisions away from government. The irony of the contract approach is that while it helps an autonomy-oriented public enterprise meet its goal, it may weaken the incentives for the firm to discontinue uneconomic operations, capital programs, and labor practices in sectors

14. The best-known treatment of government-enterprise contracts is France's Nora Report. See John Sheahan, "Experience with Public Enterprise in France and Italy," in William Shepherd, ed., *Public Enterprise: Economic Analysis of Theory and Practice* (Lexington Books, 1976), pp. 156–68.

where government offers subsidies instead. Canadian National Railways illustrates such a corporate adaptation. Rather than pressing for a complete adaptation, CN often settles for compensation, turning over both financial losses and political risks to its owner.

Finally, while public enterprise can be quite compatible with industrial adjustment, it is likely to be effective in *accelerating* industrial change only under special circumstances. As the cases of Conrail and Canadian National Railways show, autonomy-oriented enterprises can cut and disinvest in unprofitable operations and increase productivity very much like private sector firms. But like those firms, they will be reluctant to make high-risk or low-yield investments that might endanger their financial independence. Similarly, they will be reluctant to reduce capacity in a declining market when the benefits thereof cannot be captured by the firm. If nationalization combines the operations of several firms, managers' incentives will be different from those of their predecessor firms. Managers may seek to cut their least efficient productive capacity to lower their financial dependence on government. In general, however, an autonomy-oriented public enterprise will pursue a market-oriented course and a security-oriented firm a protectionist one, unless they receive consistent incentives and commands from government to pursue accelerationist policies. In both the United States and Canada, the federal governments are unable to consistently pursue accelerationist objectives themselves, let alone transmit such objectives to public enterprise.

Index

Accelerationist policy, 142; and Amtrak and Conrail, 88, 121; and compensation schemes, 18; and industrial change, 32–33, 85, 271, 275; and industrial policy analysis, 6–7, 9, 11, 12–13, 14; and nationalization, 67, 168–69; and political constraints, 15–19; rail adjustment policy and failure of, 57–61; requirements for, 19–24, 269; in United States and Canada, 25. *See also* Industrial adjustment policy

Adams, Brock, 53n, 102, 104n, 239n

Adjustment policies. *See* Industrial adjustment policy

Administrative policy instruments, 64–68

Aggarwal, Vinod K., 12n

Aharoni, Yair, 154n, 156n, 165n, 279n

Aitken, Hugh G. H., 75n

Alaska Railroad, 29

Allen, Benjamin J., 47

American High Speed Rail Corporation (AHSR), 250

Amtrak Improvement Act of *1978*, 97, 232, 242

Amtrak Improvement Act of *1981*, 236

Amtrak (National Railroad Passenger Corporation), 4, 40, 44; and accelerationist policy, 60, 61; and appointment process, 282; and capital expenditures (investment), 247–51; command structure, 231–37; and Congress, 92–94, 95, 96, 97, 231, 232–34, 235–36, 240–44, 245–47, 254–55; and Conrail development, 215, 217, 222; and corporate strategy, 237–40; corridor projects, 248–51, 252, 253, 254; creation of, 88–97, 120–21, 229–30; and DOT, 90, 97, 121, 231–33, 234, 235, 238, 239, 241, 242–44, 246, 249, 253, 254, 255, 266; and employment, 251–54; financial constraints, 230–31; growth strategy, 239; ICC and intercity service, 59n; and industrial adjustment policy, 266–67; as nationalization avoidance strategy, 87–88; and policy choice, 123–25, 126–27; and policy conflict, 254–55; as public enterprise, 280, 282; subsidies for, 55;

unprofitable operations, 240–47; and USRA, 230n

Amtrak Reorganization Act of *1979*, 236, 244, 246, 252–53

Anastassopolous, Jean-Pierre, 165n

Arnold, R. Douglas, 272n

Association of American Railroads (AAR), 93

Aucoin, Peter, 166n

Autonomy (decisionmaking authority): and CN, 182, 191, 199, 206; and Conrail, 216, 218–19; and public enterprise, 153–54, 158, 159, 168, 278–79, 279–80, 281, 282n, 284; and VIA Rail Canada, 237

Axworthy, Lloyd, 181, 260, 263

Baldwin, John, 67n, 155n, 161n

Baldwin, Robert E., 7n

Bandeen, Robert, 180n, 183–84, 188n, 195, 280

Bankruptcies: Canadian railroad, 131; Conrail and railroad, 99–100, 101, 102, 103

Bankruptcy Act (U.S.), 37

Barnum, John, 235n

Bayh, Birch, 245n

Belanger, Gerard, 165n

Bennett, R. B., 173

Bennett, William, 197

Berger, Stephen, 213n

Blanchette, Robert, 245n, 273n

Bohn, Glenn, 198n

Borden, Robert Laird, 130–34, 145

Botterell, Robert, 80n

Boulding, Kenneth E., 149n

Boyd, Alan, 237, 238, 244, 245n, 249n, 250, 253

Branch lines, 45–46, 52

Break, George, 69n

Brinegar, Claude, 101n, 103n, 105n, 106

Brown, Roger C., 131n, 133n

Bryan, Jay, 194n

Bussières (Les Entreprises Bussières Ltée), 194

Byrd, Robert, 240, 245

285